Prenatal Development of Postnatal Functions

PRENATAL DEVELOPMENT OF POSTNATAL FUNCTIONS

Edited by
Brian Hopkins and Scott P. Johnson

Advances in Infancy Research

Westport, Connecticut
London

Library of Congress Cataloging-in-Publication Data

Prenatal development of postnatal functions / edited by Brian Hopkins and Scott P. Johnson.

  p. cm. -- (Advances in infancy research)
  Includes bibliographical references and indexes.
  ISBN 0-275-98126-6 (alk. paper)
  1. Prenatal influences. 2. Fetal behavior. 3. Fetus—Growth. 4. Fetus—Development. 5. Maternal-fetal exchange. I. Hopkins, Brian, 1940– II. Johnson, Scott P., 1959– III. Advances in infancy research.

RG622.P746 2005
618.2'4--dc22   2005003456

British Library Cataloguing in Publication Data is available.

Library of Congress Catalog Card Number: 2005003456
ISBN: 0-275-98126-6

First published in 2005

Praeger Publishers, 88 Post Road West, Westport, CT 06881
An imprint of Greenwood Publishing Group, Inc.
www.praeger.com

Printed in the United States of America

The paper used in this book complies with the Permanent Paper Standard issued by the National Information Standards Organization (Z39.48–1984).

10 9 8 7 6 5 4 3 2 1

This book is dedicated to the memories of Jean-Pierre Lecanuet and Jan Winberg

CONTENTS

INTRODUCTION

Brian Hopkins and Scott P. Johnson

In the past, most textbooks on developmental psychology tended to ignore the functional significance of prenatal life for postnatal development, despite admonitions from the likes of Carmichael (1954) that such an omission would result in an impoverished understanding of ontogenetic development. To be fair, there was little encouragement at the time for developmental psychologists in general and infancy researchers in particular to regard human prenatal development as anything more than a period of rapid physical growth during which an array of age-related spinal reflexes became established. It was almost as if the ten lunar months of human pregnancy constituted a sort of developmental limbo or suspended state of animation from which the fetus was released only after birth. Paradoxically, the grand theories of development articulated by Piaget and others drew heavily on embryological principles of growth as a means of deriving metaphors for understanding the psychological development of infants and children. Beyond such metaphorical applications, development continued to be portrayed as a process of behavioral change from birth onward.

Such a myopic vision of development began to be dispelled in the early 1980s with evidence of fetal learning derived from ingenious and carefully controlled studies in both humans and other species. At about the same period, real-time ultrasound made its incursion as a research tool for studying fetal behavior under physiological conditions. In addition, developmental neurobiologists were revealing additional complexities in neurogenesis and synaptogenesis across a variety of vertebrate species that removed once and for all notions of prenatal development as consisting of only a succession of hardwired reflex circuits at the spinal level. All told, these achievements have led to a radical reappraisal of the ways in which developmental psychologists think about the origins of development. As a consequence, there has been a renascence in trying to understand the postnatal consequences of structural and functional development as well as experiential effects during prenatal life. What, then, has this renascence delivered, and how best should we interpret any evidence in favor of meaningful continuities between prenatal and postnatal development?

These sorts of overarching questions have been addressed from a diversity of viewpoints in the chapters of the present volume. Accordingly, they range from molecular events that determine corticogenesis and the role of sensory experience in shaping cortical connectivity through perceptual and motor learning, to how adverse circumstances operating on the mother during pregnancy may express themselves in disordered developmental outcomes. Such a coverage, which is by no means exhaustive in scope, entails evaluating the application of animal models and findings from human studies to arrive at conclusions that inform us about the nexus between prenatal and postnatal development. Without doubt, this is one of the most fundamental issues in the developmental sciences and one that continues to challenge existing beliefs about the nature of ontogenetic development.

The first chapter, by Sarah Pallas, addresses how studies of gene expression and those involving the manipulation of sensory experience inform us about prenatal corticogenesis. In attempting to find the middle ground between the extremes of *genetic pre-specification* and *extrinsic specification,* she brings together a rich corpus of evidence indicating that molecular markers of gene expression ensure *inter-areal specificity* of thalamic projections to the cortex, while subsequent neural activity transported via these axons serves to determine areal fates. This developmental scenario brings with it two important suggestions. First, inter-areal specificity may not rely on activity-dependent mechanisms, such as Hebbian rules of correlation-based synaptic changes, but rather on as yet unidentified area-specific cues in the cortex that attract thalamic axons to their target areas in the cortex (Lopez-Bendito & Molnar, 2003). Second, once thalamocortical pathways have been established, it becomes possible for sensory inputs to begin inducing plastic changes in the brain, something that will take place sooner in the auditory compared to the visual system because the former has earlier access to extrinsic stimulation than the latter. In humans, connections between thalamic nuclei and the cortex are not evident until about five months of gestational age, and thus any form of auditory learning in the fetus, such as being able to discriminate between maternal and other voices, cannot be expected before this time.

The role of sensory patterns in shaping cortical functions is illustrated by Pallas in a number of ways, while at the same time she takes care to point out species differences in this respect. One is through the aegis of the cortical re-wiring of thalamocortical projections in the neonatal ferret, an experimental paradigm to which Pallas and her colleagues have made major contributions. In brief, the paradigm involves re-routing retinal inputs from their usual destination (namely, the lateral geniculate body) to the auditory medial geniculate nucleus in the thalamus. Subsequent recordings from the auditory cortex revealed visual responses, including selective orientation to visual stimuli. This intriguing finding not only emphasizes the considerable cross-modal plasticity of the developing brain at early stages of development but also the limited role played by intrinsic molecular mechanisms (i.e., genetic pre-specifications) in ensuring cortical regionalization. If such plasticity is a feature of the fetal brain, then it should not be too surprising that the fetus is capable of rather more advanced forms of learning, ensuring appropriate adaptation to the postnatal environment that go beyond mere habituation. And if sensory-induced plasticity means that cortical areas are interchangeable when one of them is damaged, then this finding has important ramifications for treatment therapies involving brain-damaged infants.

A final comment on this chapter refers back to the role of activity-dependent processes that influence the strength of synaptic connections between neurons, the chief mechanisms of which are considered to be *long-term potentiation* (LTP) and its close cousin, *long-term depression* (LTD). LTP, first discovered in 1966, is widely regarded as being the cellular basis for learning and memory. While a number of different models of LTP have been proposed, controversy persists about whether both pre- and postsynaptic cells are involved in its induction, and even with regard to its relationships with learning and memory (Shors & Matzel, 1997).

As for LTD, a weakening of synapse connectivity that can last from hours to days, its discovery during the early 1980s in cerebellum (and later knowledge of its existence in other structures such as the hippocampus) led to the supposition that it is implicated in motor learning (Ito, 1986), a topic addressed from a developmental perspective in the chapter by Robinson and Kleven. The precise roles that LTD play in learning and memory, especially procedural memory, have yet to be elucidated to the same degree as for LTP. Furthermore, mechanisms other than LTP and LTD that are age-specific in nature may be involved in the developmental plasticity of the brain, a point that is made clear by Pallas.

In the second chapter, Jean-Pierre Lecanuet, Carolyn Granier-Deferre, and Anthony DeCasper continue the theme of prenatal sensory experience and learning, particularly within the context of auditory modality. In doing so they provide a critical evaluation of previous work on these topics, a brief that is broadcast in the title of their chapter. Among other things, the potentially detrimental effect of overexposing the fetus to sounds considered appropriate for mature auditory systems is highlighted with evidence from the development of the mammalian cochlea, whose receptors change from an initial sensitivity to low frequency, to sensitivity for sounds with a higher frequency. Such a discontinuity in fetal hearing should warn parents against the unfettered use of commercially available gadgets that are purported to promote brain development *in utero* via auditory stimulation. Such warnings are at last beginning to be found in textbooks on human development (e.g., Bjorklund & Pellegrini, 2003). A lack of knowledge about what constitutes effective stimulation also becomes evident in studies on the influence of maternal speech on prenatal and postnatal auditory discrimination, which often do not take account of fetal *behavioral state* (a topic also dealt with by de Vries and Hopkins in their chapter). Consequently, we do not yet know the most effective state in which such learning takes place, or if in fact there is one such state. While the authors refer to findings in favor of transnatal continuities in different types of learning, they emphasize the inherent difficulties in disentangling the longer-term effects of prenatal auditory experience on speech and language development from other nonmaternal sources of auditory stimulation occurring after birth. In this regard, they conclude that a fetal differential psychology capable of addressing this, and other, issues has yet to be achieved.

A somewhat controversial issue concerning continuities between prenatal and postnatal development centers on the functioning of the *vestibular system*. It is known that structurally this system matures early in prenatal life, but it has been held that it only becomes functional after birth. Support for the claim that the vestibulum is functionally inhibited in the prenatal human is derived from a study in which the maternal abdomen was shaken from side to side when the fetus was in state 1F (i.e., quiet sleep with low heart rate variability), a maneuver that failed to alter the fetal heart rate pattern or induce movement in the near-term fetus (Visser, Zeelenberg, de Vries, & Dawes, 1983; see, however, Issel, 1983). Research reported by Lecanuet et al., and carried out by the first author, found that vestibular stimulation in the same fetal state induced a transient increase in a heart rate of moderate amplitude. In this study, pregnant mothers were subjected to lateral swaying and fore-and-aft rocking motions while reclining in a chair. This difference in mode of vestibular stimulation might explain the contrast in findings. Shaking the mother's abdomen could have selectively impinged on the semicircular canals that detected angular acceleration as consequence of this maneuver engendering rotary movements of the fetal head. Rocking the mother, especially in a fore-and-aft direction, would provide linear acceleration that is detected by the utricle and saccule. Thus, one conclusion to be drawn from these two studies is that the otoliths become functional before birth, which may not be the case for the semicircular canals. The speculative nature of this conclusion should be emphasized in the light of a persisting lack of any further knowledge about the functional development of the vestibular system in the human fetus. Not to place too fine of a point on it, there is an outstanding need for further research on vestibular functioning that crosses the prenatal-postnatal divide.

Chapters 3 and 4 focus on the acquisition of olfactory (and gustatory) prenatal preferences and their effects on behavior after birth. The sense of smell consists of two distinct systems: the main *olfactory system*, which is attuned to sensing volatile compounds; and the *vermeronasal system*, which detects stimuli mostly associated with pheromones. Both chapters are chiefly concerned with the main olfactory system. Before considering this system, it is worthwhile to reiterate some of its unique properties that set it apart from other sensory modalities.

The first unique feature of the olfactory system is that it has no thalamocortical relay between its neurons and the primary sensory cortex, as it is directly routed to the periform cortex in the temporal lobe (i.e., the primary olfactory cortex), and from here to the hypothalamus and the orbitofrontal cortex. Second, along with the hippocampus, the olfactory bulb is the only CNS structure that continues generating sensory neurons and axonal outgrowth throughout life. While both olfactory and taste cells are continuously replaced, there is one important difference between them: olfactory cells have true axons and form axodendritic synapses in contrast to taste cells, which possess no axons or dendrites (Farbman, 1990). Third, olfaction is different from vision, audition, and touch in that it is represented in multimodal neurons in the limbic system and paralimbic region (Gottfried & Dolan, 2003). As a consequence, olfaction could function on the basis of different neural processes than those governing other sensory systems, particularly in instances of cross-modal integration.

These distinctive features of the olfactory system should be kept in mind while reading the third and fourth chapters. Another point to consider is that there are two types of odor perception: the *orthonasal route* via the nose, in which odors are perceived as emanating from the external environment; and the *retronasal route* involving the nasopharynx toward the roof of the mouth, which delivers the perception of odors as coming from the mouth. In the mammalian fetus, both types will be perceived as any chemical substance enters both the nasal and oral passages. Thus, it is impossible to distinguish whether fetal chemosensation is due to olfaction or taste.

The contribution by Benoist Schaal ranges across both human and animal studies, with reference to his own pioneering work on the development of olfactory learning in evaluating the "odor bridging" or *transnatal chemosensory continuity* (TCC) hypothesis. According to this hypothesis, prenatal experience with the contents of amniotic fluid and maternal diet prime the establishment of postnatal olfactory preferences, both at the species and individual level. One way in which this link might be achieved is through the chemical similarity of volatile compounds that abound in amniotic fluid and in breast milk (i.e., colostrum) immediately after birth as a consequence of maternal dietary preferences. This, and other features of the TCC hypothesis, gives rise to six testable predictions concerning its biological validity. However, Schaal is careful to point out that it is one of a number of possible scenarios that can account for perinatal continuity in olfactory perception. One of these alternative hypotheses forms the centerpiece of the next chapter (namely, labor-induced effects on odor preferences in the newborn). A concluding comment in Schaal's thorough review echoes that made about fetal auditory learning by Lecanuet and colleagues; namely, the need to gain insights into longer-term effects of prenatal olfactory experience that go beyond the newborn period and early infancy. Another issue relates to the ever-present *binding problem* in the study of perception: the lack of current knowl-edge about how the process of olfactory bridging is integrated with other sensory modalities in order to enable successful adaptations to the postnatal environment. As referred to previously, the attainment of cross-modal integration between olfaction and vision for the pur-poses of object and event localization may be a product of different neural processes between audition and vision. Certainly, humans are relatively poor at localizing the source of an odor without the accom-paniment of visual (or somatosensory) cues (Kobal, van Tuller, & Hummel, 1989).

Turning to the contribution by Richard Porter, Jan Winberg, and Heili Varendi, we find much that complements the previous chapter. The nub of their chapter stems from their own intriguing research on the effects of labor and delivery on the preferences (and aversions) of a human newborn for particular odors. Evidence suggests that the birth process, and labor contractions in particular, trigger a cascade of excitatory catecholamines (including norepinephrine), and an acti-vation of the locus coeruleus in the brain stem, whose axons have a widespread distribution at all levels of the neuroaxis (namely, the cerebral cortex, the cerebellum, the hypothalamus, and the spinal cord). The consequence of such neurochemical events is an alert state lasting a few hours after birth in which the newborn is very sensitive to sensory stimulation, a phenomenon first fully reported in the 1960s (Desmond et al., 1963). Thus, the effect of a vaginal delivery accom-panied by uterine contractions is to create a "window of opportunity" (or sensitive period) for rapid postnatal olfactory learning. But why specifically for olfactory learning? The mechanisms by which such a selective effect is achieved are not clear, but it is known that in rats many norepinephrine neurons in the locus coeruleus project to the olfactory bulb. As for humans, clever experimentation by Porter et al. revealed that, in two groups of newborns delivered by cesarean sec-tion, those who experienced uterine contractions performed above chance level in a task requiring discrimination between a familiar and a novel odor, which was not the case for the group that lacked expo-sure to such contractions. Added to this outcome was the finding that the blood-based level of norepinephrine was higher in those infants who demonstrated a preference for the familiar odor.

There is much more to be gleaned from this chapter about what is involved in chemosensory perception during early development.

Another insight is that classical conditioning of human newborns to associate an odor with tactile stimulation resulted in a head-turning preference for that odor. This preference was not evident in those exposed to smelling or stroking separately. Such a finding indicates that olfaction and touch are cross-modally integrated in full-term newborns, thereby facilitating the localization of odors. Given that the evidence for discriminating the conditioned odor was based on head turning to one side of the body, the question arises as to when in development olfactory perception becomes lateralized. Relevant in this respect is that such perception in adults, and especially its emotional and hedonic components, is more lateralized to the right hemisphere (Brand, Millot, Saufaux, & Morand-Villneuve, 2002). For newborns, however, at least one study suggests that their response to what are attractive odors is a function of the left hemisphere (Olko & Turkewitz, 2001).

Moving from olfactory to motor learning during the prenatal period brings us to the chapter by Scott Robinson and Gale Kleven. In this rich, informative review, the authors draw attention to the premise that prenatal motor development is not only driven by the spontaneous activity of dedicated *central pattern generators* (CPGs) in the nervous system, but that it also depends just as importantly on proprioceptive feedback arising from movements. This contention represents stage three in the history of research on fetal motility; the first being that it is an outcome of the chaining of reflexes activated to perform in sequence only when elicited by external stimulation, and the second ascribing it solely to the output of CPGs mainly situated in the spinal cord. Hardwired CPGs have been portrayed as consisting of excitatory glutamergic projections and networks of inhibitory GABAergic interneurons. Working in tandem, they are supposed to produce rhythmic movements at a variety of different frequencies. With regard to interneurons, there is a current upsurge of interest in neuroscience to deal with the long-standing problem of classifying the neurochemical diversity and functional sophistication of the many different subclasses of interneurons (Whittington & Traub, 2003). If it is achieved, there may be some adjustments to existing views on the processes by which interneurons contribute to the functioning of CPGs.

As for motor learning during prenatal development, Robinson and Kleven draw upon findings from their program of research, using what they refer to as the "interlimb yoke training paradigm." When exposed to such training that consists of linking the legs by means of threads attached to the ankles, fetal rats exhibited more coordinated hind-limb movements as detected with the aid of 3-D movement registrations. The inference drawn is that the rat fetus can use proprioceptive feedback to modify interlimb coordination of the yoked limbs, with the effect persisting for up to thirty minutes after the yoke is removed. Other studies showed that the ability to respond to yoking with increases in interlimb coordination corresponded to the age at which muscle spindles in the fetal rat become functional; actually a rather late achievement in its prenatal development.

One important conclusion drawn from the findings of this research, and the writings of others, is that developing motor systems are not just activity-dependent, but also experience-dependent. Consequently, spontaneous neural activity, sensory feedback, and forms of extrinsic stimulation should all contribute to their development. In this way, they more fully prepare the developing organism for the essential task of rapidly adjusting to motor-based experiences after birth.

Movement is one of the main themes of the next chapter, by Johanna I. P. de Vries and Brian Hopkins. The focus is almost entirely devoted to human development, and once again emphasis is given to the spontaneous generation of movements through the medium of the CPG concept. While this concept has been criticized as a neural abstraction that does not account for what is actually observed in developing organisms (Thelen & Smith, 1994), it serves as a useful counterpoint to interpretations derived from the now discredited paradigm of *reflexology*. In the past, this paradigm depicted the development of motor control as a process of forming concatenations between spinal reflexes. We now know that the spinal cord is more than just a neural substrate for the production of reflexes (Poppele & Bosco, 2002). Its circuitry has the capability to solve some complex problems in motor control, such as the *inverse dynamics problem* (deriving forces from kinematics) and the biomechanical *degrees-of-freedom problem* (a problem addressed by Robinson and Kleven).

Also addressed in this chapter is the prenatal to postnatal development of posture, a topic that has suffered neglect relative to the study of movement patterns in this context. The authors offer the maintenance of a head position relative to the torso as an example of posture. They report that, like the attainment of stable behavioral states, this configuration with the head turned to the right in most fetuses is another late-occurring event in human prenatal development and is sustained for some two to three months after birth. This developmental course suggests that in some way this posture stands for an ontogenetic adaptation ensuring an appropriate passage of the fetal head through the birth canal. The same may apply to some of the fifteen movement patterns so far identified in the human fetus (i.e., they serve as adaptations to life in the womb, but may be unnecessary or even incompatible with those required for the postnatal environment). While the concept of ontogenetic adaptation is not without its problems when applied to human behavioral development, it does have a certain heuristic value in challenging us to question any suggestions of straightforward continuities between prenatal and postnatal life in both the motor and perceptual domains (a note of warning echoed in other chapters of the book). As for the future of research on human motor development *in utero*, much will depend on progress with 3-D dynamical recordings and subsequent opportunities to make longer continuous registrations than those that are currently available.

The final chapter, by Vivette Glover and Thomas O'Connor, affords an enlightening overview of research addressing the relatively new issue of how *maternal stress and anxiety* during pregnancy can adversely affect postnatal developmental outcomes in children, with effects still being realized in adulthood. As with Robinson and Kleven's chapter, there are necessary extrapolations from animal experiments in order to pinpoint the mechanisms involved. The authors outline two possible mechanisms. The first derives from the finding that maternal stress hormones, of which glucocorticoids appear as the most prominent, are conveyed through the placenta to the fetus. The second derives from evidence that maternal anxiety during pregnancy is related to impaired uterine blood flow. Empirical support for both mechanisms has been found, some of which stems from Glover's own work. A commonality between them is that they are both associated with *fetal growth restriction*, which in severe cases has well-documented deleterious effects on various aspects of postnatal development (Thureen, Anderson, & Hay, 2001). One provocative finding to emerge from Glover's involvement in a British longitudinal study is that elevated levels of maternal anxiety at eighteen weeks of pregnancy, but not postnatally, are connected with cases of children judged to display *mixed-handedness* at about three and one-half years of age. This atypical handedness, rather than a left-hand preference, has a higher incidence among children with developmental disorders such as autism and dyslexia. This outcome, among others, is construed by the authors as additional evidence that "fetal programming" occurs in humans.

The *fetal programming*, or fetal origins of adult disease, hypothesis has become an increasingly attractive medium for trying to understand the origins of developmental disorders. Starting with findings from retrospective epidemiological studies in the 1990s (Barker, 1992), it holds that prenatal insults arising, for example, from defects in the placental supply of nutrients or severe instances of *hypermesis gravidum* (i.e., "morning sickness") can give rise to permanent effects on the structure, physiology, and metabolism of organ systems that become evident through susceptibility to a range of diseases and disorders in children and beyond. Initially, such susceptibility encapsulated cardiovascular and metabolic diseases, but it has since been extended to include cognitive and behavioral dysfunctions, as witnessed in the chapter by Glover and O'Connor and elsewhere (Sandman et al., 1999). In essence there is nothing new about this hypothesis, except that it exerts a stronger emphasis on the long-term effects of prenatal and perinatal complications on morbidity and mortality. Moreover, it has not escaped some degree of criticism (Susser & Levin, 1999). One paradox, or what has been termed the "double-edged sword" (McEwen, 1998), that has to be contended with is the claim that fetal stress in the form of, for example, *pre-eclampsia* can result in the acceleration of both brain and lung maturation (Amiel-Tison et al., 2004). Whether such seemingly counterintuitive effects are necessarily beneficial in the long term, and how one operationalizes the degree of stress imposed, are issues to be answered by proponents of this alternative hypothesis using larger scale data sets than have previously been the case.

ACKNOWLEDGMENTS

Appreciation is extended to Anne Bekoff, Bob Lickliter, Julia Mennella, Mary Schneider, and Rachel Wong for their valuable help in reviewing chapters in this volume.

REFERENCES

Amiel-Tison, C., Cabrol, D., Denver, R., Jarreau, P.H., Papiernik, E., & Piazza, P.V. (2004). Fetal adaptation to stress. Part I: Acceleration of fetal maturation and earlier birth is triggered by placental insufficiency in humans. *Early Human Development, 78,* 15–27.
Barker, D.J.P. (Ed.). (1992). *Fetal and infant origins of adult disease.* London: BMJ Books.

Bjorklund, D.F., & Pellegrini, A.D. (2002). *The origins of human nature: Evolutionary developmental psychology.* Washington, DC: American Psychological Association.

Brand, G., Millot, J.L., Saufaux, M., & Morand-Villneuve, N. (2002). Lateralization in human nasal chemoreception: Differences in bilateral electrodermal responses to olfactory and trigeminal stimulation. *Behavioral and Brain Research, 133,* 205–210.

Carmichael, L. (1954). The onset and early development of behavior. In L. Carmichael (Ed.), *Manual of child psychology* (pp. 60–185). New York: Wiley.

Desmond, M.M., Franklin, R.R., Vallbona, C., Hill, R.M., Plumb, R., Arnold, H., & Watts, J. (1963). The clinical behavior of the newlyborn. I. The term baby. *Journal of Pediatrics, 62,* 307–325.

Farbman, A.I. (1990). Olfactory neurogenesis: Genetic or environmental controls? *Trends in Neurosciences, 13,* 362–365.

Gottfried, J.A., & Dolan, R.J. (2003). The nose smells what the eye sees: Cross-modal visual facilitation of human olfactory perception. *Neuron, 39,* 375–396.

Issel, E.P. (1983). Fetal response to external mechanical stimuli. *Journal of Perinatal Medicine, 11,* 232–243.

Ito, M. (1986). Long-term depression as a memory process in the cerebellum. *Neuroscience Research, 3,* 531–539.

Kobal, G., van Tuller, S., & Hummel, T. (1989). Is there directional smelling? *Experientia, 45,* 130–132.

Lopez-Bendito, G., & Molnar, Z. (2003). Thalamocortical development: How are we going to get there? *Nature Reviews Neuroscience, 4,* 276–289.

McEwen, B.S. (1998). Protective and damaging effects of stress mediators. *New England Journal of Medicine, 338,* 171–179.

Olko, C., & Turkewitz, G. (2001). Cerebral asymmetry of emotion and its relationship to olfaction in infancy. *Laterality, 6,* 29–37.

Poppele, R., & Bosco, G. (2002). Sophisticated spinal contributions to motor control. *Trends in Neurosciences, 26,* 269–276.

Sandman, C.A., Wadhwa, P., Glynn, L., Chicz-Demet, A., Porto, M., & Garite, T.J. (1999). Corticotrophin-releasing hormones and fetal responses in human pregnancy. *Annals of the New York Academy of Sciences, 897,* 66–75.

Shors, T.J., & Matzel, L.D. (1997). Long-term potentiation: What's learning got to do with it? *Behavioral and Brain Sciences, 20,* 597–655.

Susser, M., & Levin, B. (1999). Ordeal for the fetal programming hypothesis. *British Medical Journal, 318,* 885–886.

Thelen, E., & Smith, L.B. (1994). *A dynamic systems approach to the development of cognition and action.* Cambridge, MA: MIT Press.

Thureen, P.J., Anderson, M.S., & Hay, W.W. (2001). The small-for-gestational infant. *Neuroreviews, 2,* 139–149.

Visser, G.H.A., Zeelenberg, H.J., de Vries, J.I.P., & Dawes, G.S. (1983). External physical stimulation of the human fetus during episodes of low heart rate variation. *American Journal of Obstetrics and Gynecology, 145*, 579–584.

Whittington, M.A., & Traub, R.D. (2003). Interneuron diversity series: Inhibitory interneurons and network oscillations in vitro. *Trends in Neurosciences, 36*, 676– 682.

CHAPTER 1

PRE- AND POSTNATAL SENSORY EXPERIENCE SHAPES FUNCTIONAL ARCHITECTURE IN THE BRAIN

Sarah L. Pallas

ABSTRACT

On simultaneous fronts, molecular biologists and systems neurobiologists are elucidating the steps involved in the development and patterning of cerebral cortex, and the mechanisms underlying them. Perhaps owing to the nature of their experimental approaches, molecular biologists have emphasized the intrinsic, genetic instructions that specify cortical regions, whereas systems neurobiologists have concentrated their efforts on the role of neuronal activity delivered to the cortex through extrinsic, sensory experience. Of interest to infant development researchers, it is becoming increasingly clear that prenatal and early postnatal experience can play a significant role in shaping cortical connectivity and function. Experiments on cross-modal plasticity have shown that changing the modality of input to the cortex, without changing the thalamocortical pathway carrying the information, can completely change the functional identity of cortex, allowing, for example, the auditory cortex to detect and process visual input, and mediate visual behavior. Parallel studies in deaf and blind humans using psychophysical and brain imaging techniques show that cross-modal plasticity in the form of sensory substitution occurs naturally in these patients. Such evidence suggests that directed stimulation of infants in the womb could have profound effects on both normal development and on compensation for developmental deficits in sensory pathways.

INTRODUCTION

An important goal of infant brain research is to promote maximal intellectual potential and mental health. Therefore it is important to know to what extent prenatal care and other forms of intervention can influence future outcome. To what extent can an infant's brain be shaped by perinatal experience? The perennial argument over heredity-driven versus nurturance-driven ideas in child rearing practices (Bruer, 1999; Gopnik, Meltzoff, & Kuhl, 1999) is paralleled by the continuing debate over the intrinsic-versus-extrinsic-control hypotheses of cortical development. Other chapters in this volume deal with prenatal development of motor systems and olfaction in human infants. This chapter reviews studies, primarily from animal models, that are beginning to elucidate the relative roles of "nature and nurture" in perinatal cortical development and concentrates on the *visual* and *auditory* systems.

Genetics is a powerful force in behavioral development. Indeed, early cortical development depends entirely on intrinsic, primarily genetic, influences out of necessity. This dependency is because in humans the cerebral cortex is not connected to the sensory relay nuclei in the thalamus until the fifth month of gestation, two months after the *retina* is wired to the *thalamus.* Thus, there is no opportunity for sensory experience to influence the cortex until after this time point. In humans and other anthropoid primates, this programmed *sensory deprivation* is prolonged by the fact that birth occurs at a relatively late stage of cortical development, after the eyes and ear canals open. It is important for the clinician to realize that humans are rather unusual in this regard. Results of studies on early postnatal, non-primate animals often reflect developmental stages that occur prenatally in humans (Clancy, Darlington, & Finlay, 2001). Thus, results from studies of research animals such as rodents and carnivores may not be strictly comparable to those from humans, due to the varying access to sensory stimuli at different developmental time points. The presence of spontaneous, patterned neuronal activity in the prenatal brain, however, may at least partially correct this disparity.

The *cerebral cortex* starts out as a relatively uniform, undifferentiated sheet of cells. During the course of brain development, the brain is progressively subdivided into multiple structurally and functionally distinct areas, within which are modules specialized for processing particular subclasses of information handled by that cortical area. This process is called the development of *areal fate,* or *arealization.*

Although it has been clear for centuries that the cortex exhibits this *regionalization of function*, there is still much disagreement over the mechanism(s) responsible for the arealization process. The question can be asked whether *visual cortex* is visual simply because it's hooked up to the eyes, or whether it is hooked up to the eyes because it's pre-defined, perhaps genetically, as visual. If the eyes could be surgically redirected to the auditory pathway, would the *auditory cortex* be responsive to visual stimulation (James, 1890)? Would light then be perceived as sound? These questions can now be approached more directly using *gene expression* and *gene knockout* studies, and the *cross-modal re-wiring paradigm*.

GENE EXPRESSION STUDIES

There is a significant amount of intrinsic patterning information present in early cortex. Several genes are differentially expressed within the cortical epithelium in such a way that they might be in a position to influence or even control the fate, or "identity," of different cortical regions (Donoghue & Rakic, 1999a, 1999b; Dyck et al., 1998; Rubenstein et al., 1999; Sestan, Rakic, & Donoghue, 2001). Some exhibit a graded or region-specific pattern prior to and/or in the absence of thalamocortical innervation (Bishop, Goudreau, & O'Leary, 2000; Miyashita-Lin, Hevner, Wasserman, Martinez, & Rubenstein, 1999; Nakagawa, Johnson, & O'Leary, 1999). Proof that *areal fate* is under intrinsic, genetic control could be obtained if expression of distinct marker genes or proteins predicted the future boundaries of cortical areas. At the time of this writing, however, no naturally-occurring genes express only in one cortical area, although one experimentally-created *transgene* called *H2Z1* is restricted to presumptive *somatosensory cortex* (Cohen-Tannoudji, Babinet, & Wassef, 1994; Nothias, Fishell, & Ruiz i Altaba, 1998). Other markers show discontinuities in the region of presumptive areal boundaries (Sestan et al., 2001). An added difficulty is that much of the work in this area has been done with *gene knockout* methods.

Mice with knockout of the patterning genes thought to be involved in arealization generally die at birth, before cortical areas can be defined using anatomical or physiological methods and before cortical features such as cytoarchitecture, local connectivity, and circuit formation—the very features most typically thought of as defining cortical areal identity—can be examined. For example, two research groups have demonstrated that knockout of the *homeobox genes Pax6* and *Emx2* leads to a loss of expression of downstream genes that are usually restricted to those areas where the upstream genes are highly expressed (Bishop et al., 2000; Mallamaci, Muzio, Chan, Parnavelas, & Boncinelli, 2000). If the downstream genes are in fact defining the boundaries of specific cortical areas, then the knockout results would be convincing evidence that the genes specify areal identity, but so far this has not been demonstrated. If the *gene expression patterns* specify *areal identity*, they may pre-specify other aspects of cortical organization as well, possibly reducing the opportunity for clinical intervention in cases of perinatal brain damage and without employment of gene manipulation strategies. Alternatively, perhaps the role of the marker *gene gradients* is simply to direct the proper sensory afferents to innervate individual areas, after which those afferents and their activity patterns can direct further cortical differentiation. Many studies have shown the specific, targeted nature of the *thalamocortical projections* (e.g., Crandall & Caviness, 1984; Ghosh, Antonini, McConnell, & Shatz, 1990; Miller, Windrem, & Finlay, 1991).

Perhaps the most convincing evidence that levels of expression of *morphogens* can control cortical fate comes from an elegant study by Elizabeth Grove and colleagues (Fukuchi-Shimogori & Grove, 2001). The authors of this study employed the *gene electroporation technique* in mice to "knock-in" a high concentration of *fibroblast growth factor 8* (FGF8) in a location rostral to its normal region of high expression in the somatosensory whisker "barrel" cortex. Remarkably, the new FGF8 region exhibited morphological characteristics of the *barrel cortex*, suggesting that a second barrel cortex had been induced to form. It will be both necessary and fascinating to find out whether the putative second barrel cortex forms as a result of anomalous somatosensory thalamic innervation induced by the FGF8 expression.

The picture painted by these gene expression studies suggests a hardwired, unchanging cortex pre-specified by genetic "blueprints." However, the cortex is a very plastic brain structure, even into adulthood, and is tremendously responsive to changing environmental conditions and new information. The evolution of the cerebral cortex has resulted in more individual areas containing increasingly specialized processing circuits, which are correlated with the learning capacity of the animal (Darlington, Dunlop, & Finlay, 1999; Finlay & Darlington, 1995; Kaas, 1995). Anatomical and physiological studies suggest that an important role of the mammalian cerebral cortex is to allow the animal to adapt to its environment through learning.

If this were the case, then it would seem that the cortex should develop in such a way that its circuits are not pre-specified beyond a bare bones scaffold, so that the environment could maximally shape the outcome of circuit-building processes. The possibility that developmental patterns established through gene expression can then be altered by sensory activity has not been well-explored and would be of great interest.

SENSORY MANIPULATION STUDIES

Electrical activity communicated via synapses can alter the location, number, and strength of synaptic connections between neurons. In adults, *long-term potentiation* (LTP) and its correlate *long-term depression* (LTD) are activity-dependent processes that influence synaptic strength through N-methyl-D-aspartate (NMDA) receptor function or other calcium-dependent processes, in turn triggering a signal cascade that signals the pre-synaptic cell to change its connection efficacy (Malinow & Malenka, 2002), or even to form new synapses (Nudo, 1999; Pons et al., 1991; Trachtenberg et al., 2002; but see Grutzendler, Kasthuri, & Gan, 2002). In young brains, a similar mechanism may be at work (Constantine-Paton & Cline, 1998), but perhaps with greater effect, given the increased malleability of circuits at earlier stages. Early experiences can also facilitate later learning, forming a "memory trace" in the brain that can be reactivated with repeated exposure to specific experiences (Knudsen, Zheng, & DeBello, 2000; Linkenhoker & Knudsen, 2002). There may also be additional activity-dependent mechanisms for synapse formation and plasticity in young brains that cease to operate with age. Thus, neuronal activity can profoundly influence cortical development at time-points after genetic "blueprints" have had their main effects.

Intrinsic Activity

How and at what point does sensory experience influence cerebral cortical development? Can it instruct the presumptive cortex how to develop and define itself? One seemingly obvious limitation is that sense organs cannot drive cortical activity until they are functional, and their respective *thalamocortical pathways* are established. Despite the lack of sensory organ input to the early fetal brain, however, neuronal activity from the sense organs and elsewhere does influence the early brain. Neurons within the sensory pathways are spontaneously active, and this intrinsic, *spontaneous neuronal activity* is necessary for the development of proper cortical function.

With respect to the *visual system*, the *retina, lateral geniculate nucleus,* and *visual cortex* have all been shown to produce waves of coordinated, spontaneous action potentials (Chiu & Weliky, 2001; Weliky & Katz, 1999; Wong, Meister, & Shatz, 1993). Because the spatiotemporal pattern of these potentials mimics the pattern of natural stimulation to a considerable extent, it is thought that they may be used by the brain to prime the formation of sensory circuits before the sense organs can drive the cortex (Mooney, Penn, Gallego, & Shatz, 1996; Penn, Riquelme, & Shatz, 1998; Penn & Shatz, 1999; Shatz, 1994; Wong & Oakley, 1996; see Wong, 1999, for review).

The sensory cortex is characterized by its *modular organization.* In the *visual cortex,* modules code for motion, color, and binocular depth of visual stimuli; whereas in the *auditory cortex,* modules code for sound frequency, intensity, and location, among other aspects. *Spontaneous activity* appears to be necessary for guiding the brain through development. Activity blockade during the generation of spontaneous activity can negatively affect development of modules at many levels of the visual system, beyond the effects produced by *visual deprivation* or even removal of the eyes (Mooney et al., 1996; Penn et al., 1998; Ruthazer & Stryker, 1996). Spontaneous activity cannot cause the brain to adapt to abnormal environmental conditions because it is ignorant of the world outside, but it seems possible that patterns of spontaneous activity could be clinically manipulated in order to produce a particular therapeutic outcome.

Extrinsic Activity

Stimulation of the sensory organs is necessary for plasticity, as well as for the final aspects of normal cortical development. Extrinsically-driven activity from sensory organs can support and maintain typical development. Unlike spontaneous activity, sensory stimulation can also induce plastic changes that allow the brain to reflect the pattern of sensory stimulation within a *critical period* of development. The following section discusses the experimental evidence for these statements.

The ability of the fetus to make use of sensory stimuli depends first on the developmental state of the sensory organs. In humans, the *eyes* do not open until late in the second trimester. At this point, the fetus or *preterm infant* can exhibit crude avoidance responses to bright light presented through the uterine wall, mediated by midbrain and not *thalamocortical circuits* (Dubowitz, Dubowitz, Morante, & Verghote, 1980; Johnson, 1990). Even after birth, the image-forming ability of the infant eye is poor. *Color vision,* binocular *depth perception,* and maximal *acuity* mature much later: not until six months after birth (Dobson & Teller, 1978; Held, 1993; Teller & Bornstein, 1987). The newborn human is much more capable of discriminating sound stimuli than light stimuli. The *cochlea* becomes capable of transducing sound waves at eighteen weeks' gestation (Lavigne-Rebillard & Pujol, 1990; Pujol & Lavigne-Rebillard, 1995; see Fernald, 2001, for review). The ability of the fetus to be influenced by sound is not only a popular legend but has a clear scientific basis (Rauscher & Shaw, 1998; but see Steele, Brown, & Stoecker, 1999), even to the extent that a fetus and newborn can differentiate pitch and maternal vocalizations (DeCasper, Lecanuet, Busnel, Granier-Deferre, & Maugeais, 1994; Fernald & Simon, 1984).

Even after the *thalamocortical circuit* is formed, the amount of sensory stimulation that can reach the fetal cerebral cortex is limited, especially in the case of visual stimuli. Because the human fetus resides in the womb after the sensory organs become functional, the visual system necessarily lags behind in development of sensory-driven organization. Auditory stimuli have a greater opportunity to influence brain development *in utero.* The dark, cushioned environment of the womb filters out all but the brightest of light stimuli, but a wide variety of sound stimuli, particularly mid- and low-frequency sounds and the voice of the mother, can permeate the uterine membranes and reach the fetus (DeCasper et al., 1994; Hepper & Shahidullah, 1994). The *ear canal* is filled with fluid *in utero,* however, and because it is designed to work in air, sounds must be loud to be detected, therefore limiting the opportunity for auditory influences on cortical development. How do these differing levels of access affect the development of the two systems? Surprisingly, in regards to the cellular maturation of cerebral cortex and projection pathways, the visual and auditory systems develop in a nearly parallel fashion (Bayer & Altman, 1991; Gao, Newman, Wormington, & Pallas, 1999; Gao, Wormington, Newman, & Pallas, 2000; Marin-Padilla, 1988; Payne, Pearson, & Cornwell, 1988), which suggests that this aspect of development is activity-independent or controlled by spontaneous activity—not by sensory experience. However, the synaptic circuitry responsible for *stimulus recognition* requires experience to mature and may develop faster in the auditory pathway because of its earlier access to extrinsic stimulation.

Once the sensory pathway is complete, how does sensory experience influence cortical development? The answer to this question remains elusive, and the interpretation of the data gathered so far has generated substantial controversy. As stated above, the preponderance of evidence suggests that spontaneous activity can form only crude circuits, which must later be refined by external sensory cues (see Katz & Shatz, 1996; Ruthazer & Stryker, 1996; Sengpiel et al., 1998, for review). But the question of which aspects of cortical fate develop under the influence of spontaneous activity, and which aspects require extrinsic, sensory influence has not been resolved.

Sensory Deprivation Studies

Many of the studies addressing the role of sensory experience in the maturation of cortical circuits have been done in the visual pathway using *sensory deprivation*. Sensory deprivation resulting from *cataracts, amblyopia, strabismus,* or similar visual disorders in infancy can have permanent negative consequences, particularly for *acuity* and *depth perception.* The experimental model of choice for investigating possible treatments has been the development and plasticity of the *ocular dominance columns* in layer 4 of visual cortex (Daw, 2003). In adult mammals with frontally placed eyes, such as primates and carnivores, the terminals from left-eye and right-eye neurons in the visual thalamus (LGN) project in segregated fashion to layer 4, forming alternating columns or patches of cortical neurons with right- or left-eye input (see Sherman & Spear, 1982, for review). Wiesel and Hubel show that this state of affairs depends on a balance in activity between the two eyes: *monocular deprivation* during development allows the open eye to "capture" more brain territory, resulting in a shift toward wider open-eye than closed-eye columns and an absence of physiological responses to stimulation of the eye that was closed (Wiesel & Hubel, 1963, 1965; see Katz & Crowley, 2002, for review). Using transneuronal tracers, it was demonstrated that these cortical eye-specific columns form slowly during development, suggesting that balanced neuronal activity from the two eyes leads to their segregation through *activity-dependent stabilization* of coactive synapses, also termed "Hebbian learning" (LeVay, Stryker, & Shatz, 1978; Shatz & Stryker, 1978). Supporting this idea is the observation that blockade of neuronal activity (Stryker & Harris, 1986) leads to an absence of columns in adults. *Activity blockade* also prevents the deprivation-induced ocular dominance shift, as does blockade of the NMDA-type of glutamate receptor (Kleinschmidt, Bear, & Singer, 1987; Rauschecker, Egert, & Kossel, 1990; Roberts, Meredith, & Ramoa, 1998). Together, these results established the theory that ocular dominance column formation and plasticity depend on retinal activity.

Recently, a surprising result has raised questions about this theory. Crowley and colleagues, using ferrets as a model system, have found that *ocular dominance columns* still form in the visual cortex in the absence of the eyes. It is currently unknown whether spontaneous activity in thalamus or cortex is necessary to form the columns (Crowley & Katz, 1999, 2000; Katz & Crowley, 2002). This work and other studies show that the columns can form without sensory activity, but that functional retinal input to the pathway is required for maintenance and plasticity of the columns (Chapman, 2000; Crair, Horton, Antonini, & Stryker, 2001). Thus, despite over forty years of work, the role of activity in the development of ocular dominance columns is still controversial.

Cross-Modal Plasticity

The sensory deprivation studies described above can reveal whether activity is needed for cortical development at all, but not whether the type of activity is important or how it exerts its effects. In fact, the role of the type (modality) of sensory input on cortical development and patterning is also controversial. One way to ascertain the role of sensory activity in cortical patterning is by changing the type of activity by *cross-modal re-wiring* of *thalamocortical pathways*. Some interpretations of the *genetic pre-specification* model would predict that cortical fate should remain unaltered in certain critical respects by changing afferent input. Alternatively, an *extrinsic specification* model predicts that changing the modality of input would change cortical areal identity. A *balanced hypothesis* would suggest that molecular markers guide the appropriate thalamic nuclei to their normal targets, after which the spatiotemporal neuronal activity pattern carried by the thalamic axons determines the activity-dependent aspects of areal fate. In fact, the target specificity of *thalamocortical projections* is high, and the failure of most attempts to perturb it (Crandall & Caviness, 1984; Miller, Chou, & Findlay, 1993; Miller et al., 1991) supports the notion of pre-specification. On the other hand, the extreme plasticity exhibited by sensory cortex, even into adulthood (Jain, Florence, & Kaas, 2000; Pons et al., 1991) suggests that activity-driven factors are an essential aspect of cortical organization.

One way to induce a deliberate mismatch in modality of thalamic inputs and cortical targets is by *transplantation* of a cortical anlage from one area to a different location, where it will receive different thalamocortical afferents (TCAs) (see O'Leary, Schlaggar, & Tuttle, 1994, for review). Implantation of a small portion of presumptive visual cortex from late fetal donor rats into the location of presumptive somatomotor cortex in newborn host rats causes the donor visual cortex to develop the projections and modular organization characteristic of somatosensory cortex (Schlaggar & O'Leary, 1991; Stanfield & O'Leary, 1985), suggesting that cortical fate is determined by the type of TCAs it receives or by some other factor in the host environment. However, another group has found an opposite result; that the donor largely retains its original fate with respect to both modular organization and TCA innervation (Frappe, Roger, & Gaillard, 1999; Gaillard & Roger, 2000). The different results cannot be explained by differing ages of transplantation, but may be due to differences in transplant technique—particularly whether the transplant includes any part of the sub-plate region that is subjacent to the cortical plate. In any case, a drawback of these transplantation studies is that it is indeterminable whether the change in thalamocortical inputs or any of the factors present in the host area are the causative factor in any potential changes in cortical areal fate of donor tissue.

As shown in Figure 1.1, another way to accomplish *cross-modal rewiring* is by re-routing sensory axons to different thalamic nuclei, which in turn carry the new information to their usual cortical targets (Frost, 1999; Schneider, 1973; see Pallas, 2001, for review). The advantage of this approach is that the modality and spatiotemporal pattern of activity is being changed, but the identity of TCAs and host cortical tissue is not. In *hamsters*, an altricial rodent species, re-routing of retinal axons to *somatosensory thalamus* (VB) results in activation of the somatosensory cortex by light (Métin & Frost, 1989). In *ferrets*, an altricial carnivore with a gyrencephalic (fissured) cortex, re-routing of retinal axons to the *auditory thalamus* (MGN) allows the *primary auditory cortex* (A1) to respond to moving, oriented bars of light with similar tuning as in *visual cortex* (Roe, Pallas, Hahm, & Sur, 1990; Roe, Pallas, Kwon, & Sur, 1992; Sur, Garraghty, & Roe, 1988; see Pallas, 2001, for review). One question that has been subsequently addressed is whether the new input activity patterns cause a re-specification of areal fate, or whether they are taking advantage of existing, pre-specified circuits in the cross-modally rewired cortex.

NORMAL   X-MODAL

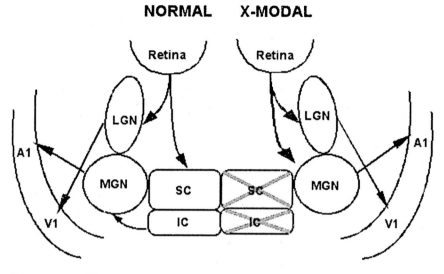

Figure 1.1. The surgery necessary to generate cross-modal plasticity is depicted. Neonatal ablation of the superior colliculus (SC) eliminates one retinal target. The other main target, the lateral geniculate nucleus (LGN), is left intact. The LGN in turn projects to the primary visual area of the cerebral cortex (V1). Ablation of the inferior colliculus (IC) eliminates the primary input to the auditory thalamic nucleus (medial geniculate [MGN]). The target-seeking behavior of the retinal axons leads them to the newly deafferented MGN, which in turn is in need of inputs. This re-routing results in an auditory thalamus that relays visual information to primary auditory cortex (A1).

The use of the altricial hamster and ferret species allows the manipulation of sensory pathways prior to their final establishment. At the developmental stage when the re-wiring procedure is carried out, thalamic axons are only beginning to innervate cortex, and the layer 4 cortical cells that will receive their input are still migrating into position. The *eyes* and *ears* are closed at birth. Ferrets are not capable of sight or hearing until one month after birth, making them an ideal model system for studies of early brain development.

Plasticity of retinal projections. Not all retinal ganglion cells are participating in the cross-modal innervation of the *thalamus*; rather it is specifically the *W class* of *ganglion cells* that are exhibiting the plasticity (Bhide & Frost, 1992; Roe, Garraghty, Esguerra, & Sur, 1993). In addition to innervating somatosensory or auditory thalamus in cross-modal hamsters and ferrets (Angelucci, Clascá, Bricolo, Cramer, & Sur,

1997; Bhide & Frost, 1999; Métin, Irons, & Frost, 1995; Pallas, Hahm, & Sur, 1994; Pallas & Sur, 1994; Roe et al., 1993), *retinal axons* are also present in the *auditory thalamus* of early deafened ferrets (Pallas & Moore, 1997), despite the fact that there are multiple synapses intervening between the cochlea and the MGN. Thus, *retinal plasticity* can be induced even when retina itself has not been target-deprived, providing another pathway for cross-modal plasticity.

Thalamocortical pathways. The spatial pattern of *thalamocortical projections* into normal *A1* is characteristically 1-D in that a sheet of axons from *MGN* projects into a slab of layer 4 target neurons in A1. This organization is reflective of the frequency-mapped *tonotopic organization* of *A1*. In *ferrets*, neurons in medial A1 are tuned to high frequencies, whereas low frequencies are represented by neurons in lateral A1 (Kelly, Judge, & Phillips, 1986). Orthogonal to the tonotopic axis is the isofrequency axis, where all neurons within a rostrocaudally-extending slab of cortical neurons are tuned to a similar frequency range. This arrangement contrasts with the 2-D organization of visual space in *V1*. The 1-D thalamocortical projection pattern of the auditory pathway is maintained in the cross-modal ferrets; the thalamocortical pathway is not converted to a 2-D organization as a result of its 2-D visual input (Pallas, Roe, & Sur, 1990). Thus, it would seem unlikely that cross-modal A1 could represent 2-D visual spatial information.

Topography in A1. Surprisingly, a 2-D map of visual space is formed in *A1* of cross-modal ferrets (Roe et al., 1990). *Visual elevation* is mapped along the tonotopic axis, whereas *visual azimuth* is mapped along the rostrocaudal, isofrequency axis. The elevational map always expresses the same polarity, but the azimuthal map can differ in polarity from one animal to the next, suggesting that an activity-dependent and somewhat random process controls its polarity. Although it appears that the second dimension does not arise by altering thalamocortical projection patterns, it may occur through any one or more of several other changes to the circuitry. It is possible that there are physiological or anatomical alterations within cortex that either suppress or enhance certain inputs in order to recreate the retinal topography in A1. Our preliminary data show that there are alterations in inhibitory circuitry intrinsic to A1 that may shape the topographic representation of visual space in auditory cortex. Further work is needed to investigate whether such alterations bear any responsibility for the changes in topography.

Response properties. Neurons in the *sensory cortex* are commonly defined by the type of stimulus they prefer. When comparing stimulus tuning of neurons in visual, somatosensory, and auditory cortices, both similarities and differences can be noted. For example, the visual, somatosensory, and auditory cortex contain neurons sensitive to the direction and rate of movement of a stimulus. However, many visual and somatosensory stimuli have 2-D spatial aspects that can be recognized and coded by visually-responsive neurons. For example, *V1 neurons* are sensitive to the orientation of a bar of light, and have simple or complex spatial substructures to their receptive fields. *A1 neurons* cannot directly exhibit such 2-D response properties, because A1 is activated during stimulation of the *cochlea* by sounds of particular frequencies, and frequency is a 1-D physical construct. However, in cross-modal *ferrets*, visual stimuli are coded by the cross-modal A1 with respect to their 2-D characteristics: *cross-modal A1 neurons* can be orientation selective and have simple or complex receptive fields (Roe et al., 1992).

The ability of auditory cortical neurons to code visual stimuli in an apparently normal fashion is remarkable and suggests that either the stimulus encoding circuitry is similar between the two cortical areas, or that the visual inputs reorganize A1's circuitry for visual object discrimination. The presence of visual circuits cannot be explained by the re-routing of extraneous visual inputs to AI as a by-product of the re-wiring surgery, other than those induced through *MGN* (Pallas et al., 1990; Pallas & Sur, 1993). MGN does not contain orientation-tuned or simple/complex receptive fields (Roe et al., 1993) and cannot provide these properties. In cross-modal *hamsters*, direction- and orientation-tuned neurons were found in similar proportions and tuning strength as in normal S1 (Métin & Frost, 1989), suggesting that similar processes may be at work in the two species.

Modular connectivity patterns. Neurons with similar stimulus preferences are often located close together spatially or are interconnected if they are in different spatial locations. Aspects of stimuli that are arranged in this modular fashion in the *visual cortex* include orientation, color, motion, and binocularity (Bartfeld & Grinvald, 1992; Daw, 1998; LeVay et al., 1978; Livingstone & Hubel, 1988). Modules in *auditory cortex* include frequency (Kelly et al., 1986; Reale & Imig, 1980) and sound location via binaural cues (Imig, Reale, Brugge, Morel, & Adrian, 1986; Kelly & Judge, 1994; Middlebrooks, Dykes, & Merzenich, 1980). In normal auditory cortex, interhemispheric (callosal) connections unite neurons with the same binaural coding characteristics along the sound frequency map (tonotopic) axis, and intracortical (horizontal) connections interconnect neurons with similar frequency tuning along the opposite anteroposterior, constant (iso-) frequency axis (Imig et al., 1986). In the normal visual cortex, neurons with similar orientation tuning are interconnected in a clustered, radial fashion from any one location (Callaway & Katz, 1990). These specific connectivity patterns arise gradually during development, under the influence of activity (Callaway & Katz, 1990; Feng & Brugge, 1983; Innocenti, Fiore, & Caminiti, 1977; Innocenti & Frost, 1979).

We examined the effect of cross-modal re-wiring of visual input on the modular connectivity pattern in the *auditory cortex* by injecting neuroanatomical tracers. What we found was a striking alteration in the pattern. Both callosal (Pallas, Littman, & Moore, 1999) and horizontal (Gao & Pallas, 1999; Sharma, Angelucci, & Sur, 2000) connections in cross-modal A1 differed substantially from normal. Rather than being organized along the tonotopic and isofrequency axes, respectively, the pattern was much more symmetrical and consisted of clusters or patches as in the visual system, instead of the elongated banded pattern typical of A1 with its usual auditory input. The altered pattern was not a result of *deafferentation*; in fact, in early-deafened animals, both callosal and horizontal projections were diffuse and unorganized (Gao, Moore, & Pallas, 1999; see Pallas, 2001, for review; Pallas et al., 1999), beyond what is seen at any developmental age (Feng & Brugge, 1983; Moerschel & Pallas, 2001).

Interestingly, the callosal and horizontal projection patterns revealed by the tracers seemed complementary: the callosally-projecting axons extended more laterally than normal, whereas the horizontally-projecting axons projected more medially. Because the animals used for these tracer injection studies were "re-wired" on only one side of the brain, we hypothesize that *callosally-projecting axons* are communicating between auditory neurons on both sides of the brain, whereas the *ipsilateral horizontally-projecting neurons* may be involved in organizing visual response properties. In this case, it would be conceivable that the early re-wiring manipulation is actually creating a new, visual cortical area and pushing the auditory area laterally. Alternatively, it is possible that A1 comes to represent both auditory and visual information, although it is difficult to imagine how a 1-D map of sound frequency could coexist with a 2-D map of visual space on the same cortical surface. Rather than bimodal neurons, there may be parcellation of A1 into islands of visual and auditory responsiveness, creating a fractured map such as is seen in mammalian *cerebellar cortex* (Gonzalez, Shumway, Morissette, & Bower,

1993) and the electrosensory system of South American electric fish (Shumway, 1989). Multimodal mapping experiments are currently underway to test these hypotheses. At any rate, the alterations in connectivity of A1 as a result of early, anomalous visual input suggest strongly that brain circuitry is dependent on the spatiotemporal pattern of early, extrinsic activity for its organizing principles, and that the genetic identity of the thalamocortical inputs or the cortical target plays a more limited role than might be expected from gene expression studies.

Inhibitory circuitry. Although the altered connectivity patterns described in the previous section may play a role in organizing visual response properties in the cross-modal A1, we have suggested that this is a result, not a cause, of the driving force behind the construction of 2-D visual response properties (Pallas, 2002). This suggestion derives from data showing that topographic mapping processes are largely activity-independent, and that stimulus tuning can be disrupted without affecting map topography (e.g. Friesen et al., 1998; Huang & Pallas, 2001; Razak, Huang, & Pallas, 2003; Weliky & Katz, 1997). One way to create the second map dimension would be to differentially suppress some of the overlapped thalamocortical inputs using retinal activity as a guiding force. *GABA* is already known to be important in shaping receptive field properties in the *visual cortex* (Allison, Kabara, Snider, Casagrande, & Bonds, 1996; Berman, Douglas, & Martin, 1992; Crook & Eysel, 1992; Crook, Kisvárday, & Eysel, 1996, 1997, 1998; Das & Gilbert, 1999; Ferster & Miller, 2000; Sato, Katsuyama, Tamura, Hata, & Tsumoto, 1995, 1996; Sillito, 1975a, 1975b). GABA regulation is also important for *activity-dependent developmental plasticity* late in development (Hensch et al., 1998; Rutherford, DeWan, Lauer, & Turrigiano, 1997; Zheng & Knudsen, 1999). Thus, it seemed a reasonable hypothesis that inhibition is involved in constructing visual response properties in the cross-modal auditory cortex. In order to explore whether visual responses in the *cross-modal A1* might be shaped by inhibitory circuitry, we examined the distribution of $GABA_A$ receptors and the distribution and morphology of different classes of *non-pyramidal GABAergic interneurons*, specifically neurons containing the calcium-binding proteins parvalbumin and calbindin (Gonchar & Burkhalter, 1997; Hendry & Jones, 1991) in cross-modal A1, and compared them to the same two classes of interneurons in normal A1 and V1.

What we found was that although receptor distributions were unchanged in adults, both the parvalbumin-containing and the calbindin-containing subclasses of GABAergic interneurons had alterations in morphology. The calbindin neurons in particular showed an increase in density and a change in both morphology and laminar distribution (Gao, Newman, et al., 1999; Gao et al., 2000; see Pallas, 2001, for review; Pallas, Booth, & Cynader, 1994). Normally these neurons are restricted to upper and lower layers of cortex and have a "double bouquet" shape of dendritic arborization, elaborating processes vertically within a cortical column (Peters & Jones, 1984). In the *cross-modal A1*, however, they are found in middle cortical layers as well, and some have arborizations that extend widely across columns. It is possible that these cells can gather information from across the isofrequency laminae, where they would be in a position to extract the second dimension of the visual map by suppressing overlapped thalamic inputs. We are currently testing this hypothesis using both anatomical and physiological methods.

Behavior. Given that visual inputs reach and activate the auditory cortex in the cross-modal *ferrets*, and that representation of the visual input is fairly normal, can the ferrets now "hear the lightning" (Swindale, 2000)? Given the dogma that sensory pathways are labeled lines, and that the percept associated with neuronal activity is determined by the label, we expected that any activity occurring in *auditory cortex* would be interpreted by the animal as auditory. However, the opposite was found (von Melchner, Pallas, & Sur, 2000; see also Merzenich, 2000). When unilaterally lesioned animals were trained in a forced-choice paradigm to discriminate light from sound stimuli using their "normal" brain hemisphere, and then tested with stimulation of the cross-modal hemisphere, they reported that light is light, even when viewed through the auditory cortex. This percept persisted when all remaining sub-cortical visual structures were ablated but disappeared when A1 was ablated. Thus, apparently the animals learn to associate a visual percept with the electrical activity in the cross-modal auditory cortex. This result is particularly surprising in light of our report that there are no A1-to-visual cortex connections induced by the manipulation; rather, A1 remains connected to other auditory structures (Pallas et al., 1990; Pallas & Sur, 1993).

This collection of results strongly supports the contention that activity patterns of cortical afferents are conveying instructions to the *sensory cortex* and are not simply acting in a permissive fashion. So does this mean that the visual activity has changed the cortical identity of A1? And if so, what is the role of intrinsic molecular signals? Cortical identity should not be thought of as a single decision; rather, there are multiple decisions made along the developmental signaling cascade that individually specify a different aspect of structure and function. A reasonable view is that intrinsic factors specify positional information or general cell identity cues that help to guide thalamo-cortical innervation; and extrinsic, activity-dependent factors, including patterned spontaneous activity, allow the cortex to develop in a way that is responsive to the environment, even to the point of reversing specification events that occurred earlier in development.

Sensory Substitution Studies

In addition to the ability of sensory cortical areas to respond to stimuli of other modalities as a result of deliberate cross-modal re-wiring, several studies have shown that *sensory deprivation* can also induce cross-modal alterations in cortical activation. This phenomenon is known as *sensory substitution,* and it has been demonstrated in animal studies in both a developmental and evolutionary context and in clinical studies using blind or deaf individuals (see Bavelier & Neville, 2002, for review).

Certain species of animals show an evolutionary reduction in a particular sensory modality. For example, in the *burrowing mole rat (Spalax ehrenbergi)*, the eyes are much reduced and are insensitive to light, and the animals communicate through vibratory and auditory signals. It has been demonstrated that the visual pathways in these animals are colonized by auditory inputs (Bronchti et al., 2002; Doron & Wollberg, 1994; Heil, Bronchti, Wollberg, & Scheich, 1991; Yaka, Yinon, & Wollberg, 1999). In congenitally deaf *cats* or cats subjected to *cochlear ablation* within a critical period, *A1* exhibits visual responses (Rebillard, Carlier, Rebillard, & Pujol, 1977). Similarly, bilateral cochlear ablation early in development in ferrets results in anomalous projections from retina to auditory thalamus (Pallas & Moore, 1997).

Our recent results show that there can also be innervation of a deafened auditory cortex by the *visual thalamus* (LGN) (Pallas, Razak, & Moore, 2002), providing a second pathway whereby visual information can reach the auditory cortex in deafened ferrets, in addition to the retino-MGN pathway. This is a surprising and important result because it counters the idea that thalamocortical projections are genetically pre-specified and raises the possibility that some aspects of cortical identity, including *thalamocortical targeting,* can be specified by extrinsic factors. It is not yet clear whether the visual-to-auditory projections in deaf animals are functional.

Krubitzer and colleagues have recently re-examined the effects of early bilateral enucleation on cortical parcellation in a marsupial rodent (Kahn & Krubitzer, 2002). Rakic and colleagues had argued (Rakic, 1988) that prenatal enucleation in macaque monkeys resulted in a new, cytoarchitecturally-defined "Area X" in the occipital cortex. Without investigating the anatomy and physiology of the purported new area, however, the results could be explained by the predicted increased *cell death* in cortical layer 4 following *deafferentation* (Finlay & Slattery, 1983). Krubitzer shows that the new Area X can be driven by auditory and somatosensory inputs, providing another piece of evidence for re-specification. This is consistent with our prediction that *A1* in cross-modal *ferrets* is subdivided into auditory and visual cortical regions with different organizational characteristics.

The animal studies on *sensory substitution* have correlates in clinical studies. In blind and deaf patients, the affected cortical area can be driven by other sensory modalities, resulting in increased ability in the other modality compared to normal, as measured psychophysically and with brain imaging methods (see Bavelier & Neville, 2002, for review). The extent of re-organization is largely dependent on the age at which the sensory deficit occurred.

CONCLUSIONS

The results from the animal and human studies discussed in this chapter demonstrate the remarkable power of the sensory environment to direct brain development, and to shape circuits in response to rearing or *in utero* conditions. But how are these data to be integrated with the data on genetic specification of cortex? What the collection of results suggests is that the immature brain is genetically influenced to develop in the way that has been predicted by its evolutionary history. Neuronal activity is not required for this aspect of development, except perhaps in a permissive way (Crair, 1999). Evidence that activity is unnecessary for setting up normal modular organization remains controversial and is difficult to incorporate into current thinking, although it is agreed that activity is required for the maintenance of patterns initially set up by early genetic instructions (Chapman, 2000). It is clear that the brain is exquisitely sensitive to unexpected stimulation patterns. Those patterns that could not have been predicted by evolution, and which must be perceived and acted upon by the animal for its survival and reproductive fitness, depend on *activity-dependent processes* to become represented, either structurally or functionally, in brain circuitry. Furthermore, specification events that are under intrinsic control initially may be modifiable or reversible at later stages by extrinsic information.

Are cortical areas interchangeable if one is damaged or deafferented during development? Our evidence and that of others suggests that appropriate stimulation, either from sensory organs or conceivably from electrical stimulation, can re-configure cortical circuits to a remarkable extent, even leading to behaviorally relevant responses in the substitute modality. Although it is not presently understood exactly when such stimulation would have to occur in human infants in order to be clinically relevant, such information should be easily obtainable by outlining the relevant *critical periods* in animal models, and then extrapolating to the timetable for human brain development (Clancy et al., 2001). We may then be in a position to offer therapy for brain injuries that occur during early development by "teaching" the remaining cortical tissue how to substitute for the damaged regions.

REFERENCES

Allison, J.D., Kabara, J.F., Snider, R.K., Casagrande, V.A., & Bonds, A.B. (1996). GABA$_B$-receptor mediated inhibition reduces the orientation selectivity of the sustained response of striate cortical neurons in cats. *Visual Neuroscience, 13*, 559–566.

Angelucci, A., Clascá, F., Bricolo, E., Cramer, K.S., & Sur, M. (1997). Experimentally induced retinal projections to the ferret auditory thalamus: Development of clustered eye-specific patterns in a novel target. *Journal of Neuroscience, 17*, 2040–2055.

Bartfeld, E., & Grinvald, A. (1992). Relationships between orientation-preference pinwheels, cytochrome oxidase blobs, and ocular dominance columns in primate striate cortex. *Proceedings of the National Academy of Sciences, USA, 89*, 11905–11909.

Bavelier, D., & Neville, H.J. (2002). Cross-modal plasticity: where and how? *Nature Reviews Neuroscience, 3*, 443–452.

Bayer, S.A., & Altman, J. (1991). *Neocortical development.* New York: Raven Press.

Berman, N.J., Douglas, R.J., & Martin, K.A.C. (1992). GABA-mediated inhibition in the neural networks of visual cortex. In R.R. Mize, R.E. Marc, & A.M. Sillito (Eds.), *Progress in brain research* (Vol. 90, pp. 443–476). New York: Elsevier.

Bhide, P.G., & Frost, D.O. (1992). Axon substitution in the reorganization of developing neural connections. *Proceedings of the National Academy of Sciences, USA, 89*, 11847–11851.

Bhide, P.G., & Frost, D.O. (1999). Intrinsic determinants of retinal axon collateralization and arborization patterns. *Journal of Comparative Neurology, 411,* 119–129.

Bishop, K.M., Goudreau, G., & O'Leary, D.D.M. (2000). Regulation of area identity on the mammalian neocortex by Emx2 and Pax6. *Science, 288,* 344–349.

Bronchti, G., Heil, P., Sadka, R., Hess, A., Scheich, H., & Wollberg, Z. (2002). Auditory activation of "visual" cortical areas in the blind mole rat (*Spalax ehrenbergi*). *Journal of Comparative Neurology, 16,* 311–329.

Bruer, J.T. (1999). *The myth of the first three years: A new understanding of early brain development and lifelong learning.* New York: Free Press.

Callaway, E.M., & Katz, L.C. (1990). Emergence and refinement of clustered horizontal connections in cat striate cortex. *Journal of Neuroscience, 10,* 1134–1153.

Chapman, B. (2000). Necessity for afferent activity to maintain eye-specific segregation in ferret lateral geniculate nucleus. *Science, 287,* 2479–2482.

Chiu, C., & Weliky, M. (2001). Spontaneous activity in developing ferret visual cortex in vivo. *Journal of Neuroscience, 21,* 8906–8914.

Clancy, B., Darlington, R.B., & Finlay, B.L. (2001). Translating developmental time across species. *Neuroscience, 105,* 7–17.

Cohen-Tannoudji, M., Babinet, C., & Wassef, M. (1994). Early determination of a mouse somatosensory cortex marker. *Nature, 368,* 460–463.

Constantine-Paton, M., & Cline, H.T. (1998). LTP and activity-dependent synaptogenesis: the more alike they are, the more different they become. *Current Opinions in Neurobiology, 8,* 139–148.

Crair, M.C. (1999). Neuronal activity during development: permissive or instructive? *Current Opinions in Neurobiology, 9,* 88–99.

Crair, M.C., Horton, J. C., Antonini, A., & Stryker, M.P. (2001). Emergence of ocular dominance columns in cat visual cortex by 2 weeks of age. *Journal of Comparative Neurology, 430,* 235–249.

Crandall, J.E., & Caviness, V.S. (1984). Thalamocortical connections in newborn mice. *Journal of Comparative Neurology, 228,* 542–556.

Crook, J.M., & Eysel, U.T. (1992). GABA-induced inactivation of functionally characterized sites in cat visual cortex (area 18): Effects on orientation tuning. *Journal of Neuroscience, 12,* 1816–1825.

Crook, J.M., Kisvárday, Z.F., & Eysel, U.T. (1996). GABA-induced inactivation of functionally characterized sites in cat visual cortex (area 18): Effects on direction selectivity. *Journal of Neurophysiology, 75,* 2071–2088.

Crook, J.M., Kisvárday, Z.F., & Eysel, U.T. (1997). GABA-induced inactivation of functionally characterized sites in cat striate cortex: Effects on orientation tuning and direction selectivity. *Visual Neuroscience, 14,* 141–158.

Crook, J.M., Kisvárday, Z.F., & Eysel, U.T. (1998). Evidence for a contribution of lateral inhibition to orientation tuning and direction selectivity in cat visual cortex: Reversible inactivation of functionally characterized sites combined with neuroanatomical tracing techniques. *European Journal of Neuroscience, 10*, 2056–2075.

Crowley, J.C., & Katz, L.C. (1999). Development of ocular dominance columns in the absence of retinal input. *Nature Neuroscience, 2*, 1125–1130.

Crowley, J.C., & Katz, L.C. (2000). Early development of ocular dominance columns. *Science, 290*, 1321–1324.

Darlington, R.B., Dunlop, S.A., & Finlay, B.L. (1999). Neural development in metatherian and eutherian mammals: Variation and constraint. *Journal of Comparative Neurology, 411*, 359–368.

Das, A., & Gilbert, C.D. (1999). Topography of contextual modulations mediated by short-range interactions in primary visual cortex. *Nature, 399*, 655–661.

Daw, N.W. (1998). Neurobiology: Columns, slabs and pinwheels. *Nature, 395*, 20–21.

Daw, N.W. (2003). Critical periods in the visual system. In B. Hopkins & S.P. Johnson (Eds.), *Neurobiology of infant vision* (pp. 43–103). New York: Praeger.

DeCasper, A.J., Lecanuet, J.P., Busnel, M.C., Granier-Deferre, C., & Maugeais, R. (1994). Fetal reactions to recurrent maternal speech. *Infant Behavior and Development, 17*, 159–164.

Dobson, V., & Teller, D.Y. (1978). Visual acuity in human infants: A review and comparison of behavioral and electrophysiological studies. *Vision Research, 18*, 1469–1483.

Donoghue, M.J., & Rakic, P. (1999a). Molecular evidence for the early specification of presumptive functional domains in the embryonic primate cerebral cortex. *Journal of Neuroscience, 19*, 5967–5979.

Donoghue, M.J., & Rakic, P. (1999b). Molecular gradients and compartments in the embryonic primate cerebral cortex. *Cerebral Cortex, 9*, 586–600.

Doron, N., & Wollberg, Z. (1994). Cross-modal neuroplasticity in the blind mole rat Spalax ehrenbergi: A WGA-HRP tracing study. *NeuroReport, 5*, 2697–2701.

Dubowitz, L.M., Dubowitz, V., Morante, A., & Verghote, M. (1980). Visual function in the preterm and fullterm newborn infant. *Developmental Medicine and Child Neurology, 22*, 465–475.

Dyck, R.H., Richards, L.J., Akazawa, C., Contos, J.J.A., Chun, J., & O'Leary, D.D.M. (1998). Graded expression of Emx-1 and Emx-2 in developing rat cortex [Abstract]. *Society for Neuroscience Abstracts, 23*, 872.

Feng, J.Z., & Brugge, J.F. (1983). Postnatal development of auditory callosal connections in the kitten. *Journal of Comparative Neurology, 214*, 416–426.

Fernald, A. (2001). Hearing, listening, and understanding: Auditory development in infancy. In G. Bremner & A. Fogel (Eds.), *Blackwell handbook of infant development* (pp. 35–70). Oxford: Blackwell.

Fernald, A., & Simon, T. (1984). Expanded intonation contours in mothers' speech to newborns. *Developmental Psychology, 20,* 104–113.

Ferster, D., & Miller, K.D. (2000). Neural mechanisms of orientation selectivity in the visual cortex. *Annual Review of Neuroscience, 23,* 441–471.

Finlay, B.L., & Darlington, R.B. (1995). Linked regularities in the development and evolution of mammalian brains. *Science, 268,* 1578–1584.

Finlay, B.L., & Slattery, M. (1983). Local differences in the amount of early cell death in neocortex predict adult local specializations. *Science, 219,* 1349–1351.

Frappe, I., Roger, M., & Gaillard, A. (1999). Transplants of fetal frontal cortex grafted into the occipital cortex of newborn rats receive a substantial thalamic input from nuclei normally projecting to the frontal cortex. *Neuroscience, 89,* 409–421.

Friesen, J., Yates, P.A., McLaughlin, T., Friedman, G.C., O'Leary, D.D.M., & Barbacid, M. (1998). Ephrin A5 (AL-1/RAGS) is essential for proper retinal axon guidance and topographic mapping in the mammalian visual system. *Neuron, 20,* 235–243.

Frost, D.O. (1999). Functional organization of surgically created visual circuits. *Restorative Neurology and Neuroscience, 15,* 107–113.

Fukuchi-Shimogori, T., & Grove, E.A. (2001). Neocortex patterning by the secreted signaling molecule FGF8. *Science, 294,* 1071–1074.

Gaillard, A., & Roger, M. (2000). Early commitment of embryonic neocortical cells to develop area specific thalamic connections. *Cerebral Cortex, 10,* 443–453.

Gao, W.J., Moore, D.R., & Pallas, S.L. (1999). Bilateral cochlear ablation in neonatal ferrets prevents refinement of horizontal connectivity in primary auditory cortex [Abstract]. *Society for Neuroscience Abstracts, 25,* 1771.

Gao, W.J., Newman, D.E., Wormington, A.B., & Pallas, S.L. (1999). Development of inhibitory circuitry in visual and auditory cortex of postnatal ferrets: Immunocytochemical localization of GABAergic neurons. *Journal of Comparative Neurology, 409,* 261–273.

Gao, W.J., & Pallas, S.L. (1999). Cross-modal reorganization of horizontal connectivity in auditory cortex without altering thalamocortical projections. *Journal of Neuroscience, 19,* 7940–7950.

Gao, W.J., Wormington, A.B., Newman, D.E., & Pallas, S.L. (2000). Development of inhibitory circuitry in visual and auditory cortex of postnatal ferrets: immunocytochemical localization of calbindin and parvalbumin-containing neurons. *Journal of Comparative Neurology, 422,* 140–157.

Ghosh, A., Antonini, A., McConnell, S.K., & Shatz, C.J. (1990). Requirement for subplate neurons in the formation of thalamocortical connections. *Nature, 347,* 179–181.

Gonchar, Y., & Burkhalter, A. (1997). Three distinct families of GABAergic neurons in rat visual cortex. *Cereberal Cortex, 7,* 347–358.

Gonzalez, L., Shumway, C., Morissette, J., & Bower, J.M. (1993). Developmental plasticity in cerebellar tactile maps: Fractured maps retain a fractured organization. *Journal of Comparative Neurology, 332,* 487–498.

Gopnik, A., Meltzoff, A.N., Kuhl, P.K. (1999). *The scientist in the crib: Minds, brains, and how children learn.* New York: William Morrow.

Grutzendler, J., Kasthuri, N., & Gan, W.B. (2002). Long-term dendritic spine stability in the adult cortex. *Nature, 420,* 812–816.

Heil, P., Bronchti, G., Wollberg, Z., & Scheich, H. (1991). Invasion of visual cortex by the auditory system in the naturally blind mole rat. *NeuroReport, 2,* 735–738.

Held, R. (1993). Two stages in the development of binocular vision and eye alignment. In K. Simons (Ed.), *Early visual development: Normal and abnormal* (pp. 155–164). New York: Oxford University Press.

Hendry, S.H.C., & Jones, E.G. (1991). GABA neuronal subpopulations in cat primary auditory cortex: Co-localization with calcium binding proteins. *Brain Research, 543,* 45–55.

Hensch, T., Fagiolini, M., Mataga, N., Stryker, M., Baekkeskov, S., & Kash, S. (1998). Local GABA circuit control of experience-dependent plasticity in developing visual cortex. *Science, 282,* 1504–1508.

Hepper, P.G., & Shahidullah, B.S. (1994). Development of fetal hearing. *Archives of Diseases in Children, 71,* F81–F87.

Huang, L., & Pallas, S.L. (2001). NMDA receptor blockade in the superior colliculus prevents developmental plasticity without blocking visual transmission or map compression. *Journal of Neurophysiology, 86,* 1179–1194.

Imig, T.J., Reale, R.A., Brugge, J.F., Morel, A., & Adrian, H.O. (1986). Topography of cortico-cortical connections related to tonotopic and binaural maps of cat auditory cortex. In F. Lepore, M. Ptito, & H.H. Jasper (Ed.), *Two hemispheres-one brain: Functions of the corpus callosum* (pp. 103–115). New York: Alan R. Liss.

Innocenti, G.M., Fiore, L., & Caminiti, R. (1977). Exuberant projection into the corpus callosum from the visual cortex of newborn cats. *Neuroscience Letters, 4,* 237–242.

Innocenti, G.M., & Frost, D.O. (1979). Effects of visual experience on the maturation of the efferent system to the corpus callosum. *Nature, 280,* 231–234.

Jain, N., Florence, S.L., & Kaas, J.H. (2000). Growth of new brainstem connections in adult monkeys with massive sensory loss. *Proceedings of the National Academy of Sciences, USA, 97,* 5546.

James, W. (1890). *Principles of psychology.* New York: Dover.

Johnson, M.H. (1990). Cortical maturation and the development of visual attention in early infancy. *Journal of Cognitive Neuroscience, 2,* 81–95.

Kaas, J.H. (1995). The evolution of isocortex. *Brain, Behavior and Evolution, 46,* 187–196.

Kahn, D.M., & Krubitzer, L. (2002). Massive cross-modal cortical plasticity and the emergence of a new cortical area in developmentally blind mammals. *Proceedings of the National Academy of Sciences, USA, 99*, 11429–11434.

Katz, L.C., & Crowley, J.C. (2002). Development of cortical circuits: Lessons from ocular dominance columns. *Nature Reviews Neuroscience, 3*, 34–42.

Katz, L.C., & Shatz, C.J. (1996). Synaptic activity and the construction of cortical circuits. *Science, 274*, 1133–1138.

Kelly, J.B., & Judge, P.W. (1994). Binaural organization of primary auditory cortex in the ferret (*Mustela putorius*). *Journal of Neurophysiology, 71*, 904–913.

Kelly, J.B., Judge, P.W., & Phillips, D.P. (1986). Representation of the cochlea in primary auditory cortex of the ferret (*Mustela putorius*). *Hearing Research, 24*, 111–115.

Kleinschmidt, A., Bear, M.F., & Singer, W. (1987). Blockade of "NMDA" receptors disrupts experience dependent plasticity of kitten striate cortex. *Science, 238*, 355–358.

Knudsen, E.I., Zheng, W., & DeBello, W.M. (2000). Traces of learning in the auditory localization pathway. *Proceedings of the National Academy of Sciences, USA, 97*, 11815–11820.

Lavigne-Rebillard, M., & Pujol, R. (1990). Auditory hair cells in human fetuses: Synaptogenesis and ciliogenesis. *Journal of Electron Microscopy Techniques, 15*, 115–122.

LeVay, S., Stryker, M.P., & Shatz, C.J. (1978). Ocular dominance columns and their development in layer IV of the cat's visual cortex: A quantitative study. *Journal of Comparative Neurology, 179*, 223–244.

Linkenhoker, B.A., & Knudsen, E.I. (2002). Incremental training increases the plasticity of the auditory space map in adult barn owls. *Nature, 419*, 293–296.

Livingstone, M., & Hubel, D.H. (1988). Segregation of form, color, movement, and depth: Anatomy, physiology, and perception. *Science, 240*, 740–749.

Malinow, R., & Malenka, R.C. (2002). AMPA receptor trafficking and synaptic plasticity. *Annual Review of Neuroscience, 25*, 103–126.

Mallamaci, A., Muzio, L., Chan, C.H., Parnavelas, J., & Boncinelli, E. (2000). Area identity shifts in the early cerebral cortex of $Emx^{-/-}$ mutant mice. *Nature Neuroscience, 3*, 679–686.

Marin-Padilla, M. (1988). Early ontogenesis of the human cerebral cortex. In A. Peters & E.G. Jones (Eds.), *Development and maturation of cerebral cortex* (pp. 1–33). New York: Plenum Press.

Merzenich, M.M. (2000). Seeing in the sound zone. *Nature, 404*, 820–821.

Métin, C., & Frost, D.O. (1989). Visual responses of neurons in somatosensory cortex of hamsters with experimentally induced retinal projections to somatosensory thalamus. *Proceedings of the National Academy of Sciences, USA, 86*, 357–361.

Métin, C., Irons, W.A., & Frost, D.O. (1995). Retinal ganglion cells in normal hamsters and hamsters with novel retinal projections. I. Number, distribution, and size. *Journal of Comparative Neurology, 353*, 179–199.

Middlebrooks, J.C., Dykes, R.W., & Merzenich, M.M. (1980). Binaural response-specific bands in primary auditory cortex (AI) of the cat: Topographical organization orthogonal to isofrequency contours. *Brain Research, 181,* 31–48.

Miller, B., Chou, L., & Finlay, B.L. (1993). The early development of thalamocortical and corticothalamic projections. *Journal of Comparative Neurology, 335,* 16–41.

Miller, B., Windrem, M.S., & Finlay, B.L. (1991). Thalamic ablations and neocortical development: Alterations in thalamic and callosal connectivity. *Cerebral Cortex, 1,* 241–261.

Miyashita-Lin, E.M., Hevner, R., Wasserman, K.M., Martinez, S., & Rubenstein, J.L.R. (1999). Early neocortical regionalization in the absence of thalamic innervation. *Science, 285,* 906–909.

Moerschel, D.J., & Pallas, S.L. (2001). Early postnatal formation of clustered horizontal connections in ferret auditory cortex [Abstract]. *Society for Neuroscience Abstracts, 27,* 903–908.

Mooney, R., Penn, A.A., Gallego, R., & Shatz, C.J. (1996). Thalamic relay of spontaneous retinal activity prior to vision. *Neuron, 17,* 863–874.

Nakagawa, Y., Johnson, J.E., & O'Leary, D.D.M. (1999). Graded and areal expression patterns of regulatory genes and cadherins in embryonic neocortex independent of thalamocortical input. *Journal of Neuroscience, 19,* 10877–10885.

Nothias, F., Fishell, G., & Ruiz i Altaba, A. (1998). Cooperation of intrinsic and extrinsic signals in the elaboration of regional identity in the posterior cerebral cortex. *Current Biology, 8,* 459–462.

Nudo, R.J. (1999). Recovery after damage to motor cortical areas. *Current Opinions in Neurobiology, 9,* 740.

O'Leary, D.D.M., Schlaggar, B.L., & Tuttle, R. (1994). Specification of neocortical areas and thalamocortical connections. *Annual Review of Neuroscience, 17,* 419–439.

Pallas, S.L. (2001). Intrinsic and extrinsic factors shaping cortical identity. *Trends in Neurosciences, 24,* 417–423.

Pallas, S.L. (2002). Cross-modal plasticity as a tool for understanding ontogeny and phylogeny of cerebral cortex. In A. Shüz & R. Miller (Eds.), *Cortical areas: Unity and diversity* (pp. 245–272). London: Harwood.

Pallas, S.L., Booth, V., & Cynader, M. (1994). Development and plasticity of GABA circuitry in primary visual and primary auditory cortex in ferrets [Abstract]. *Society for Neuroscience Abstracts, 20,* 875.

Pallas, S.L., Hahm, J., & Sur, M. (1994). Morphology of retinal axons induced to arborize in a novel target, the medial geniculate nucleus. I. Comparison with arbors in normal targets. *Journal of Comparative Neurology, 349,* 343–362.

Pallas, S.L., Littman, T., & Moore, D.R. (1999). Cross-modal reorganization of callosal connectivity in auditory cortex without altering thalamocortical projections. *Proceedings of the National Academy of Sciences, USA, 96,* 8751–8756.

Pallas, S.L., & Moore, D.R. (1997). Retinal axons arborize in the medial geniculate nucleus of neonatally deafened ferrets [Abstract]. *Society for Neuroscience Abstracts, 23,* 1994.

Pallas, S.L., Razak, K.A., & Moore, D.R. (2002). Cross-modal projections from LGN to primary auditory cortex following perinatal cochlear ablation in ferrets [Abstract]. *Society for Neuroscience Abstracts, 28,* 220.

Pallas, S.L., Roe, A.W., & Sur, M. (1990). Visual projections induced into the auditory pathway of ferrets. I. Novel inputs to primary auditory cortex (AI) from the LP/Pulvinar complex and the topography of the MGN-AI projection. *Journal of Comparative Neurology, 298,* 50–68.

Pallas, S.L., & Sur, M. (1993). Visual projections induced into the auditory pathway of ferrets. II. Corticocortical connections of primary auditory cortex with visual input. *Journal of Comparative Neurology, 337,* 317–333.

Pallas, S.L., & Sur, M. (1994). Morphology of retinal axon arbors induced to arborize in a novel target, the medial geniculate nucleus. II. Comparison with axons from the inferior colliculus. *Journal of Comparative Neurology, 349,* 363–376.

Payne, B.R., Pearson, H., & Cornwell, P. (1988). Development of visual and auditory cortical connections in the cat. In E.G. Jones & A. Peters (Eds.), *Development and maturation of cerebral cortex* (pp. 309–389). New York: Plenum Press.

Penn, A.A., Riquelme, P.A., & Shatz, C.J. (1998). Competition in retinogeniculate patterning driven by spontaneous activity. *Science, 279,* 2108–2112.

Penn, A.A., & Shatz, C.J. (1999). Brain waves and brain wiring: The role of endogenous and sensory driven neural activity in development. *Pediatric Research, 45,* 447–458.

Peters, A., & Jones, E.G. (1984). *Cerebral cortex: Cellular components of the cerebral cortex* (Vol. 1). New York: Plenum Press.

Pons, T.P., Garraghty, P.E., Ommaya, A.K., Kaas, J.H., Taub, E., & Mishkin, M. (1991). Massive cortical reorganization after sensory deafferentation in adult macaques. *Science, 252,* 1857–1860.

Pujol, R., & Lavigne-Rebillard, M. (1995). Sensory and neural structures in the developing human cochlea. *International Journal of Pediatric Otorhinolaryngology, 32,* S177–S182.

Rakic, P. (1988). Specification of cerebral cortical areas. *Science, 241,* 170–176.

Rauschecker, J., Egert, U., & Kossel, A. (1990). Effects of NMDA antagonists on developmental plasticity in kitten visual cortex. *International Journal Development Neuroscience, 8,* 425–435.

Rauscher, F.H., & Shaw, G.L. (1998). Key components of the Mozart effect. *Perceptual and Motor Skills, 86,* 835–841.

Razak, K.A., Huang, L., & Pallas, S.L. (2003). NMDA receptor blockade in the superior colliculus increases receptive field size without altering velocity and size tuning. *Journal of Neurophysiology, 90,* 110–119.

Reale, R.A., & Imig, T.J. (1980). Tonotopic organization in auditory cortex of the cat. *Journal of Comparative Neurology, 192,* 265–291.

Rebillard, G., Carlier, E., Rebillard, M., Pujol, R. (1977). Enchancement of visual responses in the primary auditory cortex of the cat after an early destruction of cochlear receptors. *Brain Research, 129,* 162–164.

Roberts, E.B., Meredith, M.A., & Ramoa, A.S. (1998). Suppression of NMDA receptor function using antisense DNA blocks ocular dominance plasticity while preserving visual responses. *Journal of Neurophysiology, 80,* 1021–1032.

Roe, A.W., Garraghty, P.E., Esguerra, M., & Sur, M. (1993). Experimentally induced visual projections to the auditory thalamus in ferrets: Evidence for a W cell pathway. *Journal of Comparative Neurology, 334,* 263–280.

Roe, A.W., Pallas, S.L., Hahm, J., & Sur, M. (1990). A map of visual space induced in primary auditory cortex. *Science, 250,* 818–820.

Roe, A.W., Pallas, S.L., Kwon, Y., & Sur, M. (1992). Visual projections routed to the auditory pathway in ferrets: Receptive fields of visual neurons in primary auditory cortex. *Journal of Neuroscience, 12,* 3651–3664.

Rubenstein, J.L.R., Anderson, S., Shi, L., Miyashita-Lin, E., Bulfone, A., & Hevner, R. (1999). Genetic control of cortical regionalization and connectivity. *Cerebral Cortex, 9,* 524–532.

Ruthazer, E.S., & Stryker, M. (1996). The role of activity in the development of long-range horizontal connections in area 17 of the ferret. *Journal of Neuroscience, 16,* 7253–7269.

Rutherford, L.C., DeWan, A., Lauer, H.M., & Turrigiano, G.G. (1997). Brain-derived neurotrophic factor mediates the activity-dependent regulation of inhibition in neocortical cultures. *Journal of Neuroscience, 17,* 4527–4535.

Sato, H., Katsuyama, N., Tamura, H., Hata, Y., & Tsumoto, T. (1995). Mechanisms underlying direction selectivity of neurons in the primary visual cortex of the macaque. *Journal of Neurophysiology, 74,* 1382–1394.

Sato, H., Katsuyama, N., Tamura, H., Hata, Y., & Tsumoto, T. (1996). Mechanisms underlying orientation selectivity of neurons in the primary visual cortex of the macaque. *Journal of Physiology, 494,* 757–771.

Schlaggar, B.L., & O'Leary, D.D.M. (1991). Potential of visual cortex to develop an array of functional units unique to somatosensory cortex. *Science, 252,* 1556–1560.

Schneider, G.E. (1973). Early lesions of the superior colliculus: Factors affecting the formation of abnormal retinal projections. *Brain, Behavior and Evolution, 8,* 73–109.

Sengpiel, F., Gödecke, I., Stawinski, P., Hübener, M., Löwel, S., & Bonhoeffer, T. (1998). Intrinsic and environmental factors in the development of functional maps in cat visual cortex. *Neuropharmacology, 37,* 607–621.

Sestan, N., Rakic, P., & Donoghue, M.J. (2001). Independent parcellation of the embryonic visual cortex and thalamus revealed by combinatorial Eph/ephrin gene expression. *Current Biology, 11,* 39–43.

Sharma, J., Angelucci, A., & Sur, M. (2000). Induction of visual orientation modules in auditory cortex. *Nature, 404,* 841–847.

Shatz, C.J. (1994). Role for spontaneous neural activity in the patterning of connections between retina and LGN during visual system development. *International Journal of Developmental Neuroscience, 12,* 531–546.

Shatz, C.J., & Stryker, M.P. (1978). Ocular dominance in layer IV of the cat's visual cortex and the effects of monocular deprivation. *Journal of Physiology, 281,* 267–283.

Sherman, S.M., & Spear, P.D. (1982). Organization of visual pathways in normal and visually-deprived cats. *Physiological Review, 62,* 738–855.

Shumway, C.A. (1989). Multiple electrosensory maps in the medulla of weakly electric gymnotiform fish. I. Physiological differences. *Journal of Neuroscience, 9,* 4388–4399.

Sillito, A.M. (1975a). The contribution of inhibitory mechanisms to the receptive field properties of neurons in the striate cortex of the cat. *Journal of Physiology, 250,* 305–329.

Sillito, A.M. (1975b). The effectiveness of bicuculline as an antagonist of GABA and visually evoked inhibition in the cat's striate cortex. *Journal of Physiology, 250,* 287–304.

Stanfield, B.B., & O'Leary, D.D.M. (1985). Fetal occipital cortical neurons transplanted to the rostral cortex can extend and maintain a pyramidal tract axon. *Nature, 313,* 135–137.

Steele, K.M., Brown, J.D., & Stoecker, J.A. (1999). Failure to confirm the Rauscher and Shaw description of recovery of the Mozart effect. *Perceptual and Motor Skills, 88,* 843–848.

Stryker, M.P., & Harris, W.A. (1986). Binocular impulse blockade prevents the formation of ocular dominance columns in cat visual cortex. *Journal of Neuroscience, 6,* 2117–2133.

Sur, M., Garraghty, P.E., & Roe, A.W. (1988). Experimentally induced visual projections into auditory thalamus and cortex. *Science, 242,* 1437–1441.

Swindale, N.V. (2000). Cortical development: Lightning is always seen, thunder is always heard. *Current Biology, 10,* R569–R571.

Teller, D., & Bornstein, M.H. (1987). Infant color vision and color perception. In P. Salapatek & L. Cohen (Eds.), *Handbook of infant perception* (pp. 185–235). Orlando, FL: Academic Press.

Trachtenberg, J.T., Chen, B.E., Knott, G.W., Feng, G., Sanes, J.R., Welker, E., et al. (2002). Long term in vivo imaging of experience-dependent synaptic plasticity in adult cortex. *Nature, 420,* 788–794.

von Melchner, L.S., Pallas, S.L., & Sur, M. (2000). Visual behavior induced by retinal projections directed to the auditory pathway. *Nature, 404,* 871–875.

Weliky, M., & Katz, L.C. (1997). Disruption of orientation tuning in visual cortex by artificially correlated neuronal activity. *Nature, 386,* 680–685.

Weliky, M., & Katz, L.C. (1999). Correlational structure of spontaneous neuronal activity in the developing lateral geniculate nucleus in vivo. *Science, 285,* 599–604.

Wiesel, T.N., & Hubel, D.H. (1963). Single cell responses in striate cortex of kittens deprived of vision in one eye. *Journal of Neurophysiology, 26,* 1003–1017.

Wiesel, T.N., & Hubel, D.H. (1965). Comparison of the effects of unilateral and bilateral eye closure on cortical unit responses in kittens. *Journal of Neurophysiology, 28,* 1029–1040.

Wong, R.O.L. (1999). Retinal waves and visual system development. *Annual Review of Neuroscience, 22,* 29–47.

Wong, R.O.L., Meister, M., & Shatz, C.J. (1993). Transient period of correlated bursting activity during development of the mammalian retina. *Neuron, 11,* 923–938.

Wong, R.O.L., & Oakley, D.M. (1996). Changing patterns of spontaneous bursting activity of on and off retinal ganglion cells during development. *Neuron, 16,* 1087–1095.

Yaka, R., Yinon, U., & Wollberg, Z. (1999). Auditory activation of cortical visual areas in cats after early visual deprivation. *European Journal of Neuroscience, 11,* 1301–1312.

Zheng, W., & Knudsen, E. (1999). Functional selection of adaptive auditory space map by $GABA_A$ mediated inhibition. *Science, 284,* 962–965.

FURTHER READING

Chenn, A., Braisted, J., McConnell, S.K., & O'Leary, D.D.M. (1997). Development of the cerebral cortex: Mechanisms controlling cell fate, laminar and areal patterning, and axonal connectivity. In W.M. Cowan, T.M. Jessell, & S.L. Sipursky (Eds.), *Molecular and cellular approaches to neural development* (pp. 440–473). Oxford: Oxford University Press.

Daw, N.W. (1995). *Visual development.* New York: Plenum.

Debski, E.A., & Cline, H.T. (2002). Activity-dependent mapping in the retinotectal projection. *Current Opinion in Neurobiology, 12,* 93–99.

Eliot, L. (1999). *What's going on in there?* New York: Bantam Books.

Katz, L.C. (1999). What's critical for the critical period in visual cortex? *Cell, 99,* 673–676.

Katz, L.C., & Shatz, C.J. (1997). Synaptic activity and the construction of cortical circuits. *Science, 274,* 1133–1138.

Sanes, D.H., Reh, T.A., & Harris, W.A. (2000). *Development of the nervous system.* San Diego: Academic Press.

Wilson, S.W., & Rubenstein, J.L.R. (2000). Induction and dorsoventral patterning of the telencephalon. *Neuron, 28,* 641–645.

CHAPTER 2

ARE WE EXPECTING TOO MUCH FROM PRENATAL SENSORY EXPERIENCES?

Jean-Pierre Lecanuet, Carolyn Granier-Deferre,
and Anthony DeCasper*

ABSTRACT

In the last two decades or so much knowledge has been gained concerning the potential for learning in the human fetus. We now know that the prenatal environment is rich with a textured array of sensible stimuli. Our understanding of how/whether the fetus makes "sense" of these opportunities for learning about their world is, so far, quite incomplete. If, however, prenatal sensory experience impacts later learning and cognitive processes, then the experience probably occurs late in fetal development in the human. Such is the case with the different forms of auditory learning that is the main, but not exclusive, focus of the present contribution. Having come so far in demonstrating the existence of continuities in learning from prenatal to postnatal life, now is an opportune time to return to some of the fundamental questions that motivated the emerging field of fetal psychology in the first place. A number of such questions are considered for which we as yet have no definitive answers, such as the influence of behavioral

---

*Our friend and colleague Jean-Pierre Lecanuet played an instrumental role in the formation of the study of prenatal sensory stimulation. He had developed a draft of this chapter before his untimely death in 2002. We have produced a finished version while trying to be faithful to his plan for the chapter and to his opinions about the title he had given it. Whatever the reader finds interesting and useful undoubtedly appeared in the draft version, and any shortcomings are the responsibility of those who modified it.

states on prenatal perception. This "return to basics" brings with it some critical comments that will hopefully serve as debating points with regard to what constitutes further progress in the field. Perhaps the most basic question is whether fetal sensory experiences have any impact on the development of individual differences in cognition that can be observed later in life.

INTRODUCTION

Consider the following proposition: differences in fetuses' prenatal sensory experiences (PSEs) and learning histories can cause differences in prenatal central nervous system (CNS) development, which in turn can cause individual differences in later cognitive functioning. The proposition has adherents, with varying degrees of commitment, among contemporary scientists, clinicians, and laypersons alike. It implies that an individual's PSE exerts a salient influence on his/her emotional and cognitive functions much later after birth. How did such a proposition arise, what is the actual state of affairs, and are we expecting PSE to account for too much of the variance in individual differences?

FROM BELIEFS TO OBSERVATIONS ABOUT PRENATAL SENSORY EXPERIENCE

The wisdom of Western cultures has a long history of beliefs about the significance of prenatal development, events that could affect it, and its influence on later life. It was common knowledge centuries ago that traumatic events that befell a pregnant woman could "mark" her fetus, or that unmet maternal needs would affect the appearance and even the personality of her baby. Opinion leaders served to establish the credibility of such notions. For example, Jeanne d'Albret, Queen of Navarre (1528–1572), went out of her way to surround herself with good music and pleasant sights so that her son, Henry, born in 1553, would grow to be of good humor and have an appropriate royal sense of good taste when he ascended to the throne. Clearly the queen believed that prenatal experience could affect both the disposition and perceptions of her son. It is unclear whether the queen believed that the world she created would affect her son directly or indirectly via the effects that the experiences had on her. It is also unclear whether her experiences were just a bit beyond the norm or were truly extraordinary, both in frequency and in kind. Her son, Henry IV, King of

France (1589–1610), lived a life rich with varied postnatal experiences, and he served France well in his last decade. He was reputed to be gallant, witty, and humane, and he was among the most popular kings of France. He wanted his subjects to be able to eat a "poule au pot" each Sunday. Did he select this dish because his mother ate a lot of it during her pregnancy? We don't know. We will never know whether his mother's very early efforts to influence his behavior as king had any effect; however, his story provides us with a convenient vehicle for posing some of the issues addressed in this chapter.

The question about whether the fetus is open to direct influence from the world has been resolved over the past century, as has the question of whether those influences are beneficial. In 1827, Xavier Bichat (1771–1802) stated that the human fetus lived in a world all but isolated from stimulation. Then, in 1882, Wilhelm Preyer considered that, while the fetus was relatively isolated, it was exposed to minimal levels of sensory stimulation and profited from them. Forty years later, Feldman (1920) wrote that every sensory system, with the exception of vision and olfaction, received appropriate prenatal stimulation. Klosovski (1963) stated that vestibular, cutaneous, and chemical stimulation played a major role in brain development. The chapters in this volume offer evidence that all senses are open to stimulation before birth, and that PSE can have both positive and negative effects on development. Nevertheless, we are still faced with questions about the significance of an individual's PSE for functioning in later life and questions about the appropriate or optimal level of those experiences.

The issue of whether a pregnant woman's responses to her world can affect fetal development has also been answered. In particular, there is a significant body of research devoted to clarifying the role of maternal stress and depression on postnatal personality and socioemotional behavior (e.g., DiPietro, Hilton, Hawkins, Costigan, & Pressman, 2002). The issue of how a pregnant woman's reaction to the world affects postnatal personality and emotion remains outside the scope of this chapter (see chapter 7 by Glover & O'Connor); however, questions about the interaction between cognition and emotion are fundamental ones for psychology. Perhaps future research on the development of those interactions will extend into the prenatal period, where both cognition and emotion have their roots.

Contemporary understanding of prenatal development, including PSE, has come a long way by using conventional concepts and modern technologies (but advances in functional genetics will likely reshape our thinking). Because contemporary scientific knowledge is based on conventional concepts, it has been relatively easy for the data to be absorbed into the realm of common knowledge. The internet has become a widely accepted distributor of such knowledge, and a common belief seems to be that if information can be found on the internet, then it must be true. A search for the term "human prenatal sensory experience" via the Google search engine turned up more than 9,000 entries, many of which were commercial. A cursory examination of these sites informs the layman that prenatal sensory stimulation will, for example, increase neural growth; decrease the rate of prenatal cell death; stimulate dendritric growth; and facilitate the development of memory, learning, thinking, and social interactions, including maternal bonding. Many sites also indicate how the pregnant mother-to-be can provide specific forms of stimulation and extra stimulation to produce even greater and long-lasting benefits. Unfortunately, common knowledge often reflects an incorrect understanding of the data, often appears as half-truths, and almost never acknowledges the caveats that scientists take for granted (e.g., extra stimulation may not be better than the usual amount and under certain conditions may actually be harmful). Moreover, the continuum between minimally appropriate and excessive stimulation is probably not linear and is likely to involve issues of the nature of the stimulus, its intensity, frequency of its occurrence, and its timing during early development.

Our current understanding of prenatal development and learning is the most recent instance of the advances in the scientific understanding of child development that have occurred during the last half of the twentieth century. Along the way we have refined the concepts of emotional and cognitive functioning and have operationalized them. One result was that evidence for the basic competencies seemed to appear at earlier and earlier stages of development. First children, then toddlers, then infants and newborns appeared to be more competent than was previously thought, and they also seemed to profit from experience.

Even though our measures of cognitive functioning have become more useful, we have not been able to discern much evidence of individual stability in general cognitive function during the first postnatal years of typical children. Indeed, two characteristics of the data in this area stand out: the degree of stability in an individual's cognitive functioning increases as the time between measurements decreases, and it increases as the age when the earliest measure was taken increases. Thus, the rank of individuals as young infants does not predict their place in their childhood peer group: the variance in children's cognitive functioning that can be explained by their level of infantile functioning may, from time to time, be statistically significant, but it is functionally trivial with an R^2 value of about 4% (e.g., Lécuyer, 1989). Another approach in this area attempts to relate performance of specific cognitive functions in early infancy (e.g., *habituation* and attention) to performance of comparable cognitive functions later in life. Studies here tend to find slightly higher correlations (e.g., Tsao, Liu, & Kuhl, 2004). Unsurprisingly, studies also find that many different concurrent experiences (e.g., the amount of maternal speech to the infant, its linguistic properties, and its context) account for additional variance (Bornstein, 1989; Rose, 1989).

Currently we are able to observe the fetus, and we continue to find surprising competencies and learning abilities that have been revealed by studies of PSE. However, we do not think there is likely to be any discernable variance in later cognitive functioning that can be explained by variation in the prenatal sensory experiences of healthy fetuses: the effects of age at first test and the time between tests will continue to influence the strength of the correlations, because, we believe, these characteristics of the data result from the nature of ontogeny. At any point in time, the functioning of an individual's cognitive system rests on multiple substrates and multiple processes whose development is inherently dynamic (not linear) and can be affected by their ever-changing environments. As Sontag (1965) opined, we will continue to seek the relation between fetal behavior and "postnatal behavior and even adolescent and adult behavior, although the extended life span of human beings makes the later objective an exotic and almost impossibly ambitious one" (p. 782). Perhaps it is time to consider some of the factors that should limit our expectations regarding the effects of PSE.

THE CONCEPT OF PRENATAL SENSORY EXPERIENCE

In this chapter, a PSE is said to occur when a change in some aspect of the physical world activates a sensory receptor. A consequence of that activation can be observed in a response that is mediated by CNS/ANS (e.g., evoked motor potentials or cardiac responses). The relevant human data will focus on experiences in the auditory modality after thirty-six weeks gestational age (GA) when *behavioral states* are clearly differentiated (see chapter 6 by de Vries & Hopkins). Behavioral states are important because they reflect differently organized conditions of the nervous system. Just as other psychologists usually study awake subjects because the state of wakefulness reflects an underlying organization of the nervous system, so too should prenatal investigators be aware of the underlying state of their fetal subjects. Indeed, one of the challenges facing prenatal research is to flesh out the development of the various states and how they might modulate the effects of PSE.

What stimuli are available to directly stimulate fetal receptors? The basic features of physical stimuli that can activate the senses are understood, and we know that these stimuli can occur within the fetal compartment. Mechanical forces (weak to strong), changes in temperature, and even painful stimuli can come into contact with the fetal skin to provide exteroceptive somesthetic stimulation. Also, *proprioceptive stimulation* may arise from passive movements caused by the mother or from self-initiated fetal movement. Maternal blood and *amniotic fluid* carry numerous chemosensory molecules that can stimulate the olfactory and gustatory receptors. Frequent changes in the orientation of the fetal head, and changes in velocity of its movement through space, can stimulate the vestibular senses. The inner ear, bone, tissues, and fluids can vibrate at frequencies and amplitudes that stimulate the auditory hair cells, thus providing the opportunity for auditory experiences. Finally, energy waves at frequencies able to stimulate *fetal visual receptors* can penetrate the fetal compartment. By the time of birth, all the senses are functional to some extent (e.g., Bradley & Mistretta, 1975; Lecanuet, Granier-Deferre, & Busnel, 1989). Because human sensory systems develop in order—cutaneous and proprioceptive senses, chemical senses, vestibular senses, audition, then vision—some characteristics of the effects of these potential activating stimuli are also ordered.

As previously mentioned, most of this discussion will focus on audition, with the intent of providing a model for considering the effects of PSE in the other modalities. However, to begin we will illustrate the concepts just discussed with a recent study on the issue of *prenatal vestibular stimulation*. This issue has been a contentious one, mainly because relevant experimental data are sparse. Lecanuet and Jacquet (2002) seated a pregnant woman motionless in a chair and then moved the chair with either a lateral or antero-posterior passive rocking motion. The fetuses were at least thirty-eight weeks GA and were in state 1F. The researchers observed that the onset of rocking elicited a transient heart rate increase of moderate amplitude (6–8 bpm). This increase is presumably the result of a vestibular response to changes in the velocity and direction of movement. This is the clearest experimental evidence to date showing that the vestibular system is operative, at least late in gestation. While similar experiences occur throughout gestation, we do not yet know whether or how they might affect ongoing and subsequent functioning (cf. Ronca & Alberts, 1995).

What auditory stimuli reach the fetus? Airborne sounds between about 0.4–0.5 kHz that enter the fetal compartment by crossing maternal tissue are attenuated as a function of frequency: the higher the frequency, the greater the attenuation (~3 dB/octave). The components of these sounds at or above 70 dB, *ex utero*, are considered to be above near-term fetal auditory absolute threshold, and are thus likely to produce an auditory PSE. This attenuation function implies that all of the acoustic characteristics of an airborne signal that activate the inner hair cells (e.g., extra uterine speech sounds) will not be available to the fetus. In contrast, the mother's vocal sounds and biological sounds are privileged in that they reach fetal inner ear without attenuation (Lecanuet et al., 1998). The intrauterine acoustic characteristics of an object vibrating directly against the maternal abdomen are not the same as those reaching the fetus when the object vibrates in air. An informative example here is that of the *electronic artificial larynx* (EAL). This vibro-acoustic stimulus produces low frequencies that are about 80 dB measured in air. When this stimulus is applied directly to the maternal abdomen, as it often is during quick assessments of fetal hearing, its overall intrauterine sound level is highly amplified (~120–130 dB), and it elicits *fetal stress reactions*, including *micturition* (Gerhardt, Abrams, Kovaz, Gomez, & Conlon, 1988; Zimmer et al., 1993). Moreover, the acoustic properties of the fetal compartment itself are not homogeneous. Measurements made within a man-made rubber "uterus," and from within the uterus of an unconscious ewe, indicate that the resonance characteristics of a liquid-filled vessel can create significant differences between the signals that are transmitted and those that occur within (Gerhardt et al., 1988; Lecanuet et al., 1998). Complicating matters even more is the fact that the location of the recording microphone, or *fetal ear*, determines which signals—frequency, amplitude, and/or phase—are registered. Therefore, we do not know with certainty the nature of the effective stimulus that activates a maturing fetal auditory system that is inside a liquid-filled chamber containing an ever-growing fetus and a decreasing volume of amniotic fluid, and whose receptors are changing position until the end of gestation approaches (see chapter 6 by de Vries & Hopkins). In general, if we are to consider the effects of prenatal sensory stimulation, we should be concerned with our understanding of the effective stimulus' character.

STRUCTURAL AND FUNCTIONAL CONSEQUENCES OF PRENATAL SENSORY EXPERIENCE

What kinds of experiences can the fetal sensory systems provide? Sensory systems development involves increasingly elaborate coding of the stimulus and increasing integration of the afferent and efferent pathways. For example, all mammalian studies indicate that the initial cochlear responses are restricted to the lower-middle frequencies, *temporal coding* is poor, and there is no frequency selectivity (Pujol & Uziel, 1986). Subsequently, the entire range of frequencies to which a species responds will activate highly tuned receptor cells, and temporal coding will be precise. One consequence of this developmental pattern is that receptor cells that initially responded to a low-frequency stimulus will not respond to it later, and will respond only to a higher frequency sound (Romand, 1997; Rubel & Ryals, 1983). Thus, not only will different peripheral receptors and auditory fibers be activated by the same stimulus, but the increasingly mature higher-order functions will produce a more elaborated expression of the stimulus.

One can now consider the possibility that the properties of a fetus' sensory experience is the result of the interaction between a changing effective stimulus, an increasingly mature sensory system and increasingly mature central structures (e.g., Bourgeois, Goldman-Rakic, & Rakic, 1994). For completeness one may also want to note that the effect of specific experiences may be modulated by non-sensory fetal variables such as behavioral state, and by maternal factors such as stress level, changing glucose levels and hormones.

The image of fetal sensory experience created thus far is a dynamic one. What kind of effects, both short- and long-term, might dynamic sensory experiences have? For one, sensory stimulation has the general effect of enabling and maintaining an adequate (and perhaps optimal) level of functioning of sensory systems' peripheral and central structures. For example, animal studies that minimize auditory input (deprivation and lesion studies) have shown that afferent input is necessary to establish and maintain appropriate signal processing at each field receptor level (peripheral, brain stem nuclei, and higher centers). Deprivation effects, their reversibility, and also the effects of prolonged exposure to selectively enriched sound environments vary as a function of timing (e.g., Granier-Deferre & Lecanuet, 1987; Moore, 1985; 2002). Animal studies also find that there is a *critical period* when the developing ear is highly susceptible *to acoustic trauma*: sounds that are innocuous to a mature auditory apparatus may permanently damage the inner hair cells of an immature apparatus (e.g., Pujol & Uziel, 1986; Rubel & Ryals, 1982). Thus, we may conclude that *auditory stimulation* of the human fetus contributes to the structural and functional development of the auditory system, but that the nature of stimulation effects depends upon the level of anatomo-cellular maturation and level of functioning the system has attained at the time.

Prenatal Experience and Learning

One expression of structural and functional developments like those discussed above is the ability to learn. Indeed, one class of behavioral consequences of prenatal sensory stimulation can be placed under the rubric of "learning." Three types of learning experiences have been documented to result from prenatal sensory stimulation by chemosensory and auditory stimuli: habituation, associative learning, and exposure learning. However, unlike the structural and physiological effects of PSE described above, it is less clear that PSE is required to enable and/or maintain these learning processes or indeed, what role PSE plays in their development. When the effects of prenatal learning are observed in postnatal behavior, they constitute clear instances of transnatal continuity in sensory experiences.

Habituation. Taken to be a simple form of learning, *habituation* is defined as a decrement in reactivity to an often-repeated stimulus. It has been demonstrated in fetal mammals with auditory stimuli. A classic example is that of Vince (1979), who exposed fetal guinea pigs to the vocalization of a bantam hen (a natural predator). After birth, the prenatally stimulated subjects showed reduced reactivity to the vocalization relative to the reactivity of controls that had no prenatal experience with the vocalization.

Stimulus-Stimulus Associative Learning (Classical Conditioning). This type of learning has also been demonstrated. Here, the classic example is that of Stickrod, Kimble, and Smotherman (1982), who demonstrated *aversive conditioning* with chemosensory stimuli. Rat fetuses were exposed just once to a paired presentation of a taste-odor stimulus (CS) and nausea (US) resulting from injection of a toxic agent. Sixteen days after birth, these animals showed an aversion to the taste/odor stimulus, but the relevant control animals did not. Most recently, a conditioned association between an auditory stimulus (CS) and a vibro-acoustic stimulus (US) has been demonstrated in a chimpanzee fetus (Kawai, Morokuma, Tomonaga, Horimoto, & Tanaka, 2003). Thus, transfer of a learned association from the womb is possible.

Stimulus Learning through Mere Exposure. Prenatal learning about a specific stimulus after exposure to it has been shown with chemosensory stimuli and auditory stimuli. The introduction of flavors through the mother's diet into the amniotic pool results in a clear preference for that flavor after birth. Such prenatal exposure effects may also explain why newborns are attracted to the complex odor of their amniotic fluid (Schaal, Marlier, & Soussignan, 1998, 2002; see also chapters 3 and 4 in this volume). To date, the research on *mere exposure* to an auditory stimulus indicates that it can become, because of repeated sensory experiences with it in the absence of obvious reinforcers, perceptually discriminable from otherwise similar but novel sounds. That is to say, some features of the stimulus have been learned or have become familiar.

Familiarity Effects. The effect of stimulus familiarity after prenatal exposure has been observed in the human fetus. Fetuses show different basal heart rates when exposed to their mother's voice or that of another female (Kisilevsky et al., 2003; Lecanuet, Manéra, & Jacquet, 2002). They display a significant cardiac orienting response to a prose passage their mother often recited but not to a passage she had not recited before, demonstrating they can discriminate between the two (DeCasper, Lecanuet, Busnel, Granier-Deferre, & Maugeais, 1994).

Familiarity effects have also been observed after birth in newborns. DeCasper and Fifer (1980) demonstrated that newborns would more readily learn to emit a specific instrumental sucking response if it was reinforced by their mother's voice rather than by the voice of another female. Thus, prenatal exposure to the maternal voice enhanced its potency as a postnatal reinforcer of newborn behavior. Mere exposure to other maternally generated vocal stimuli such as a sung melody, a short story, and native language sounds, also increases their reinforcing potency after birth (DeCasper & Spence, 1986; Moon, Panneton-Cooper, & Fifer, 1993; Panneton, 1985). The consensus among researchers is that the prosodic features of maternally generated vocal and speech sounds had become familiar.

Because the reinforcing properties of the familiar stimulus was directly contrasted with a comparable but unfamiliar stimulus in these studies, we can say that newborns preferred the prenatally familiarized stimulus. Thus, the prenatally familiarized stimuli acquired positive affective valence. Interestingly, all the PSE learning studies conducted to date indicate that, all else equal, prenatal experience with a stimulus causes that stimulus to acquire positive affective valence. Although we noted earlier that we would not discuss the emotional consequences of prenatal experiences, there is a pervasive emotional aspect to the effects of PSE.

Another interesting consequence of *prenatal sensory learning* is shown by Mastropieri and Turkewitz (1999). Recall that newborns can discriminate between their mother's language and another language. Their study showed that mere exposure to normally occurring maternal speech before birth enabled newborns to discriminate between "happy" and "sad" expressions of an utterance spoken in their mother's language. The infants did not discriminate between "happy" and "sad" expressions of an utterance that were spoken in another language. Thus, *mere exposure* permitted a conditional discrimination: newborn's discrimination between different prosodic moods of an utterance that occurs within a language required prenatal familiarity with the language in which the prosodic differences were embedded.

The last study of mere exposure in the auditory modality to be discussed is of special interest because it demonstrates the longevity of mere exposure effects in a precise way. Granier-Deferre, Bassereau, Ribeiro, Jacquet, and Lecanuet (2003) exposed fetuses between thirty-five to thirty-eight weeks GA to a simple descending melody for two minutes (twenty-four repetitions) at 80 dB SPL, twice a day. Testing of the fetuses occurred on a day following exposure to the stimulus. That is to say, without interruption of their daily routine. Test stimuli were delivered when the fetuses were in state 1F, which corresponds to "quiet" sleep in the newborn. The experimental fetuses had no cardiac reaction to the familiar descending sequence, but showed the usual brief cardiac deceleration to the control stimulus, which was an ascending version of the descending melody. This later response was expected because moderately intense stimuli are known to elicit the cardiac component of the orienting response. Control infants responded with the typical deceleration to both the ascending and descending sequences. Thus, the most straightforward explanation of the absence of reaction by the experimental fetuses to the familiarized

descending sequence is that they had habituated to daily presenta-
tions of that sequence.

The fetuses were never again exposed to the melody before or after
birth. They were tested again when they were five week-old infants.
A second age-equivalent control group was also tested. Infants were
tested in quiet sleep with the stimuli delivered at 60 dB/SPL. The
control infants reacted to the ascending and descending melodies
with a brief cardiac deceleration, like that typically observed in fetuses.
The experimental infants also reacted to the control melody with
similar brief deceleration. However, the descending sequence they
had heard as fetuses elicited a cardiac deceleration that was about
twice great. Thus, mere exposure of a near-term fetus to a simple
melody for a total of no more than eighty-four minutes (1,008 repetitions) at 80 dB *ex utero* over a three-week period can produce a familiarity effect that lasts for at least five weeks after birth. Because the
quantity and timing of the prenatal experience and the retention
interval are known, these data provide a starting point for future
investigations of how the amount and distribution of a prenatal auditory stimulus are related to the kind of *familiarity effects* that can occur
and to their duration.

SOME CLOSING ON THE QUESTION THAT IS THE TITLE OF THIS CHAPTER

First, it is clear that there is *transnatal continuity of human prenatal
sensory experiences* (see chapter 3 by Schaal), including evidence that
PSE can facilitate early postnatal instrumental learning. It was primarily these data combined with the strong cultural propensity to
impute great significance to early experience that allowed some individuals to induce the general proposition that opened this chapter.
We, however, do not believe that the existing data, human and animal, can reasonably support this general proposition.

We know that prenatal sensory stimulation serves the general
function of enabling and maintaining an adequate level of functioning
during the maturation of peripheral and central structures. So far in
the evolution of the species, normally occurring experiences seem
perfectly appropriate for this role. Nevertheless, it is reasonable to
ask if augmenting or controlling PSE can enhance or facilitate development. For example, controlling PSE may have clinical utility. However, given the wisdom of evolution, the absence of compelling need,
the large gaps in current knowledge, and the real possibility that

augmented stimulation can be harmful rather than helpful, we strongly suggest that explicit attempts to significantly augment prenatal sensory stimulation should be avoided under normal circumstances.

We asserted that the fetuses' *behavioral state* should be considered during PSE learning and also when evaluating the effects of PSE. Animal research shows that prenatal associative learning can occur when the fetus is in an active behavioral state (Kawai et al., 2003), and that associative learning and its retrieval after birth are not state dependent (Cheour et al., 2002). However, we know of no human studies that have controlled for state during the times of PSE learning. So, in fact, we do not yet know whether or how the fetal state during PSE modulates learning in humans. We have controlled state when testing for the effects of PSE, however. We have done so for three reasons: state strongly modulates neonatal (Berg, Berg, & Graham, 1971) and fetal reactions to non-startling stimuli, and fetuses are more reactive in 2F than in 1F. It is easier to see the effects of PSE on prenatal (and postnatal) cardiac reactions when the basal heart rate variability is low, as it is during 1F. And, knowing state at the time of testing allows meaningful interpretation of the results and comparison among studies. At this juncture, we will simply reassert that fetal state must remain an important consideration when investigating fetal perceptive abilities, as it reflects modulation of the CNS processes that mediates the experience.

The study by Granier-Deferre et al. (2003) is the only human experiment on long-term retention (five weeks) of a prenatal experience that has, in fact, restricted the relevant sensory experience to the prenatal period *per se*. It will be very difficult to isolate the longer-term effects of prenatal experience with the maternal voice and speech sounds *per se*, because those specific prenatal experiences begin to be overlaid by other similar and relevant experiences immediately after birth. We should remember that other sensory experiences also continue immediately after birth, some of which are very similar to those occurring before birth.

The study of auditory PSE in humans has, in its relatively short history, revealed some remarkable phenomena: fetuses habituate to repetitive stimulus events, they can remember them, and they can discriminate them from other similar events. The effects of PSE are transnatal: newborns (and young infants) remember specific prenatally experienced stimuli, newborns attend to them and display positive affect toward them, they can discriminate them from other similar but unfamiliar stimuli, and newborn instrumental learning is facilitated when familiar stimuli are used as reinforcers (DeCasper & Spence, 1991). These phenomena, however, are of limited use for evaluating the assertion that an individual fetus' specific PSE has long-lasting effects. Some effects of a specific PSE are likely to be general in that they would occur with any appropriate PSE (e.g., experience with the human characteristics of the maternal voice that might be important for language development and social bonding). Other PSE effects are likely to reflect the nature of a specific PSE *per se* (e.g., increased reinforcing properties of the maternal voice *per se* might facilitate the first postnatal adaptations).

Upon reflection, the expectation that PSE will have subsequent effects on general linguistic, intellectual, and social functioning is really the expectation that early infant (or fetal) measures of intelligence will show stability in inter-individual differences over time. We noted that the nature of development does not lend itself to such an approach. We believe the same holds true in a search for general, long-term effects of PSE: at any point in time, the functioning of an individual's linguistic competencies and social behavior rests on multiple substrates and multiple processes, in which development is inherently dynamic (not linear) and can be affected by their ever-changing environments. Sontag's (1965) opinion (as previously described) also applies.

So far, human research has demonstrated the existence of a variety of PSE effects and some of their consequences. This work will surely continue, but it is not too soon to encourage a more embryological approach, as well. Future research that is guided by the principles of developmental embryology offers a disciplined way to ponder the key question posed in this chapter. In general, the development of a sensory system (or any other phenotypic characteristic) proceeds by increasing differentiation of the system itself and by increasing integration of the system with other sensory systems and other central structures. In the main, the effects of sensory experience will be most significant when they occur at times when the sensory system itself, and other systems that interact with it, are undergoing significant developmental change: sensory stimulation before or after this time will have a lesser impact. Because the various sensory systems become functional in a regular order and become integrated, the possibility exists that stimulating one modality can affect the functioning of another modality. For example, auditory learning of the maternal call by bobwhite quails occurs via mere *exposure learning* in the perinatal period. However, if the later developing visual system is stimulated during the period of auditory development, then the usual auditory learning does not occur (Foushee & Lickliter, 2002). Similarly, if extra stimulation of the earlier maturing tactile/vestibular systems coincides with the onset of auditory functioning, then the maternal call is not learned as usual. In contrast, if the tactile/vestibular systems are stimulated after the onset of auditory function, then chicks learn the maternal call as usual (Honeycutt & Lickliter, 2003). Finally, the effects of PSE can also be significantly modulated when a sensory system becomes integrated with other processes, such as learning and memory. For example, in Hall and King's study (1990), rat pups were habituated to an odor while using only one nostril (the other was blocked) at a time before the *anterior commissure* had developed (day 6). They could subsequently perform the learned response with the educated nostril both before and after the commissure had developed, but the other nostril was always ineffective. However, if the pups learned the response with one nostril after the commissure had developed (day 12), then they could later perform the task with either nostril, even if the commissure was severed. A similar embryological approach to human PSE research will encourage more analytical studies to help to understand the nature of the developmental processes that underlie the effects of PSE.

CONCLUSIONS

Experimental research has established the fact of transnatal effects of PSE in animals and man and has established some of its fundamental consequences and limitations. Despite the progress that has been made, it is our opinion that we have yet to establish whether PSEs have any impact on the development of individual differences that can be observed later in life. However, if and when we attempt to do so, there will not likely be any significant direct correlations between PSE and subsequent cognitive and social functioning. Future research, guided by an embryological approach, will undoubtedly reveal more about the mechanisms of PSE effects and, thus, realistic expectations about their expression and longevity. The purpose of this chapter has been to curb unbridled expectations about the significance of PSE for later life but not the enthusiasm for researching its significance during ontogeny.

REFERENCES

Berg, K.M., Berg,W.K., & Graham, F.K. (1971). Infant heart rate response as a function of stimulus and state. *Psychophysiology, 8,* 30–44.

Bichat, M.F.X. (1827). *Physiological researches upon life and death*. Boston: Richardson and Lord.

Bornstein, M.H. (1989). Stability in early mental development: From attention and information processing in infancy to language and cognition in childhood. In M.H. Bornstein & N.A. Krasnegor (Eds.), *Stability and continuity in mental development: Behavioral and biological perspectives* (pp. 145–170). Hillsdale, NJ: Erlbaum.

Bourgeois, J.-P., Goldman-Rakic, P.S., & Rakic, P. (1994). Synaptogenesis in the prefrontal cortex of rhesus monkeys. *Cerebral Cortex, 4*, 78–96.

Bradley, R.M., & Mistretta, C.M. (1975). Fetal sensory receptors. *Physiological Review, 55*, 352–382.

Cheour, M., Martynova, O., Naatanen, R., Erkkola, R., Sillanpaa, M., Kero, P., et al. (2002). Speech sounds learned by sleeping newborns. *Nature, 415*, 599–600.

DeCasper, A.J., & Fifer, W.P. (1980). Of human bonding: Newborns prefer their mother's voice. *Science, 208*, 1174–1176.

DeCasper, A.J., Lecanuet, J.-P., Busnel, M.-C., Granier-Deferre, C., & Maugeais, R. (1994). Fetal reactions to recurrent maternal speech. *Infant Behavior and Development, 17*, 159–164.

DeCasper, A.J., & Spence, M.J. (1986). Prenatal maternal speech influences newborns' perception of speech sounds. *Infant Behavior and Development, 9*, 133–150.

DeCasper, A.J., & Spence, M.J. (1991). Auditorially mediated behavior during the perinatal period: A cognitive view. In M.S. Weiss & P.R. Zelazo (Eds.), *Newborn attention: Biological constraints and the influence of experience* (pp. 142–176). Norwood, NJ; Ablex.

DiPietro, J.A., Hilton, S.C., Hawkins, M., Costigan, K.A., & Pressman, E.K. (2002). Maternal stress and affect influence fetal neurobehavioral development. *Developmental Psychology, 38*, 659–668.

Feldman, W.M. (1920). *Principles of ante-natal and post-natal child physiology*. New York: Longmans.

Foushee, R.D., & Lickliter, R. (2002). Early visual experience affects postnatal auditory responsiveness in bobwhite quail (Colinus virginianus). *Journal of Comparative Psychology, 116*, 369–380.

Gerhardt, K.J., Abrams, R.M., Kovaz, G.M., Gomez, K.J., & Conlon, M. (1988). Intrauterine noise levels in pregnant ewes produced by sound applied to the abdomen. *American Journal of Obstetrics and Gynecology, 159*, 228–232.

Granier-Deferre, C., Bassereau, S., Ribeiro, A., Jacquet, A.-Y., & Lecanuet, J.-P. (2003, August). *Cardiac "orienting" response in fetuses and babies following in utero melody-learning*. Paper presented at XI European Conference on Developmental Psychology, Milan, Italy.

Granier-Deferre, C., & Lecanuet, J.-P. (1987). Influence de stimulations auditives precoces sur la maturation anatomique et fonctionnelle du systeme auditif [Influence of precocial auditory stimulation on the anatomical and functional maturation of the auditory system]. *Progress in Neonatology*, 7, 236–249.

Hall, W.G., & King, C. (1990). Developmental change in unilateral olfactory habituation is mediated by anterior commissure maturation. *Behavioral Neuroscience*, 104, 796–807.

Honeycutt, H., & Lickliter, R. (2003). The influence of prenatal tactile and vestibular stimulation on auditory and visual responsiveness in bobwhite quail: A matter of timing. *Developmental Psychobiology*, 43, 71–81.

Kawai, N., Morokuma, S., Tomonaga, M., Horimoto, N., & Tanaka, M. (2003). Associative learning and memory in a chimpanzee fetus: Learning and long-lasting memory before birth. *Developmental Psychobiology*, 44, 116–122.

Kisilevsky, B.S., Hains, S.M.J., Lee, K., Xie, X., Huang, H., Ye, H.-H., et al. (2003). Effects of experience on fetal voice recognition. *Psychological Science*, 14, 220–224.

Klosovski, B.N. (1963). *The development of the brain.* Oxford: Pergamon.

Lecanuet, J.-P., Gautheron, B., Locatelli, A., Schaal, B., Jacquet, A.-Y., & Busnel, M.-C. (1998). What sounds reach fetuses: Biological and non-biological modelling of the transmission of pure tones. *Developmental Psychobiology*, 33, 203–220.

Lecanuet, J.-P., Granier-Deferre, C., & Busnel, M.-C. (1989). Sensorialité foetale: Ontogenèse des systèmes sensoriels, conséquences de leur fonctionnement foetal [Fetal sensoriality: ontogeny of sensory systems, consequences of their fetal functioning]. In J.P. Relier, J. Laugier, & B.L. Salle (Eds.), *Médecine périnatale* (pp. 201–225). Paris: Médecine-Sciences Flammarion.

Lecanuet, J.-P., & Jacquet, A.-Y. (2002). Fetal responsiveness to maternal passive swinging in low heart rate variability state: Effect of stimulation, direction and duration. *Developmental Psychobiology*, 40, 57–67.

Lecanuet, J.-P., Manéra, S., & Jacquet, A.-Y. (2002, April). *Fetal cardiac responses to mother's voice and to another woman's voice.* Paper presented at the International Conference on Infant Studies (ICIS Meeting), Toronto, Canada.

Lécuyer, R. (1989). *Bébés astronomes, bébés psychologues: L'intelligence de la première année* [Baby astronomers, baby psychologists: Inteliigence in the first year]. Liège: Mardaga.

Mastropieri, D.P., & Turkewitz, G. (1999). Prenatal experience and neonatal responsiveness to vocal expressions of emotion. *Developmental Psychobiology*, 35, 204–214.

Moon, C., Panneton-Cooper, R.K., & Fifer, W.P. (1993). Two-day-olds prefer their native language. *Infant Behavior and Development*, 16, 495–500.

Moore, D.R. (1985). Postnatal development of the mammalian central auditory system and the neural consequence of auditory deprivation. *Acta Otolaryngologica*, 421, 19–38.

Moore, D.R. (2002). Auditory development and the role of experience. *British Medical Bulletin, 63,* 171–181.

Panneton, R.K. (1985). *Prenatal auditory experience with melodies: Effects on postnatal auditory preferences in human newborns.* Unpublished doctoral dissertation, University of North Carolina at Greensboro, North Carolina.

Preyer, W. (1882). *Dies Seel Des Kinder [The mind of the child].* Lepizig: Fernau.

Pujol, R., & Uziel, A. (1986). Auditory development: Peripheral aspects. In P.F. Timiras & E. Meisami (Eds.), *Handbook of human biologic development* (pp. 109–130). Boca Raton: CRC Press.

Romand, R. (1997). Modification of tonotopic representaion in the auditory system during development. *Progress in Neurobiology, 51,* 1–17.

Ronca, A.E., & Alberts, J.R. (1995). Maternal contributions to fetal experience and the transition from prenatal to postnatal life. In J.-P. Lecanuet, W.P. Fifer, N.A. Krasnagor, & W.P. Smotherman (Eds.), *Fetal development: A psychobiological perspective* (pp. 331–350). Hillsdale, NJ: Erlbaum.

Rose, S. (1989). Measuring infant intelligence: New perspectives. In M.H. Bornstein & N.A. Krasnegor (Eds.), *Stability and continuity in mental development: Behavioral and biological perspectives* (pp. 171–188). Hillsdale, NJ: Erlbaum.

Rubel, E.W., & Ryals, B.M. (1982). Patterns of hair cell loss in chick basilar papilla after intense auditory stimulation: Exposure duration and survival time. *Acta Otolaryngologica, 93,* 31–41.

Rubel, E.W., & Ryals, B.M. (1983). Development of the place principle: Acoustical trauma. *Science, 219,* 512–514.

Schaal, B., Marlier, L., & Soussignan, R. (1998). Olfactory function in the human fetus: Evidence from selective neonatal responsiveness to the odour of amniotic fluid. *Behavioral Neuroscience, 112,* 1438–1449.

Schaal, B., Marlier, L., & Soussignan, R. (2002). Human foetuses learn odours from their pregnant mother's diet. *Chemical Senses, 25,* 729–737.

Sontag, L. (1965). Implications of fetal behavior and environment for adult personalities. *Annals New York Academy of Sciences, 134,* 782–786.

Stickrod, G., Kimble, D.P., & Smotherman, W.P. (1982). In utero taste/odor aversion conditioning in the rat. *Physiology and Behavior, 28,* 5–7.

Tsao, F.-M., Liu, H.-M., & Kuhl, P. (2004). Speech perception in infancy predicts language development in the second year of life: A longtudinal study. *Child Development, 75,* 1067–1084.

Vince, M.A. (1979). Postnatal consequences of prenatal sound stimulation in the guinea-pig. *Animal Behaviour, 27,* 908–918.

Zimmer, E.Z., Chao, C.R., Guy, G.P., Marks, F., & Fifer, W.P. (1993). Vibroacoustic stimulation evokes fetal micturition. *Obstetrics & Gynecology, 8,* 178–180.

FURTHER READING

Birnholz, J.C., & Benacerraf, B.B. (1983). The development of the human fetal hearing. *Science, 222,* 516–518.

Gottlieb, G.G. (2001). A developmental psychobiological systems view: Early formulation and current status. In S. Oyama, R. Gray, & P. Griffiths (Eds.), *Cycles of contingency* (pp. 41–54). Cambridge, MA: MIT Press.

Hepper, P. (2003). Prenatal psychological and behavioural development. In J. Valsiner & K. Connolly (Eds.), *Handbook of developmental psychology* (pp. 91–113). London: Sage.

Jeffery, N., & Spoor, F. (2004). Prenatal growth and development of the modern human labyrinth. *Journal of Anatomy, 204,* 71–92.

Joseph, R. (1999). Fetal brain and cognitive development. *Developmental Review, 20,* 81–98.

Kisilevsky, B.S., & Low, J.A. (1998). Human fetal behavior: 100 years of study. *Developmental Review, 18,* 1–29.

Lai, C.H., & Chan, Y.S. (2001). Development of the vestibular system. *Neuroembryology, 1,* 61–71.

Madison, L.S., Madison, J.K., & Adubato, S.A. (1986). Infant behavior and development in relation to fetal movement and habituation. *Child Development, 57,* 1475–1482.

Schaal, B., Lecanuet, J.-P., & Granier-Deferre, C. (1999). Sensory and integrative development in the human fetus and perinates: The usefulness of animal models. In M. Haug & R.E. Whalen (Eds.), *Brain, behavior and cognition: Animal models and human studies* (pp. 119–142). Washington, DC: American Psychological Association.

Wakai, R., Leuthold, A., & Martin, C. (1996). Fetal auditory evoked responses detected by magnetoencephalography. *American Journal of Obstetrics and Gynecology, 74,* 1484–1496.

CHAPTER 3

FROM AMNION TO COLOSTRUM TO MILK: ODOR BRIDGING IN EARLY DEVELOPMENTAL TRANSITIONS

Benoist Schaal*

ABSTRACT

This chapter focuses on the roles of olfaction in the adaptive responsiveness of newborns around birth. It starts with the facts that (1) the fluids that normally contact the nasal chemoreceptors *in utero* (amniotic fluid) and in the postnatal niche (colostrum and milk) carry odors that are attractive to newborns, and (2) no distinctive orientation responses are displayed when the odors of these fluids are presented to newborns in a paired-choice paradigm. Accordingly, these perinatal substrates are interpreted as being treated by newborns in an equivalent manner on either sensory or motivational grounds. Various physiological and behavioral mechanisms in the mother-infant unit give credit to the notion of a chemical overlap between amniotic and lacteal niches. These results, obtained in newborns from different mammalian species, point to a general means of

*I would like to thank the numerous collaborators who contributed to the gathering of the results reported in this chapter: Jean-Louis Brazier, Maurice Chastrette, Henri Cohen, Olivier Defaux, Michel Desage, Gérard Coureaud, Tao Jiang, Dominique Longlois, Jean-Pierre Lecanuet, Luc Marlier, Anne-Sophie Moncomble, Raymond Nowak, Pierre Orgeur, Christian Rognon, and Robert Soussignan. I also acknowledge inspiration from fruitful discussions with Eliott Blass, Carolyn Granier-Deferre, Elisabeth Hertling, André Holley, Jean-Pierre Lecanuet, David Lewkowicz, Pascal Poindron, Gilles Sicard, Jacob Steiner, and Richard Tremblay. The constructive comments of Bob Lickliter and Brian Hopkins on a previous draft are gratefully acknowledged.

adaptive responsiveness to early transitions in development. Specifically, they raise the hypothesis that newborns are prepared to attend certain odor stimuli through their experience in the prenatal niche. Several testable predictions raised by this hypothesis led to corroborative evidence: (1) the degree of amniotic-lacteal similarity appears to be higher right after birth, (2) fetal odor experience results in a selective orientation response to that same odor after birth, and (3) the disruption of the perinatal odor continuity induces measurable consequences in neonatal behavior. Thus, the fetal brain registers uterine odor stimuli and mediates positive orientation when these odorants are re-encountered in the newborn's environment. While neonatal odor responses are canalized through fetal experience, neonates also bear the pervasive ability to acquire novel odor information in associative and non-associative contexts. A range of mechanisms are surveyed that do not necessarily rely on the transnatal chemosensory continuity, but which are facilitatory or complementary of it. All told, multiple, redundant processes promote the early learning of the odor properties of the postnatal environment, some operating in anticipation (pre-functional responses, fetal learning), while others work in the immediacy of postnatal constraints. Thus, organisms are born with a draft version of the odor environment they will face later as newborns or weanlings. This fetal draft of the postnatal environment is rapidly revised and changed in content as knowledge is being expanded in the physical and social worlds.

INTRODUCTION

Among psychobiological discontinuities that pace early development—namely, birth, weaning, motor autonomy, and puberty—the former is certainly the most dramatic in its multiple and vital consequences. The psychobiological impact of birth remains poorly understood, however (Dawes, 1968; Hofer, 1981; Lagercrantz & Slotkin, 1986). One may admit that it represents a sequence of species-specific microtransitions that recruit all reactive resources of the nascent creature to maintain homeostasis. During the hours of ongoing labor, the "birthing" organism passes through episodes of regulatory turmoil in metabolic (relative hypoxia, hypercapnia and acidosis, hypothermia), physical (waves of bodily compression, especially of the head), and ecological (sharp alterations in the intensity, timing, and novelty of the sensory environment) conditions. This unsteady episode also massively resonates on neuroendocrine processes (Lagercrantz, 1996) that influence brain systems underlying arousal and initial cognitive activity (Ronca & Alberts, 1995).

For newborn organisms, one way to efficiently face the upheavals of the birth transition is to actively bring to it a set of sensory, cognitive, and motor competences that foster the engagement of initial attention, investigation, recognition, and decision for directed actions. These inaugural abilities for perception and action are rapidly completed and renewed through the infant's ability to encode and retain unprecedented sources of information and to use them according to the changing requirements of the environment and of the organism itself. However, though newborn organisms have the final "word" in any behavioral decision leading to adapted responses, they cannot be considered separately from the parental contribution. In all mammals, females have been selected to provide passive (physiological) and/or active (behavioral) assistance to complement their offspring's reactive and proactive capacities. One of the strategies that is most conserved among mammalian females is to carry over (into the newly born offspring's surroundings) stimuli that were present in the fetal environment, and at the same time boost the infant up into states of activation within a background of balanced emotion.

Recent research has documented how prenatal development contributes to prepare sensorimotor abilities to function *ex utero* as systems of "perceptual beaconing"; namely, sensory specializations attuned for the extraction of given cues from the complex flow of postnatal information (e.g., Alberts, 1987; Smotherman & Robinson, 1987, 1995). This beaconing is actualized in neonatal sensory expectations, the satisfaction of which evokes positive orientation and searching responses, settles distress, and in the longer run promotes metabolic optimization and adapted growth, and cognitive integration. Among candidates for such transnatal sensory beacons in human *perinates*, one may mention some which emerge in the individual-specific environment, such as soft tactile stimulations (e.g., Scafidi et al., 1990), dietary odors transferred into the amniotic fluid, milk, and other maternal biological secretions (e.g., Schaal, Marlier, & Soussignan, 1995a, 1998; Sullivan & Toubas, 1998), and maternal voice or environmental noise (e.g., DeCasper & Fifer, 1980; DeCasper & Spence, 1986; Fifer & Moon, 1995; Hepper, 1988a). Other such perinatal sensory beacons may result from *functional canalization* in the species-specific uterine environment. They can be defined as the fraction of stimuli to which any fetus of a given species has been unavoidably exposed.

These beacons may include thermotactile cues of comfort and body containment, physiological noises (DeCasper & Sigafoos, 1983; Salk, 1962), and possibly certain odors derived from the normal metabolism of the fetal-maternal unit.

The newborn brain also contains pre-organized[1] information about highly predictable aspects of the environment. These pre-organized perceptual competences are linked with specific motor abilities expressing attention or approach, and they arise without specific input from species- or individual-specific experience in the fetal or postnatal environments (cf. Morton & Johnson, 1991). Among such processes that have been best documented so far, one may include visual attraction to human faces (e.g., Farah, Rabinowitz, Quinn, & Liu, 2000; Johnson, Dziurawiec, Ellis, & Morton, 1991; Simion, Valenza, & Umiltà, 1998) and gazing eyes (Farroni, Csibra, Simion, & Johnson, 2002), as well as positive responses to sweet taste (e.g., Blass & Ciaramito, 1994; Rao, Blass, Brignol, Marino, & Glass, 1997; Steiner, 1979; Steiner, Glaser, Hawilo, & Berridge, 2001) and to certain odorants evolved for specialized communicative purposes (e.g., Schaal et al., 2003). Yet another way through which prenatal experience might impinge on neonatal expectations is through *amodal mechanisms*, especially those related to the perception of environmental intensity (Turkewitz, Lewkowicz, & Gardner, 1983) or variability (e.g., Turkewitz, 1994). For example, the fetal encoding of the generally low-intensity stimulations that normally take place in the uterine environment may determine later preferences for stimuli matched in intensity with those received *in utero* (Schneirla, 1965).

In this chapter, we will focus on the role of olfaction in the responsiveness of mammalian neonates during the transition from the prenatal to the postnatal environment. More specifically, we shall highlight some ways in which prenatal olfactory experience prepares selective responsiveness to the odor environment in neonates. A comparative approach will be presented—mainly based on studies conducted in human perinates, but also in rat, rabbit, and ovine counterparts—to examine to what extent odor cues acquired *in utero* can govern the rapid expression of adaptive responses after birth.

---

[1] Bob Lickliter suggested that such information could also be labeled as "currently unexplained" or "insufficiently researched."

NEWBORNS ARE ATTRACTED TO THE ODORS OF AMNIOTIC FLUID AND MILK

The fact that newborn mammals respond to milk by attraction and readiness to ingest has been known for long time. Traditional pastoralists certainly used that tendency to lure young animals for centuries (e.g., Evans-Pritchard, 1937). One of the earliest "experimental" records on neonatal attraction for milk is certainly Galen's (129–199 BP) trial with a goat kid that survived one of his renowned fetal dissections. This kid was taken from the female and left in a storeroom containing vessels filled with wine, oil, honey, milk, and various cereals and fruits. "'We first noticed,' described Galen, 'this little kid go on foot as if it knew that legs served to walk. Then we saw it shaking the remaining wetness from the mother, and scratching its flank with one leg; it snuffled at each vessel in the room, and after having sniffed them all, absorbed the milk. At this moment, we uttered that *Hippocrates* was right in foretelling that animals' natures do not need to be taught'" (author's translation; Daremberg, 1856, as cited in Grmek, 1997, pp. 31–32).

More recent experiments refined Galen's insight in demonstrating that volatile compounds carried in homospecific lacteal secretions, including *colostrum* and transitional and mature milks, generally evoke attention and appetitive responses in mammalian newborns. Indeed, newly born lambs are attracted to a cloth impregnated with ovine milk as compared to a scentless, humid cloth (Schaal & Orgeur, unpublished data). Likewise, rabbit milk carries various odor cues, to which rabbit pups respond very reliably by activation, orientation, and oral seizing (Coureaud & Schaal, 2000; Keil, von Stralendorff, & Hudson, 1990). In addition, human infants evince attraction or mouthing to the odor of human milk obtained from either their own mother (Marlier & Schaal, 1997) or from an unfamiliar lactating woman (Marlier & Schaal, 2001; Soussignan, Schaal, Marlier, & Jiang, 1997).

Parallel evidence was obtained for positive reactions of newborns to birth fluids. This was first assessed empirically in the rat (Blass & Teicher, 1980; Teicher & Blass, 1977). Newborn pups generally express searching and oral grasping of a nipple when they are put in contact with the abdomen of a lactating female rat. But when the female's abdomen is washed to remove natural odor cues, the pups refuse to orally grasp the nipple to which they are directed. If such washed nipples are thereafter painted with amniotic fluid, then normal oral seizing performance recovers. Thus, it was assumed that a prenatal odor cue can govern the release of the initial nipple attachment in rat pups. In the normal course of events, such amniotic traces are spread on the female's abdominal fur by her self-licking activity during parturition (Roth & Rosenblatt, 1966) and certainly also by direct deposition through the newly born pups' searching motions.

Positive responsiveness to the odors of substrates from the prenatal environment (namely, amniotic fluid or placenta) was later confirmed in a wide array of mammalian newborns, including *rat and mouse pups* (Hepper, 1987; Kodama, 1990, 2002; Kodama & Smotherman, 1997), *rabbit pups* (Coureaud, Schaal, Hudson, Orgeur, & Coudert, 2002), and *lambs* and *piglets* (Parfet & Gonyou, 1991; Schaal et al., 1995a). Human infants have also been shown to detect, and positively react to, the odor of their own *amniotic fluid* presented either as a single stimulus (Soussignan et al., 1997) or in a double-choice test (Marlier, Schaal, & Soussignan, 1994; Schaal, Marlier, & Soussignan, 1995b). This finding has been corroborated in a later study (Varendi, Porter, & Winberg, 1996). Thus, odors from either salient fluid that normally contact the nasal chemoreceptors at the fetal or neonatal stages elicit general attraction or positive pre-feeding behavior in the newborn organism when presented in isolation from other stimuli.

CHEMOSENSORY CONTINUITY ACROSS BIRTH IN MAMMALIAN INFANTS: A WORKNG HYPOTHESIS

We wondered then how newborns would behave when introduced to a *simultaneous* choice between the odor of their amniotic environment and that of their mother's *colostrum* or milk. Two-day-old *breast-fed human infants* exposed to such a choice test did not appear to respond differentially in terms of head (nose) orientation to either stimulus (Marlier, Schaal, & Soussignan, 1998a), as shown in Figure 3.1. Thus, at least in a choice paradigm that consisted of presenting frontally paired odors to active infants isolated from the familiar cues afforded by their mother, no distinctive relative response was noted in terms of average appetitive head-turning duration. This nondifferential orientation response to apparently distinct odor stimuli may be explained either in terms of nondetection, of nondiscrimination, or finally of positive discrimination but without hedonic differentiation. As mentioned in the previous section, the choice tests opposing each of the above odorous stimuli with scentless control stimuli allowed

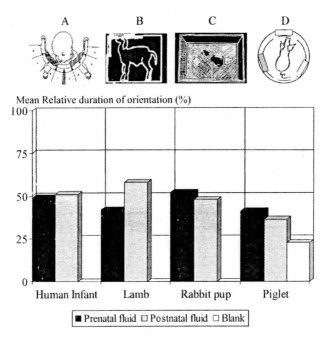

Figure 3.1. Mean relative duration of head (nose) orientation of diverse mammalian newborns when simultaneously exposed to the odor of the last substrate they contacted before birth—amniotic fluid—and the first salient odor substrate they contacted after birth contingently with oral and ingestive satisfaction—colostrum or milk. (A) Head orientation response of two-day-old breast-fed human infants exposed to their own amniotic fluid and to their mother's colostrum in two-choice test of two minutes (n = 23). (*Source*: From Marlier, Schaal, & Soussignan, 1998a.) (B) Nuzzling response of newborn lambs within two hours after birth to the odor of their own amniotic fluid and their dam's colostrum in a five-minute, two-choice test (n = 14). (*Source*: Original data from Schaal & Orgeur, 1992.) (C) Body orientation response of newborn rabbit pups to the odor of placenta from their litter and colostrum from their doe in a two-minute choice-test (n = 20). (*Source*: From Coureaud, Schaal, Hudson, Orgeur, & Coudert, 2002.) (D) Nosing response of newborn piglets exposed to a three-choice test (duration: five minutes) opposing the odors of their own birth fluids, of the sow's milk, and of a blank stimulus (n = 68). (*Source*: From Parfet & Gonyou, 1991.)

us to exclude the possibility that the infants were eventually unable to detect them. But the other two alternatives cannot be properly addressed with the experimental paradigm used here. The critical experiment would be to habituate an orientation response criterion with one of the odorants and dishabituate it with the second odorant. Without going deeper into the discussion of the perceptual processes underlying the observed phenomenon, we will first consider that two-day-old breast-fed newborns treat the odors of *amniotic fluid* and *colostrum* in an equivalent manner on either chemosensory and/or motivational grounds, at least in regards to the *head orientation response*. Other experiments using the odors of amniotic fluid and milk, but focusing on different response systems, also indicated non-differential treatment of both stimuli (Soussignan et al., 1997). These responses involved the autonomous nervous system (respiratory rate) and oro-facial effectors (facial muscle activity and/or mouthing movement).

The hypothesis of an equivalence response between two stimuli implies that the *human newborn* has the ability to assess the qualitative and/or quantitative distance between them. Deriving a single category from different versions of a stimulus has been termed "extraction of invariants" (Antell, Caron, & Myers, 1985) or "perceptual equivalence categorization" (Bornstein, 1984) in vision research. Such neonatal abilities for invariance extraction have also been shown in the olfactory domain. Engen and Lipsitt (1965) found that three-day-olds had the capacity to discriminate the odor of pure odorants from that of their mixture. They habituated the infants' respiratory response (variation in respiratory rhythm) with the odors of an anise-asafoetida mixture, and thereafter obtained dishabituation with the asafoetida compound but not with the anise compound. Judgments of similarity by adults suggested that the odor of the mixture was dominated by the anise compound, indicating that the newborns had difficulties in discriminating between pure anise and its mixture. The experiment was then repeated with another binary blend using a pure compound (isoamyl acetate and heptanal), which had more balanced contributions to the mixture. In this case, after habituation with the mixture, either pure odorant became efficient to dishabituate the respiratory response. In addition, the dishabituation efficiency of each component's odor was proportional to its dissimilarity from the mixture's odor as assessed by adults. This approach not only confirmed that three-day-old newborns have subtle discriminative abilities for odorants, but it also suggested that they perceive the qualitative distance between those odors in a similar way to adults. Neonatal ability to extract invariants from qualitatively distinct (to adult noses) odorant mixtures was also confirmed using the odors of various milks (Soussignan, Schaal, & Marlier,

1999). In particular, newborns were able to generalize the chemosensory features of a familiar *formula milk* to a similar, but qualitatively different (to adults), formula they had never encountered before.

Can the undifferentiated orientation patterns exhibited by human infants facing the amniotic fluid-milk odor contrast be observed in other mammalian newborns? In the handful of mammalian species investigated so far, neonates evinced comparable responses when they were simultaneously exposed to the homologous choice between the salient odors from the prenatal and postnatal environment (Fig. 3.1). For example, *newborn rabbits* introduced into a two-choice arena, which is presenting simultaneously the odors of placenta and conspecific milk, orient randomly to either compartment (Coureaud et al., 2002). Likewise, right after birth, ingestion-naïve *lambs* display undifferentiated nuzzling toward two pieces of cloth presented in the same time, one being impregnated with their own amniotic fluid and the other with their mother's colostrum (Schaal & Orgeur, unpublished data). Finally, newly born *piglets* exposed to a three-choice test opposing water, colostrum, and birth fluids exhibit higher but equal durations of exploration and nosing toward the latter two stimuli (Parfet & Gonyou, 1991). Thus, the newborns of various mammalian species also display equivalent attention to either perinatal fluids, as expressed by searching responses such as general orientation movements, head turning, and olfactory or gustatory exploration.

Based on current empirical evidence, the general hypothesis can be proposed that mammalian perinates are exposed to a relative continuity in the chemosensory and/or motivational properties of the biological substrates they are obligatorily contacting in the late prenatal and early postnatal niches. This *transnatal chemosensory continuity hypothesis* has two facets. First, it implies continuity in the organism's ability to detect and process odor information *in utero* and to memorize it from the fetal to neonatal stages of development. This point has been discussed at length elsewhere, and the reader is referred to various published reviews for a more complete discussion on perinatal sensory matters (e.g., Schaal, 1988a, 1988b; Schaal & Orgeur, 1992; Schaal, Orgeur, & Rognon, 1995; Smotherman & Robinson, 1987, 1995). Second, the above hypothesis implies that a (partial) chemical overlap exists between the late amniotic and the early postnatal niche. This point will be discussed at more length later in this chapter.

WHAT IS THE DEGREE OF SIMILARITY BETWEEN AMNIOTIC FLUID AND MILK?

Chemosensory Bases

The nondifferential treatment of both perinatal fluids by newborns may be first explained in terms of their chemosensory resemblance. In late pregnancy and early lactation, the fetal, amniotic, and mammary compartments are indeed contemporaneously exposed to the same chemical entries in the form of compounds introduced by the female's ingestion, inhalation, or skin care, or produced by the normal metabolic or immunogenetic functioning of the mother-fetus dyad.

The most obvious pathway to chemical overlap is the direct, simultaneous transfer of odorigenic compounds from maternal diet into the amniotic (i.e., extra-embryonic fluid), fetal (i.e., the fetal-placental blood stream), and lacteal compartments. *Amniotic fluid* has indeed been repeatedly shown to be permeated by aroma compounds from the mother's diet in humans (Hauser, Chitayat, Berns, Braver, & Muhlhauser, 1985; Korman, Cohen, & Preminger, 2001; Mennella, Johnson, & Beauchamp, 1995; Snell, 1973), as well as in various nonhuman mammals (Bilko, Altbäcker, & Hudson, 1994; Coureaud et al., 2002; Nolte, Provenza, Callan, & Panter, 1995; Schaal, Orgeur, Desage, & Brazier, 1994).

The transfer of dietary aromas operates from the mother's blood stream to colostrum/milk, as shown in various mammalian females either by chemical analyses (Desage, Schaal, Orgeur, Soubeyran, & Brazier, 1996) or by measuring the impact on subsequent flavor preferences in weaning animals (e.g., Bilko et al., 1994; Capretta & Rawls, 1974; Galef & Henderson, 1972; Le Magnen & Tallon, 1968; Mainardi, Poli, & Valsecchi, 1989; Moio, Rillo, Ledda, & Addeo, 1996; Schaal et al., 1994; Wuensch, 1975). Curiously, comparable studies are still rare in human females, although the alteration of milk odor after the ingestion of strongly flavored meals is often mentioned by midwives and obstetricians (e.g., Barrois & Larouzé, 1991; Baum, 1981; Font, 1990). Experiments by Mennella and Beauchamp (1991a, 1991b, 1996, 1999) provide empirical evidence that aromas from various foods (e.g., garlic, vanilla, alcohol, carrot) easily pass into milk. By regularly sampling milk after human mothers have ingested garlic capsules and presenting them to adult judges, they revealed changes in the odor intensity of milk that culminate two to three hours after ingestion. These odor changes are detectable to nurslings as well, as they observably modify their sucking pattern at the breast and amount of milk consumed.

Other pathways are also very influential on the olfactory profile of either perinatal fluid. *Maternally-inhaled odorants* are transferred with a very brief delay to blood, and then to amniotic fluid and milk. For example, volatile compounds from the *mother's diet* (Dougherty et al., 1962), from *perfumes* (Jirowetz, Jäger, Buchbauer, Nikiforov, & Raverdino, 1991), and from combusting tobacco (Karmowski et al., 1998; Lambers & Clark, 1996; Svensson, 1997) simultaneously pass into the fetal, amniotic, and mammary compartments. The transfer of the odorous compounds from *tobacco smoke* into milk can be clearly sniffed out by adult noses (Mennella & Beauchamp, 1998), and they may likely affect neonatal responses. Furthermore, the passage of odorigenic compounds has been attested from perfumes or varied cosmetic products applied directly on the mother's skin, with a chemically detectable transfer into milk (Liebl, Mayer, Ommer, Sonnichsen, & Koletzko, 2000; Rimkus & Wolf, 1996) and certainly into amniotic fluid as well.

Processes associated with *maternal physical exercise* might also exert simultaneous influence on the chemosensory properties of amniotic and lacteal fluids. Physical activity of the mother clearly affects the chemical composition of bodily fluids (Carey, Quinn, & Goodwin, 1997; Duffy, 1997; Wallace & Rabin, 1991). *Lactic acid* is the only metabolic marker investigated so far, but it is very likely that many other compounds bearing chemosensory impact are fluctuating as a function of maternal state and activities. Such exercise-induced changes in milk composition are detected by the nursling, who expresses increasing refusal of *maternal milk* as a function of the intensity of the effort performed by the mother (Wallace, Inbar, & Ernsthausen, 1992). In the same way, stressful situations can transitorily alter the chemosensory properties of the prenatal environment, either by acute transfer of stress-related compounds from mother to fetus through reduced rates of amniotic clearance by the placenta and correlative accumulation of metabolic by-products, or by direct fetal response to stressful stimuli. Such stimulations (e.g., high-intensity vibro-acoustic stimulation) have been shown to modify fetal states with a sharp emptying of the bladder into the amniotic pool (Zimmer, Chao, Guy, Marks, & Fifer, 1993), thus probably changing its chemical profile. Compounds bearing chemosensory impact might in this way be momentarily released and transferred toward the mother's bloodstream, where they may be collected in the *colostrum*.

The possibility of such subtle, bi-directional, fetal-maternal passages of chemosensory compounds is further documented with (as yet unidentified) volatile compounds generated by the fetal and maternal immunogenetic systems (i.e., *major histocompatibility complex* [MHC]). In *mice*, odorants reflecting the MHC of the fetus are externalized in the *pregnant mother's urine* (Beauchamp, Yamazaki, Currant, Bard, & Boyse, 1994), and most probably in her skin secretions and milk. The same phenomenon has been examined in our own species. In a first test, urine samples collected in the same women before and after delivery were clearly differentiated by rats used as trained "noses." That this olfactory discrimination between pre- and postnatal urine reflected the influence of the fetal genotype was assessed by mixing maternal postpartal urine with urine from either own or alien newborns. In this case, the discriminator rats responded more positively to the mother plus own newborn urine mixture rather than to the mother plus alien newborn urine mixture, which implies that fetal MHC-related odors contributed to the scent of mother's urine before birth (Beauchamp et al., 1995; Yamazaki, Currant, & Beauchamp, 2000). Such reciprocally transferred compounds may therefore contribute to the matching of the odor cues that are distributed into both perinatal fluids.

Finally, there is no reason to exclude the possibility that all the chemosensory-levelling processes mentioned above operate synergistically, leading to a multiply-determined chemosensory resemblance between the odor profiles encountered by the young organism prenatally, in amniotic fluid; and postnatally, in either *colostrum* or milk. One may note that mutual odor transfers between the conceptus and the mother lead to scent-matching processes that might also work on the parental side. Human mothers and fathers exposed to the odor of their offspring's amniotic fluid agreed that it was reminiscent both of the current odor of their newborn and of the mother's usual body odor before delivery (Schaal & Marlier, 1998).

Chemical Bases

Chemical analyses on the transfer of dietary aromas into both perinatal, biological compartments remain scarce, but they provide additional evidence for their chemical overlap. One preliminary gaschromatographic study was conducted to characterize the compounds shared by the *amniotic fluid* and milk obtained from the same women (Stafford, Horning, & Zlatkis, 1976). But this study has little value for the immediate postnatal period, because the sample of milk analyzed was collected on postpartum day thirty. Nevertheless (and not surprisingly), it could still identify some volatiles that were common in amniotic fluid and thirty-day milk. Other investigations targeted on given compounds demonstrated that volatiles bearing very strong olfactory impact are shared in amniotic and lacteal fluids. This is the case for at least volatile amines carrying strong animal odors (Lichtenberger, Gardner, Baretto, & Morris, 1991), and for several organic acids (Nichols, Hähnel, & Wilkinson, 1978; Ng, Fresen, & Bianchine, 1982; Rognon & Chastrette, 1992; Shimoda, Yoshimura, Ishikawa, Hayakawa, & Osajima, 2000).

Some analyses followed the transfer of markers of aroma into both amniotic fluid and milk after maternal ingestion by coupled gas chromatography-mass spectrometry. When ewes were fed a cumin-odorized diet, or were injected with cumin extract during the last days of gestation, several key odorants from *cumin* could be pinpointed in both maternal and fetal bloodstream, amniotic fluid, and milk (Desage, Schaal, Orgeur, et al., 1996; Schaal et al., 1995). A similar cumin ingestion experiment in human mothers indicated that some of these same markers were detectable in the amniotic fluid (Table 3.1; Desage, Schaal, Orgeur, et al., 1996). Moreover, the mothers

Table 3.1: Results of Chemical Analyses on Samples of Amniotic Fluid (AF)

Aroma Marker	AF1	AF2	AF3	AF4	AF5	AF6	AF7	AF8
β-pinene	–	–	–	–	–	–	–	–
p-cymene	–	–	–	–	–	–	–	–
Cineole	++	++	+	+	+	+	+	+
Limonene	–	–	++	++	–	++	+	++
γ-terpinene	–	+	+	–	–	–	–	–
Cuminaldehyde	++	++	–	–	–	–	–	–

The results were collected from eight different parturient women who, for the last two weeks of pregnancy, ingested capsules daily that contained powdered cumin. Six typical markers of the odor of cumin were extracted by solid phase micro-extraction and dosed by mass-spectrometry targeted on the characteristic ionic fragments of each compound. (–) represents the value below the detection threshold; (+) represents traces above the detection threshold, but below the quantification threshold; (++) represents more important traces. The dietary volatile compounds are variably transferred as a function of their nature and individual mother-fetus dyads.
Source: Original data from Desage, Schaal, Defaux, Cohen, & Brazier (1996).

participating in this experiment reported that the characteristic odor of cumin was detectable on the skin of their palms and forearms, indicating that odorants from diet may have been externalized into eccrine sweat or sebum. This suggests an additional way to generate chemosensory similarity between the amniotic environment and the body surface to which the infant is confronted.

TRANSNATAL OLFACTORY CONTINUITY: PREDICTIONS ON THE INFLUENCES OF PRENATAL EXPERIENCE ON POSTNATAL ODOR RESPONSIVENESS

If the hypothesis of transnatal chemosensory continuity has some biological validity, it should raise a series of predictions. Several of these predictions and their empirical assessment are outlined below.

Prediction 1. Newborns Should Selectively Recognize the Odors of Their Familiar Amniotic Fluid and Milk

It is a prerequisite of the above hypothesis that newborns are sensitive enough to recognize the peculiar quality of the odors of either fluid they contact perinatally. Regarding amniotic odor, mammalian infants from different species have been shown to orient to any sample of amniotic fluid from their own species (Schaal et al., 1995a, 1998; Teicher & Blass, 1977). In addition, they selectively oriented their nose to their own amniotic fluid when given the simultaneous choice between their familiar and an unfamiliar amniotic fluid. This was the case in murine (Hepper, 1987), ovine (Schaal et al., 1995b; Vince & Billing, 1986), and human newborns (Schaal et al., 1998). Thus, mammalian newborns respond at two levels to their amniotic odors: at a species-specific level and at an individual-specific level.

To our knowledge, a selective response to the odor of *maternal milk* has only been reported so far in human newborns. *Breast-fed infants* aged four days showed longer *head orientation* in response to the *odor of their mother's milk* when it was paired with milk collected from another woman who was in the same lactational stage (Marlier & Schaal, 1997). Previous studies using cotton pads applied to the mother's breast, hence collecting the entire exocrine secretion of that region, with milk presumably being the main substrate, provided convergent results (Macfarlane, 1975; Russell, 1976; Schaal et al., 1980).

The above results suggest an early ability of newborns to express selective responses to fluids from prenatal or postnatal origin; however, little is known regarding how these responses develop as a function of chemosensory maturation or direct exposure to these essential fluids. Although some data are indicative of discrimination between maternal and nonmaternal breast odors (i.e., Macfarlane, 1975; Russell, 1976; Schaal et al., 1980), they provide little information about the responses of newborns who are ingestively naïve. The following experiment described in prediction 2 shows that these responses may be highly dynamic in the first days after birth, particularly as a function of ingestive experience.

Prediction 2. Transnatal Chemosensory Similarity Should Be Maximal in the First Postnatal Days

It is likely that the olfactory similarity between amniotic fluid and lacteal secretions is maximal right after birth, when both media are under the contemporaneous influence of the same causes of variation. It should be recalled that *colostrum* is already present in the mammae in the last days or weeks of pregnancy, something that is also referred to as "prepartum mammary secretion" (Neville, 1995). Thus, it is as much exposed to the input of exogenic aroma compounds as is the amniotic pool. Due to its relative richness in proteins and lipids, colostrum may even have more affinity with certain lipophilic odorous compounds than *amniotic fluid*. Accordingly, a higher degree of chemosensory overlap between both perinatal fluids should occur in the first days after birth and hence result in less differentiated responses in newborns (especially those tested before their first colostrum intake). In the following days (namely, within postpartum days three through five), as the lactation process begins to set in, one may expect amniotic fluid to be increasingly discriminated and/or hedonically distinguished from lacteal secretions.

These predictions have been examined in the human infant over the five first postnatal days and, hence, over the sequence of changes affecting the makeup of milk in the human female. Within the first two days, the composition of *colostrum* remains relatively stable, enters in a transitional phase at day three, and by days four to five the neosecretion of milk increasingly replaces colostrum (Patton, Huston, Montgomery, & Josephson, 1986). These changes have been related to modifications in the olfactory properties of the lacteal fluids. To assess how infants differentiate their *amniotic fluid* odor from the evolving content of their mother's lacteal secretion, five groups of infants were exposed between days one and five to a choice-test pairing the odor of their amniotic fluid and the odor of their mother's colostrum/milk of the day (Marlier, Schaal, & Soussignan, 1997). Two phases in the pattern of neonatal response became apparent in these conditions (Fig. 3.2). First, between days one and three, the infants did not show evidence for olfactory differentiation of both substrates; second, by day four the infants not only differentiated, but they displayed longer durations of head turning toward their *mother's milk odor* as compared to the odor of their own amniotic fluid. This finding is in line with the hypothesis of a progressive shift in the infant's perception of the odor quality of milk relative to that of amniotic fluid, from a period of nondifferentiation to a period of clear differentiation.

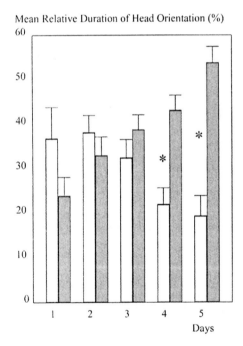

Figure 3.2. Relative duration of head orientation (±5% confidence interval) in five independent groups of (breast-fed) infants during their first five days of life. The subjects were simultaneously exposed to the odors of their amniotic fluid and of their mother's lacteal secretion of the day (within-group comparisons of relative duration of head orientation: *: $p < 0.01$). (*Source*: From Marlier, Schaal, & Soussignan, 1997.)

Prediction 3. Transnatal Chemosensory Similarity Cannot Exist between Amniotic Fluid and Artificial Formula Milks

Following the logic of the above argument, the degree of chemosensory continuity between human amniotic fluid and formulas derived from bovine milk cannot rival that of the degree between the amniotic and lacteal fluids of the same woman. Consequently, *bottle-fed infants* should orient differentially to the odors of their amniotic fluid and of their habitual formula milk.

This prediction was addressed in exposing two-day-old, bottle-fed infants to a two-choice test between the odor of both relevant substrates. These infants clearly differentiated the stimuli, with a more insistent head orientation to the prenatal, rather than postnatal, odor (Marlier, Schaal, & Soussignan, 1998b). Thus, in contrast with their two-day-old, breast-fed counterparts, who treated both stimuli nondifferentially in terms of relative duration of head turning (cf. prediction 1), bottle-fed infants expressed that their familiar prenatal fluid was different from, and had stronger reinforcing value than, heterospecific milk with which they were satiated several times prior to the test.

Prediction 4. The Exposure to an Aroma *In Utero* Should Lead to a Selective Response to the Same Pure Aroma *Ex Utero*

The transnatal continuity in odor cues may depend on species-specific or individual-specific factors pertaining to the fetus or the female. Species-specific factors designate compounds that are invariant across individual mother-fetus dyads, while individual-specific cues are idiosyncratic or shared by segments of a same population (culture) of individuals. To our knowledge, species-specific cues carried in amniotic fluid or milk have not been characterized so far in humans. But the above-reported neonatal differentiation of familiar and non-familiar amniotic fluids or milks (prediction 1) points to the fetal impact of individual-specific influences due to the females' ingestive choices.

Several experimental manipulations of the chemical composition of amniotic or lacteal fluids suggest that neonatal discrimination and preferences can be based on which simple compounds dominated quality in the prenatal environment. This effect was first demonstrated by injecting concentrated odor solutions into the amnion and testing fetuses thereafter *in utero* (Smotherman & Robinson, 1987) or *ex utero* (Pedersen & Blass, 1982; Smotherman, 1982a, 1982b;

Stickrod, Kimble, & Smotherman, 1982). In a second wave of less intrusive investigations, the composition of the amniotic fluid was manipulated by altering the diet of the pregnant female. In this way, *rat pups* born to females that had consumed either garlic, orange, or ethanol during the last days of gestation revealed a preference for that same flavor at the age of twelve days (Chotro & Molina, 1990; Hepper, 1988b). The same result was achieved with *newborn rabbits* exposed to various odor mixtures (*cumin, juniper, thyme*) transferred into the fetal compartment from the mother's diet (Coureaud et al., 2002; Hudson, Schaal, & Bilko, 1999; Semke, Distel, & Hudson, 1995). Prenatal exposure to a given odorant can have strong effects, as it can reverse spontaneous aversive reactions to it (e.g., Nolte & Mason, 1995). In the same way, *newborn lambs* displayed reduced aversion to cumin odor when they experienced it *in utero* through their mothers' diet (Schaal et al., 1995b).

Human infants born to mothers having consumed various anise-flavored foodstuffs displayed longer head orientation, more consummatory oral responses, and less facial responses of distaste when re-exposed to pure *anise odor* (anethole) on average three hours after birth (as compared to infants born to mothers who did not consume such flavors). Interestingly, the positive head orientation response to anise persisted for at least four days after birth in the anise-exposed group (Schaal, Marlier, & Soussignan, 2000), suggesting that fetal experience with odorants fosters memories upon which newborns can rely in the key period when they face their first pre-ingestive and ingestive experiences. Further results in favor of the postnatal impact of prenatal exposure to a given odorant have been found in the human neonate with respect to the following flavors: garlic (Hepper, 1995), carrot (Mennella, Jagnow, & Beauchamp, 2001), and alcohol (Faas, Sponton, Moya, & Molina, 2000).

Prediction 5. The Exposure to an Aroma in the Amniotic Context Should Lead to a Selective Response to the Same Aroma in the Milk Context

The olfactory analyzers of the newborn should be able to pick out sensory information that is common to distinct biological substrates experienced in different developmental niches. So far, this has been tested in the neonatal rabbit only. Two groups of *rabbit pups* were obtained through differentially feeding their mothers during pregnancy: a first group of females received a cumin-added diet, while the other group was exposed to the aromas of the standard diet (Coureaud et al., 2002). On the day after birth, before any suckling experience, the pups were administered a test consisting of the successive presentation of glass-rods carrying either milk from a cumin-eating female, milk from a female fed the standard diet, or water. The response criterion was the occurrence of searching behavior directed to the glass-rod and oral grasping of the glass-rod. As a result, the pups born to either group of females were highly reactive to both conspecific milks as compared to a control stimulus (water), but they were additionally discriminatively responsive between them. While the pups exposed to cumin *in utero* grasped the glass-rod carrying milk from cumin-eating females more frequently than those carrying the milk from mothers eating the standard diet, the pattern was reversed for the pups prenatally exposed to the aroma of the standard diet (Fig. 3.3). In summary, prenatal exposure to a given odor information led to a later positive response to that same odorant without distraction by the alteration of the biological matrix carrying the odorant.

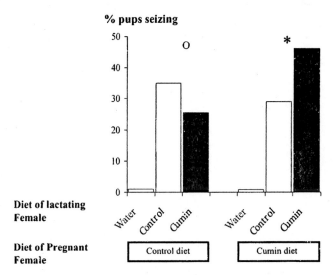

Figure 3.3. **Frequency of newborn rabbits orally seizing glass rods that convey colostrums the odor of which was either matched or mismatched with the odorous compounds that their mothers had consumed during gestation. The rabbit pups were tested before any postnatal ingestion. The colostrums were not from the pups' own mother (matched group: n = 14; nonmatched group: n = 20; within group comparisons: *: p < 0.05; °: p = 0.07). (*Source*: From Coureaud, Schaal, Hudson, Orgeur, & Coudert, 2002.)**

Prediction 6. A Disruption of Transnatal Olfactory Continuity Should Affect the Behavior of Newborns

If neonatal perception of a similarity between the amniotic and lacteal fluids has any adaptive significance, its perturbation should provoke measurable behavioral or physiological consequences. The effects of such perinatal violations to the hypothesized olfactory continuity have been approached in various ways in newborn rats, rabbits, and humans.

The survival of *rat pups* delivered prematurely (on the last day of gestation), and maintained in isolation from the dam during the first postnatal hour, depends on the nature of surrounding odors (Smotherman, Robinson, La Vallée, & Hennessy, 1987). This was shown in groups of animals put in warmed containers suffused with either: (1) amniotic odor; (2) odor of dimethyl disulfide, a compound from rat saliva; (3) a novel odorant (mint); and (4) no odor at all as a control condition. At the end of the one-hour isolation period, the survival rate was highest in condition 1 (90%), although it did not significantly differ from conditions 2 and 4 (80% and 75%, respectively). However, the introduction of the unfamiliar odorant (condition 3) was followed by a high level of pup mortality (50%), as compared with the condition in which pups were facing the familiar amniotic odor. This differential effect of the "continuous" (i.e., pups exposed to perinatal continuity) *versus* "discontinuous" perinatal environments is suggested to be mediated by the behavioral activation of the pups: while the familiar amniotic odor activated their general motor activity, the novel odorant depressed it.

In the *rabbit*, the consequence of the disruption in perinatal odor continuity was assessed by cross-fostering pups born to females exposed to an olfactorily-contrasted regimen during gestation (Coureaud et al., 2002). Immediately after delivery, half of each litter was fostered onto a female that had eaten the same diet as the biological mother, the other half being fostered onto a female that had consumed an olfactorily-distinct regimen. In this way, one group of pups was relatively "continuous" and the other relatively "discontinuous" in perinatal chemical ecologies. Both groups of pups were followed-up for their suckling success and amount of milk consumed during the first three suckling opportunities (i.e., during the first three days). The continuous pups manifested higher suckling success than the discontinuous pups at the first two nursing visits of the female (Fig. 3.4). In addition, those who acceded to the nipples in the discontinuous

% pups failing to suckle

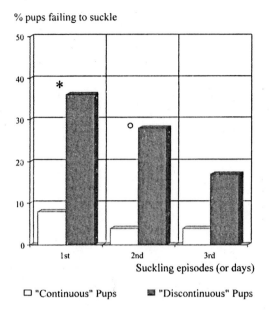

Figure 3.4. Proportion of rabbit pups that did not succeed in gaining milk in the first three sucking opportunities when exposed to perinatal odor continuity or to perinatal odor discontinuity (n = 25/group; within group comparisons: *: p < 0.05; °: p = 0.06). (*Source*: From Coureaud, Schaal, Hudson, Orgeur, & Coudert, 2002.)

group ingested on average less milk than the successful pups in the continuous group. Thus, the condition in which the olfactory properties of milk (or of the mother's belly skin secretions) are in line with the olfactory experience acquired *in utero* influencing the initial suckling performance of rabbit pups.

Finally, in the human case, breast-fed and *bottle-fed infants* can indeed be considered to be exposed to olfactorily-continuous and olfactorily-discontinuous perinatal environments, respectively. A contrasting picture appeared when both groups of infants were simultaneously presented with the odors of their own amniotic fluid and of their familiar milk, either human or formula. As already mentioned above, the relative response of *breast-fed infants* evolved from a pattern where they treated both perinatal odors as equivalent at age two days, to a pattern where they expressed a clear olfactory preference for milk over amniotic fluid (cf. prediction 2). In a functionally similar test opposing the odors of their own amniotic fluid and of their familiar *formula milk*, bottle-fed infants demonstrated a clear differential response in favor of the amniotic odor at two days of age. Thus, from this first test, both groups of infants behaved differently. Remarkably, in the same test at age four days, bottle-fed infants continued to respond more insistently to the odor of amniotic fluid presented along with formula milk (Marlier et al., 1998b), whereas their breast-fed peers displayed a clear preference for the odor of their postnatal food over the prenatal odor. In other words, when facing a preference test contrasting two salient odors experienced either prenatally or post-natally in association with satiation, breast-fed subjects developed a relative preference for the latter in a short delay, while bottle-fed infants did not follow the same pattern within the same delay.

The distinct pattern of relative preference acquisition for the post-natal food odor between different feeding categories of infants is open to several nonexclusive explanations. First, a sharp, as opposed to a progressive, olfactory transition may affect the differential engagement of neonatal learning of food. Second, *human milk* may contain olfactory factors that are intrinsically attractive to newborns. Third, human milk may carry particular substances that increase the conditionability of the odor cues contained in it. Fourth, human milk may have nonspecific biological (e.g., neurobiological, endocrine, digestive, absorptive) properties that formula milks do not have, which may differentially contribute to the faster conditioning to the lacteal food odor in breast-feeding than in bottle-feeding infants. Of relevance in this respect, *rat newborns* fed with a formula milk of hetero-specific (bovine) origin bear altered terminal fields of the *taste nerve* (cranial nerve VII) in the first-order central taste relay, as compared with pups fed rat milk (Lasiter & Diaz, 1992). Thus, being fed conspecific or heterospecific milk may condition the development of brain structures involved in chemosensory processing.

It should be borne in mind that the preceding results are *not* in line with the general principle of a positive relationship between the duration of odor exposure and subsequent preference development for that odor. They point to the fact that exposure effects may be heterogeneous in developmental time, and open the possibility that prenatal and/or perinatal periods might constitute *sensitive periods* for sensory, specifically chemosensory, acquisitions. Investigations on the postnatal durability of prenatal odor-learning conducted with nonhuman animal models clearly reveal that odors acquired *in utero* can be more, or at least equally, preferred than various odors subsequently associated with nurturance. Such a precedence effect of fetal odor learning has been noted in the *rat* during the pre-weaning period (e.g., Chotro & Molina,

1990; Hepper, 1988b), and even at adult age (Smotherman, 1982a). In the *rabbit*, an odor acquired prenatally can release as much appetitive and consummatory responses at weaning as odors acquired after birth in the context of suckling or first solid food experience (e.g., Bilko et al., 1994; Hudson et al., 1999). Moreover, in comparing the consummatory responses of mice to ortho-aminoacetophenone (a compound that is strongly repulsive to adult mice), offspring exposed to it *in utero* displayed greater acceptance, while adult mice exposed to it for the same amount of time maintained their avoidance (Nolte & Mason, 1995). As yet, comparable evidence in our own species remains equivocal.

Further Predictions in the Newborn and the Fetus

In summary, the above empirical results lend credit to the hypothesis of a *transnatal chemosensory continuity* in mammals. This hypothesis contributes to interpretive unity for available observations and provides heuristic guidance for further predictions. For example, in the conditions of the paired-choice paradigm presented above, *human newborns* would be expected not to orient differentially to *amniotic fluid* and *colostrum* taken from a same, but unfamiliar, mother-infant dyad. Rather, they should do so with the odors of alien amniotic fluid and colostrum collected from different donor women eating distinctly flavored diets, as indicated by newborn rabbits (cf. prediction 5). This relative overlap in odor quality should at least partially be corroborated by instrumental analyses (e.g., gas chromatography-mass spectrometry) and eventually by sensory analyses with panels of adults. Such analyses by adult noses conducted separately on either amniotic fluid or milk after the mothers ate garlic-filled capsules indicated consistent changes in quality and intensity of these fluids (Mennella & Beauchamp, 1991a; Mennella et al., 1995).

Another prediction would be that, at initial postnatal presentation, newborns should express stronger attraction to the odor of a milk that more closely matches their fetal odor experience. Specifically, they should favor odors that are in line with some individual- or species-specific cues sensed in the prenatal environment. Thus, *breast-fed newborns* should exhibit preference for the odor of the colostrum from their own mother relative to that of another mother in a relative preference test. In the same conditions, they should also evince stronger attraction to the odor of any *homospecific milk* over that of *heterospecific milk*. Some of the previous experiments are indicative of the fact that these two kinds of milks do not bear the same functional properties for newborns in terms of either odor properties (Russell, 1976) or impact on ingestive coordination (Johnson & Salisbury, 1977). Additionally, in keeping with the result showing neonatal odor preference for amniotic fluid over the familiar formula milk (cf. prediction 3), it may be anticipated that *bottle-fed newborns* introduced to a two-choice test opposing (non-familiar) homospecific milk and their (familiar) formula milk would also display a positive orientation bias, which would be expressed either as greater attraction toward the former over the latter or at least as equivalent attraction between both. It would also be of interest to compare the pattern of neonatal brain activation to both salient odor stimuli from the perinatal environment.

Another series of predictions can be offered on the fetal side. The fetus should react in anticipation to the chemosensory properties of conspecific colostrum or milk in a different way than it reacted to these same substrates from another species. This has been shown in the ovine fetus, which responds by increased tongue, lip, and oesophageal motility to the chemosensory properties of conspecific, but not of bovine, milk administered orally (Robinson, Wong, Roberston, Nathanielsz, & Smotherman, 1995). Fetal *lambs* also exhibit distinct responses to the oral infusion of ovine colostrum and milk (Robinson et al., 1995), indicating that the early shift in the composition of mammary secretions is detectable for the chemosensory system. The response to the peculiar properties of *colostrum* is thus already functional before direct experience with it, and it may be suggested that the amniotic-lacteal similarity may function in anticipation. Accordingly, conspecific colostrum/milk is expectedly carrying a different chemosensory quality than formulas based on soy or cow milk, and hence may induce distinct behavioral outcomes in *preterm infants.*

Although the two-choice paradigm described above relies exclusively on odors, nasal and oral chemoreceptors are normally co-stimulated in the perinatal organism, rendering the separate consideration of their functional roles in perinatal behavior artificial. Thus, to a certain extent the above argument about perinatal sensory continuity effects in nasal chemoreception may also be proposed for oral chemoreception (*gustation* and trigeminal sensation). The long-lasting impact of early taste experience in the nursing context on subsequent preferences has been repeatedly noted in human infants. For example, newborns exposed to formula milks tasting bitter, sour, or salty were more likely to consume subsequently sour-, bitter-, or salt-flavored beverages or foods (e.g., London, Snowdon, & Smithana,

1979; Mennella & Beauchamp, 2002; Vijande, Brime, Lopez-Sela, Costales, & Argüelles, 1996). Would neonates more readily consume milk carrying given sapid or odorous substances that elicit irritation mediated by the trigeminal nerve (e.g., *capsaicin* in African, or South- or Central-American infants, or *mint* in Arabic infants) if exposed to them *in utero*? Or would they ingest them more readily in food when exposed to them through milk (e.g., Kurata & Nakamura, 1994)? Even other dimensions of flavor (namely, textural or thermal properties) of amniotic fluid may be orally-sensed by fetuses, and involved in the regulation of neonatal ingestive responses.[2] Such subtle flavor differences between pre- and postnatal oral sensation may influence the initial appetitive and ingestive responses of the newborn, especially in the case of feeding with substitutive milk.

COMPLEMENTARY PROCESSES FAVOR PERINATAL CONTINUITY IN ODOR RESPONSES IN NEWBORN MAMMALS

Even though the hypothesis of chemosensory continuity accounts reasonably well for most of the empirical results that are available in the small number of species studied so far, it represents one possibility among others. Other processes certainly operate to complement the mammalian infant's use of the chemosensory match between the pre- and postnatal environments in its initial selective decisions.

Some studies may at first sight be considered as contradictory with the above hypothesis. In certain cases, neonatal organisms facing the amniotic or milk odors appear to give off distinct responses. For example, *rat pups* were reported to display only weak or no appetitive responses to milk or its odor when exposed to them on the first day after birth, despite several hours of prior contact with the mother and suckling experience. Such responses were, however, noted to develop

---

[2] Although it may be coincidental, one may note that in species where the amniotic fluid sharply decreases in volume and increases in viscosity during the last days of pregnancy (e.g., rat and rabbit; Tam & Chan, 1977), the first milk is also very viscous, while in species having abundant and watery amniotic fluid (e.g., sheep and human), the colostrum seems to have greater fluidity. One may note that human newborns presented with low-fat and high-fat formulas show more active sucking for the former (Catt, Mela, Rosenblatt, & Wells, unpublished data), which is in line with the fact that colostrum has a low fat content (Jeliffe & Jeliffe, 1978).

rapidly over the next two days as a function of increasing exposure to milk and its post-ingestive consequences (Hall, 1979; Terry & Johanson, 1987). Otherwise, rat pups successively presented (before their first feed) with amniotic fluid or milk odor on a surrogate nipple expressed the same frequency and duration of oral seizing toward both stimuli, but they indicated chemosensory differentiation by displaying a shorter latency to orally seize a nipple carrying milk than a nipple carrying amniotic fluid (Koffmann, Petrov, Varlinskaya, & Smotherman, 1998). These studies indicate a progressive development of consummatory responses for milk after birth, and a trend to distinguish milk from amniotic fluid in newborn rats. However, it can be argued that the milk used in these studies was not from rat females, but instead was "half-and-half" or heavy cream from pasteurized bovine milk, considered to mimic macronutrient composition and textural properties of mature rat milk (Hall & Rosenblatt, 1977). Although rat pups actively react to that model milk of heterospecific origin, their responses may not be representative of those they would give to homospecific milk, especially foremilk. In any case, future studies of this kind should consider using homospecific milk.

In a related experiment, cesarean-delivered *mouse pups* were shown to display mouthing when exposed to an object bearing amniotic fluid or to a mixture of it with milk from the mother. They did not respond when administered milk alone, however (Kodama, 2002). This would mean that mouse pups have the ability to olfactorily distinguish prenatal from postnatal substrates, but will respond positively to the latter only if it incorporates some elements from the prenatal environment. Such is generally the case in the natural succession of events following birth, when milk is initially sensed in the presence of the amniotic traces carried in the pup mouth or spread by the mother on her belly fur.[3]

---

[3] Another study reports distinctive responsiveness in different groups of human infants sequentially exposed immediately after birth to the odor of their own amniotic fluid, to their mother's "breast odor," or to a control stimulus (Varendi, Christenson, Porter, & Winberg, 1998). The infants exposed to the amniotic fluid odor cried for a shorter median duration relative to those exposed to the mother's "breast odor." These results were interpreted as evidence for discriminative response between amniotic and "breast odor." But the "breast odor" appeared to be only nominal, as it excluded colostrum and was obviously tainted by axillary secretions. Thus, the "breast odor" actually used in the study can reasonably be considered to be dominated by the axillary output, which is known

The studies just mentioned might at first sight disagree with aspects of the hypothesis that assumes chemosensory and/or motivational resemblance of both perinatal fluids. It may be noted, however, that these studies do not rely on *appetitive responses* between paired stimuli, but rather they rely on oral responses related to *consummatory proneness* in face of stimuli presented individually, often after stimulation of taste. It cannot be excluded that significant chemosensory stimuli can elicit a range of diverse reactions that depend on heterogeneous mechanisms of control, and which are differentially indicative of discrimination. Appetitive and consummatory behaviors have dissociated since Craig's (1918) proposal, the former taking place before the desired object is obtained, while the latter takes place after. Neonatal body or head orientations are usually considered to reflect the operation of a general appetitive mechanism of sensation-seeking, attention, and recognition memory (Kuhl, 1985), whereas oro-facial responses are seen in this early stage as reflecting the stimulus-bound operation of a selective hedonic monitor tied to ingestion (Soussignan et al., 1999; Steiner, 1979; Steiner et al., 2001). Thus, preferential responsiveness derived from a test paradigm looking for appetitive behavior may not necessarily predict the result of a test conducted in the consummatory (feeding) context (e.g., Berridge, 2000). Hence, newborn organisms may simultaneously orient nondifferentially to certain stimuli and display discriminative oral behavior to the same stimuli.

Complementary mechanisms may be envisaged for the establishment of a rapid generalization of positive responses from amniotic fluid to colostrum/milk, without both of them necessarily sharing a high degree of chemosensory resemblance or motivational equivalence. At least five of such mechanisms (as well as their combinations) may be considered.

Anointing the Postnatal Environment with Prenatal Fluid

Colostrum/milk may be qualitatively different from *amniotic fluid* and gain its attractiveness by the fact that only the familiar amniotic

---

to be quantitatively maximal and qualitatively peculiar as a consequence of physical and emotional strain (Atzmüller & Grammer, 2002; Owen, 1980; Schaal & Porter, 1991). Consequently, this armpit odor-contaminated "breast odor," carrying labor-related stress cues, may have been sensed by the infants (prior to first suckling) as being qualitatively and quantitatively novel, and as such elicited more responses of distress.

stimulus is present in the context where milk is first encountered. In normal conditions, the amniotic odor pervades the environment of the parturient mother-infant pair. In nesting mammals, the materials of the nest are impregnated with the amniotic or placental scent and play the role of odor dispenser for some time after expulsion. Likewise, mammals giving birth to precocial newborns outside a nest stay for some time on the spot where delivery occurred (Schaal, Orgeur, & Marlier, 1994). Additionally, as all just-born mammalian newborns are literally soaked with amniotic fluid, they necessarily label their way on the mother's body while seeking her mammaries. Moreover, rodent and carnivore females actively reinforce the presence of the amniotic odor in the postnatal niche by alternately licking their genital orifice, offspring, and abdominal fur (e.g., Roth & Rosenblatt, 1966). Thus, in the species-typical sequence of postnatal events, odors may gain their initial attractiveness from the fact that they were sensed for the first time contingent with the prenatal odor. This supposition is supported by several experiments in rodent newborns, in which *nipple-searching* is only expressed in the presence of amniotic fluid (Teicher & Blass, 1977), or milk becomes attractive in naïve pups only when it is mixed with amniotic fluid (Kodama, 2002; Teicher & Blass, 1977). It is also supported by the fact that the first expression of nipple attachment in rodent and lagomorph pups is under the control of particular postnatal odor cues that are matched with those already present in the amniotic fluid (Coureaud et al., 2002; Pedersen & Blass, 1982). Thus, it may be an operational rule for just-born mammals to be active in a context saturated with amniotic or placental odors, and for them to direct short-range searching to, and then orally seize and suck, objects that are anointed with the odor mixture (or a dominant note of that mixture) experienced as a fetus.

Exercising the Same Rewarding Activities in Prenatal and Postnatal Environments

Amniotic fluid and milk may be treated in the same way by newborns in simultaneous choice tests, because newborns had, prior to the tests, a chance to exercise pre-ingestive and ingestive motor patterns (i.e., searching, rooting, and sucking) in their presence. Perioral and intra-oral stimulations associated with suckling, even without obtaining fluid, constitute in themselves powerful rewards that trigger a cascade of physiological events (e.g., release of gastro-intestinal peptides; Marchini, Lagercrantz, Feuerberg, Winberg, & Uvnäs-Moberg,

1987) known to favor the development of stable odor preferences in various mammalian neonates (e.g., Blass, 1990; Brake, 1981; Hudson, Labra-Cardero, & Mendoza-Soylovna, 2002; Johanson & Hall, 1979; Kenny & Blass, 1977; Shayit et al., submitted). An association between odors carried in the amniotic fluid and sucking may already be established in the just-born infant as a consequence of sucking activity that has occurred *in utero*, as observed by ultrasonographic imaging (Miller, Sonies, & Macedonia, 2003; Nijhuis, Staisch, Martin, & Prechtl, 1984; van Woerden et al., 1988), or as a consequence of immediately postnatal sucking in the inevitable presence of amniotic odor (Schaal et al., 1995a).

Similarly, several studies demonstrate that milk becomes rewarding after it has been linked with the realization of sucking and positive post-ingestive consequences (Brake, 1981; Terry & Johanson, 1987). In the experiments mentioned previously, all mammalian newborns exposed to the prenatal-postnatal odor test paradigm had extensive sucking experience prior to the test, and both stimuli had thus been repeatedly reinforced through oral stimulation. So far, little is known about the response of neonatal organisms that have not had any obvious opportunity for postnatal sucking reward before they were exposed to the stimuli. One such experiment with ingestion-naïve human newborns indicates nondiscriminatory appetitive *head orientation* response to either *amniotic fluid* or *colostrum* from their mother (cf. Fig. 3.2). In contrast, cesarean-delivered mouse pups first show different rates of oral response to amniotic fluid and milk (Kodama, 2002). Such studies should be repeated and generalized to other species.

Delivery-Related High Arousal States Facilitate Learning of Prenatal and Postnatal Odors

Facilitated learning of the current state of the perinatal odor environments may be boosted by physiological processes linked with delivery—independent of the notion that they share sensory similarity. Episodes of relative *hypoxia* (bodily compression and hypothermia that occur during the birth process) are indeed efficient triggers of high activation states in the nascent organism, which in turn are favorable to sensory receptivity and encoding. For example, the transition from a hypoxic state to re-oxygenation in the fetus (Hepper, 1991), as well as alternating waves of bodily compression-decompression during labor (Ronca, Abel, & Alberts, 1996), have been demonstrated to favor odor acquisition in neonatal rats. Among birth-related factors, the general high arousal induced by the "stress of being born" is correlated with a massive activation of the central noradrenergic systems (Lagercrantz & Herlenius, 2002). This release of *noradrenalin* is coincident with the facilitation of odor learning in newborn *rat pups* (e.g., Rangel & Leon, 1995; Wilson & Sullivan, 1994). Similar effects may occur in human newborns in the minutes following birth (cf. chapter 4 by Porter et al.).

Such labor-related facilitation of learning does not only intervene after birth, however. A short exposure to the odors of *alcohol* or *citral* ten minutes before delivery suffices to create a positive bias toward either odor after birth (Molina & Chotro, 1991). This is confirmed when both odorants are sequentially introduced *in utero*, forty or ten minutes before delivery: the closer the odor exposure is to the actual time of expulsion, and hence maximal compression episodes, the stronger the response to the odorant will be subsequently (Chotro & Molina, 1990; Molina, Chotro, & Dominguez, 1995). Thus, the whole birth episode, through the activation of neurochemical (e.g., surge in brain catecholamines in the neonate, increase of circulating and amniotic *β-endorphin*), hormonal (e.g., high levels of the adrenocorticotrophic hormone, *ACTH* and *cortisol/*corticosterone), and physical processes (uterine contractility), constitutes a period of heightened neurosensory plasticity—specifically in the realm of odor learning (e.g., Pedersen & Blass, 1982; Sullivan, Stackenwald, Nasr, Lemon, & Wilson, 2000). It is interesting to note that the neural circuitry to process odors and brain structures involved in odor reinforcement (e.g., the *locus coeruleus*) are already well established in the fetus (Horowitz, Montmayeur, Echelard, & Buck, 1999). In the conditions of a normal delivery, this window of cognitive plasticity may be particularly efficient for the newborn brain to register both the final chemosensory image of the amniotic fluid and the salient, eventually overlapping odors that occur postnatally on the mother's body or in her milk.

Amniotic Fluid and Milk Carry Bioactive Factors Having Similar Motivational Consequences

Regardless of their chemosensory similarity, *amniotic fluid* and *colostrum/*milk may carry bioactive compounds that share similar reinforcing properties. An increasing body of data shows that both milk and amniotic fluid convey notable morphinomimetic potency, as they act as analgesics and hypnogenics. In the *rat newborn*, amniotic fluid and milk (although of bovine origin) bear similar efficiency in releasing oral grasping of an artificial nipple (Koffman et al., 1998). An intra-oral micro-infusion of milk modifies the pups' somesthesic reactivity (in terms of lengthening the latency to lift the forepaws from a warming plaque), and the power of milk to induce that response is antagonized by naloxone, indicating that the behavioral activity of milk is mediated through opioidergic pathways (Blass & Fitzgerald, 1988; Blass, Jackson, & Smotherman, 1991; Robinson & Smotherman, 1995). This mechanism is already functional in the fetus as the oral infusion of a minute amount of milk provokes the following: a behavior pattern resembling the one expressed by the suckling newborn (i.e., general extension actions, intense mouthing, and a stable change in autonomous functions) (Smotherman & Robinson, 1995); and a change in perioral or oral tactile reactivity in terms of attenuation of the avoidance response (*facial wiping*) released by irritation (Smotherman & Robinson, 1992). As in newborns, this milk-induced reduction in fetal responsiveness to noxious somesthesic stimulation is reversed by the opioid antagonist naloxone (Robinson et al., 1995; Smotherman & Robinson, 1992). Thus, from a late fetal age the functional link between the oro-nasal perception of milk and hedonic responses is well established, and it is mediated in part by opioidergic systems.

These milk-induced behavioral and physiological changes in rat fetuses seem to be more selective than in neonates, however, because they are induced only by cow milk in the former, while sucrose, lactose, corn oil, or formula milk designed for human newborns are as efficient in the latter (Smotherman & Robinson, 1996). Similar experiments conducted on *fetal lambs* reveal even narrower selectivity of oral chemoreceptors than in *rat fetuses*. While ovine fetuses do not react to mature bovine milk, they mouth and swallow actively after an oral infusion of homospecific mature milk and colostrum. Fetal lambs additionally discriminate ovine colostrum from mature ovine milk, in that they reduce oral muscle activity to *per os* administration of the former (Robinson et al., 1995). Therefore, both rat and ovine fetuses can react in anticipation to reinforcing factors they are going to encounter in colostrum/milk during their initial suckling opportunities.

Most interestingly, amniotic fluid itself is carrying milk-like pharmacological effects. *Per os* administration of rat amniotic fluid to rat fetuses externalized from the amnion generates a reduction of the *facial wiping* response normally evoked by an aversive (acid) taste (Korthank & Robinson, 1998; Robinson & Gjerde, 1998). This inhibitory effect of amniotic fluid on facial wiping does not work in fetuses pre-treated with *naloxone*, implying that amniotic fluid also engages opioid activity. Numerous compounds with opioid activity have been traced both in human amniotic fluid, and example of which is, *β-endorphins* (Kubota, Tsuzuki, & Saito, 1989), but also in milk, examples being β-casomorphins, β-casorphins, and α- and β-lactorphins (Hazum et al., 1981; Teschemacher & Koch, 1991; Teschemacher, Koch, & Brantl, 1997). Opioid agonists have also been found in the milk of other mammals such as cows (Brantl & Teschemacher, 1979), thus explaining the cross-species effects of bovine milk mentioned previously regarding the rat. Other peptides identified in bovine and human *colostrums* such as colostrinin (cf. Georgiades, Gelder, & Inglot, 1996; Janusz & Lisowski, 1993) are in higher amounts in the early period of colostral production and have been shown to promote the encoding of odors (Kruzel, Janusz, Lisowski, Fishleigh, & Georgiades, 2001; Popik, Bobula, Janusz, Lisowski, & Vetuleni, 1999).

Thus, besides the fact that amniotic and lacteal fluids may bear chemosensory resemblance, they additionally carry physiologically active compounds that trigger consummatory responses of the same nature in fetuses and newborns. Remarkably, an amniotic fluid infusion to *rat fetuses* is effective only when such fluid is taken on gestation days twenty and twenty-one, but not on day nineteen (Korthank & Robinson, 1998). This indicates that the natural opioid agonist is absent or below threshold in amniotic fluid before the last two days of gestation. It should be noted that substances with opioid activity (*β-endorphins*) were shown to rise in human plasma during labor (e.g., Hoffman, Abboud, Haase, Hung, & Goebelsmann, 1984), allowing late-gestation amniotic fluid to carry particularly active reinforcing properties, eventually favoring the emergence of preferences for any contingent stimulus.

Unconditional Attraction to Special Odorants Emitted in the Postnatal Environment

In addition to eventual pharmacological factors contained in perinatal fluids, another way to convey instantaneous preference development for the odor of lacteal fluids is to emit an unconditionally reinforcing *chemosensory* factor in the initial nursing context. In this way, continuity in chemical cues between perinatal environments may be unnecessary. Such cases have not been scrutinized often; but there are at least two of them, in which specialized odor signals are engendered by the newborn itself or by the lactating mother, may be mentioned.

Regarding the first case, recall the experiment previously described, in which *rat pups* cease to orally grasp a deodorized nipple and resume normal suckling when this nipple is re-odorized with amniotic fluid. Pup and maternal *saliva* are also efficient stimuli to reinstate suckling (Hofer, Shair, & Singh, 1976; Teicher & Blass, 1976). This can be related to the fact that pups initially contact an amniotic fluid-saliva mix deposited on the nipples by both the parturient mother licking herself and the suckling pups. Thus, salivary odor compounds become rapidly conditioned by association with amniotic fluid and/or with the realization of suckling. One constituent in pup saliva—identified as *dimethyl disulfide* (DMDS)—was effective in eliciting nipple grasping, although with half the potency of the substances that naturally coat the nipple (Pedersen & Blass, 1981). DMDS is special because it has the power to arouse behavior already in the fetus: like milk, it reduces fetal responsiveness to aversive perioral stimulation, and this effect is mediated through opioidergic processes (Smotherman & Robinson, 1992). As DMDS has apparently not been detected in amniotic fluid (Blass, 1990), one may conclude that its behavioral salience does not strongly depend on prenatal exposure.

The second case for an unconditional odor signal has been described in the rabbit. When deposited on the abdomen of a lactating doe, *rabbit pups* immediately display characteristic searching movements, and within ten seconds they locate and orally seize a nipple (Coureaud, Schaal, Langlois, & Perrier, 2001; Hudson & Distel, 1983). The same pattern of response is elicited in newborn pups by milk itself (Coureaud, Schaal, Langlois, & Perrier, 2001; Keil et al., 1990). A gas chromatographic analysis of the odor of rabbit milk resulted in the identification of a single odorous molecule, which accounts for the behavioral effect of whole milk. As this compound was ascertained to be emitted *de novo* in milk (Moncomble et al., 2002), and as it satisfied all criteria defining mammalian pheromones, it was named *mammary pheromone* (MP) (Schaal et al., 2003). It was established that the MP does not require association with labor-related activation, suckling, ingestion of milk, or contact with the mother to acquire its behavioral efficacy: pups taken away from the mother immediately after expulsion evinced maximal response to the MP at the very first presentation. Furthermore, the MP's efficiency in fetuses delivered one or two days before term, and the failure to detect it in the chemical analyses of amniotic fluid and blood from lactating females, leads to the conclusion that resultant behavioral activity does not derive from prenatal experience (Schaal et al., 2003). Accordingly, the current data indicate that in the *rabbit pup*, the MP-behavior coupling needs neither prenatal nor postnatal exposure to be specified.

In summary, certain stimuli in the postnatal environment appear to have signaling value without initial learning. Thus, pre-functional responsiveness may account for the neonates' immediate response to certain cues from the nipple or milk, without necessity for long-term storage of odor information from the prenatal niche. Recent studies indicate that the neural organization of the olfactory system has a high level of hard-wiring (Horowitz et al., 1999; Zou, Horowitz, Montmayeur, Snapper, & Buck, 2001), which is compatible with the advent of innate responsiveness to specialized odorant signals in all members of the same species.

Redundant Operations that Specify Early Olfactory Information

The above mechanisms are certainly not mutually exclusive and are not contradictory to the notion of a perinatal chemosensory continuity. The developing olfactory system is a distributed collection of sensory and neural components that were molded by evolution: they were either pre-formed by genetic programs without corrective effects of experience, constrained by predictable aspects of the species-specific environment, or modified by learning-based sensory input from the individual-specific environment. Although these pathways were addressed in isolation for the sake of clarity, they normally operate in a simultaneous or overlaying fashion in the developmental window ranging from late pregnancy to the first days or weeks following birth. Figure 3.5 illustrates how the redundant operation of these processes could concur to canalize the adaptive responsiveness of the perinatal organism, and how they can contribute to reinforce a potentially pre-existing chemosensory similarity between the prenatal and postnatal environments. For example, one may speculate that relative chemosensory similarity in both perinatal environments and common behavioral and pharmacological processes operate in synergy in the following way: the *in utero* exercise of sucking and the concurrent reception of amniotic opioid agonists can facilitate the organism's acquisition of chemosensory stimuli present in fetal fluids in late pregnancy, thus favoring the encoding of initial olfactory representations. During the process of *labor*, the high activation state of the fetus favors an actualized fine-tuning of the amniotic odor representation. This amniotic odor template will be used subsequently by the

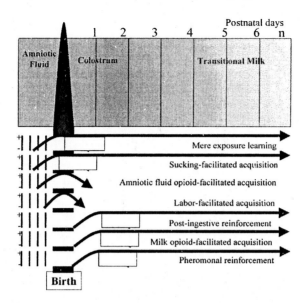

Figure 3.5. The convergent operation of hypothesized perinatal che-mosensory continuity within the context of multiply-determined learn-ing processes known to operate in newborn mammals. In the upper part of the figure, the relative similarity in amniotic and colostral odor profiles is represented in terms of gray levels: similar grays indicate overlap in chemosensory cues. In the lower part of the figure, identified psychobiological processes that potentially intervene in the early acquisition of positive responses to odorants in the prenatal and postnatal environments are pictured (see chapter text for further evidence on the action of these processes in early development). (+) and (−) denote hypothetical high or low achievement of the various learning processes.

nascent organism as he/she conveys it into the postnatal niche and as his/her mother carries it around the mammary area. This amniotic signal will support the maintenance of an optimal arousal state, favor coordinated motor activity, and thus stimulate the newborn to explore the mother's body and locate the nipple. The newborn organism may be further boosted in his/her initial suckling attempts by uncondi-tional odor signals emitted *de novo* on the nipple or in milk. Then, after the first successful oral grasping of a nipple, milk ingestion and its multiple properties can operate. Furthermore, milk opioid factors further attenuate high activity states and favor the wider sensory pro-cessing of the mother in order to progressively establish multimodal individual recognition. Finally, post-ingestive and post-absorptive consequences confirm an amniotic-like chemical image eventually carried in *colostrum*, and they contribute to re-actualizing the evolving chemosensory sensations carried in milk, the mother, and in the wider surround.

CONCLUDING REMARKS

When combined, the various strands of evidence previously reviewed are generally consistent with the view of a fetal-neonatal continuity in regards to the ability to process the chemosensory qualities of the amniotic and post-amniotic environments. In various species, the perinatal chemo-ecological continuity is obtained through different, graded ways ranging from: (1) the passive, physiological creation of an overlap in the odors generated in amniotic fluid and in colostrum/milk; (2) active behavior leading to the labeling of the postnatal environment with prenatal fluid; to (3) being exposed to the same rewarding substances or events in both perinatal environments, so that they become equally reinforcing without necessarily being chemosensorily similar (however, as amniotic fluid and milk unavoidably share odorigenic end-products of metabolism, these perinatal rewarding events tend to corroborate prenatal odor cues as signals for postnatal guidance of behavior); and (4) specialized odor signals that can be available in the postnatal niche only, wherein they can constitute unconditional stimuli for activation and learning of novel stimuli.

All of these processes may work in unison, creating a sensory chain that links the amniotic niche to the post-amniotic niche. They provide the newborn organism with redundant information at the different steps of the sequential actions, conducing to energy and immunity acquisition: getting aroused, moving in a coordinated fashion close to the female, locating the mother's nipples, orally seizing them, exerting sucking in articulation with respiration and swallowing, and ingesting milk without rejecting it because it is novel. Thus, the apparent novelty of milk and the neophobic response that is expected to go with it lose their paradoxical character when seen in the context of the functional connection between amniotic fluid and milk.

The above hypothesis calls for experimental inspection of the adaptive advantages of acquiring information in one developmental niche and the ability to treat similar information upon re-encountering it in a subsequent developmental niche. We propose that transferring sensory information acquired in a positive context in one developmental niche to the next permits the articulated interplay between emotional balance, selective attention and expression of appetitive behavior, and an extension of learning to unprecedented properties of the physical and social environment.

Regarding emotional balance, this chapter has provided abundant evidence that supports that near-term fetuses (see also Mickley, Remmers-Roeber, Crouse, Walker, & Dengler, 2000; Smotherman & Robinson, 1985) and newborn infants (cf. reviews in Rosenblatt, 1983; Schaal, 1988a) are able to differentiate odorants or tastants along the familiarity-novelty dimension. As a rule, stimuli that are endowed with familiarity *in utero* promote positive (or less negative) responsiveness in newborns, while non-familiar stimuli mainly generate avoidance and distress, or at least disinterest.

Several strategies have been selected in mammals so that their neonates attend to biologically meaningful stimuli while ignoring others. One strategy is to limit the range of effective sensory systems (Turkewitz & Kenny, 1982), while another is to specify stimuli that become salient, either by experience-sensitive or by pre-organized processes that are immune from experience. Both of these strategies for perceptual canalization provide important methods to reduce the risk of overwhelming the immature nervous system with information, and to avoid time- and energy-consuming indecision in situations of exposure to competition with littermates, predation, or colonization by deleterious micro-organisms (e.g., Gillin, Reiner, & Wang, 1983). Thus, one can predict that key stimuli encountered in the prenatal and immediately postnatal environments should be endowed with special psychobiological properties by newborn organisms: they may be detected at lower thresholds, elicit more selective attention, and be processed faster than novel stimuli in terms of recognition, decision for choice, and elicitation of selective behavior (Dukas, 1998). At least, the first prediction pertaining to reduced threshold levels for the detection of odors encountered *in utero* has received some support (e.g., Semke et al., 1995). The other aspects require further research.

In summary, the fetal-neonatal organism may be considered a specialist for the processing of certain odor stimuli. But this specialization goes hand in hand with the pervasive ability to acquire odor information through nonassociative or associative processes. Consequently, mammalian neonates are simultaneously experts in using narrowly defined information in the present occasion, and generalists who can integrate more broadly defined information that will be useful on subsequent occasions. As the effects of both of these perceptual strategies are very protracted in time, their simultaneous or sequential operation is not easily recognizable. Future investigations should consider experimental manipulations that tease apart the behavioral impacts of perceptual specializations derived from either pre-wired abilities or from abilities acquired pre- or postnatally, and how they fit together to promote adaptive trajectories of development. When the early olfactory bridging process is superposed with bridging in other modalities (such as touch and audition, as mentioned in the Introduction) or in the perception of amodal properties of the environment (e.g., intensity, rhythm, variability; cf. Bahrick & Lickliter, 2002), then one can evaluate how nascent organisms are over-determined to derive higher-level knowledge out of previous, lower-level knowledge and, hence, rapidly integrate novel experiences.

REFERENCES

Alberts, J.R. (1987). Early learning and ontogenetic adaptation. In N.A. Krasnegor, E.M. Blass, M.A. Hofer, & W.P. Smotherman (Eds.), *Perinatal development. A psychobiological perspective* (pp. 11–37). Orlando, FL: Academic Press.

Antell, S.E., Caron, A., & Myers, R.S. (1985). Perception of relational invariants by newborns. *Developmental Psychology, 21,* 942–948.

Atzmüller, A.K., & Grammer, K. (2002). The scent of fear. *Neuroendocrinology Letters, 23,* 79–84.

Bahrick, L.E., & Lickliter, R. (2002). Intersensory redundancy guides early perceptual and cognitive development. *Advances in Child Development, 30,* 153–187.

Barrois, V., & Larouzé, B. (1991). Le goût du lait [The taste of milk]. In E. Herbinet & M.C. Busnel (Eds.), *L'Aube des sens* (pp. 329–331). Paris: Stock.

Baum, J.D. (1981). Parent-offspring relations in man. *Journal of Reproduction and Fertility, 62,* 651–656.

Beauchamp, G.K., Katahira, K., Yamazaki, K., Mennella, J.A., Bard, J., & Boyse, E.A. (1995). Evidence suggesting that odortypes of pregnant women are a compound of maternal and fetal odortypes. *Proceedings of the National Academy of Sciences, USA, 92,* 2617–2621.

Beauchamp, G.K., Yamazaki, K., Currant, M., Bard, J., & Boyse, E.A. (1994). Fetal H-2 odortypes are evident in the urine of pregnant female mice. *Immunogenetics, 39,* 109–113.

Berridge, K.C. (2000). Measuring hedonic impact in animals and infants: Microstructure of affective taste reactivity patterns. *Neuroscience and Biobehavioral Reviews, 24,* 173–178. ·

Bilko, A., Altbäcker, V., & Hudson, R. (1994). Transmission of food preference in the rabbit: The means of information transfer. *Physiology & Behavior, 56,* 907–912.

Blass, E.M. (1990). Suckling: Determinants, changes, mechanisms, and lasting impressions. *Developmental Psychology, 26,* 520–533.

Blass, E.M., & Ciaramito, V. (1994). A new look at some old mechanisms in human newborns: Taste and tactile determinants of state, affect and action. *Monographs for Society of Research in Child Development, 59,* 1–81.

Blass, E.M., & Fitzgerald, E. (1988). Milk-induced analgesia and comforting in 10-day-old rats: Opioid mediation. *Pharmacology, Biochemistry and Behavior, 29,* 9–13.

Blass, E.M., Jackson, A.M., & Smotherman, W.P. (1991). Milk-induced, opioid-mediated antinociception in rats at the time of cesarean delivery. *Behavioral Neuroscience, 105,* 675–684.

Blass, E.M., & Teicher, M.H. (1980). Suckling. *Science, 210,* 15–22.

Bornstein, M.H. (1984). A descriptive taxonomy of psychological categories used by infants. In C. Sophian (Ed.), *Origins of cognitive skills* (pp. 313–338). Hillsdale, NJ: Erlbaum.

Brake, S.C. (1981). Suckling infant rats learn a preference for a novel olfactory stimulus paired with milk delivery. *Science, 211,* 506–508.

Brantl, V., & Teschemacher, H. (1979). A material with opioid activity in bovine milk and milk products. *Naunyn-Schmiedebergs Archives of Pharmacology, 306,* 301–304.

Capretta, P.J., & Rawls, A. (1974). Establishment of a flavor preference in rats: Importance of nursing and weaning experience. *Journal of Comparative Physiology and Psychology, 86,* 670–673.

Carey, G.B., Quinn, T.J., & Goodwin, S.E. (1997). Breast milk composition after exercise of different intensities. *Journal of Human Lactation, 13,* 115–120.

Catt, S.L., Mela, D.J., Rosenblatt, D.B., & Wells, J. (1998). *Infant sensory responsiveness to fat content of milk formulas.* Unpublished manuscript.

Chotro, M.G., & Molina, J.C. (1990). Acute ethanol contamination of the amniotic fluid during gestational day 21: Postnatal changes in alcohol responsiveness in rats. *Developmental Psychobiology, 23,* 535–547.

Coureaud, G., & Schaal, B. (2000). Attraction of newborn rabbits to abdominal odors of adult conspecifics differing in sex and physiological state. *Developmental Psychobiology, 36,* 271–281.

Coureaud, G., Schaal, B., Hudson, R., Orgeur, P., & Coudert, P. (2002). Transnatal olfactory continuity in the rabbit: Behavioral evidence and short-term consequence of its disruption. *Developmental Psychobiology, 40,* 372–390.

Coureaud, G., Schaal, B., Langlois, D., & Perrier, G. (2001). Orientation responses of newborn rabbits to odors emitted by lactating females: Relative effectiveness of surface and milk cues. *Animal Behaviour, 61,* 153–162.

Craig, W. (1918). Appetites and aversions as constituents of instincts. *Biology Bulletin of the Woods Hole Center, 34,* 91–107.

Dawes, G.S. (1968). *Fetal and neonatal physiology: A comparative study of the changes at birth.* Chicago: Year Book Medical Publishers.

DeCasper, A.J., & Fifer W.P. (1980). Of human bonding: Newborns prefer their mothers' voices. *Science, 208,* 1174–1176.

DeCasper, A.J., & Sigafoos, A.D. (1983). The intraterine heart beat: A potent reinforcer for newborns. *Infant Behavior and Development, 6,* 19–25.

DeCasper, A.J., & Spence, M.J. (1986). Prenatal maternal speech influences newborn's perception of speech sounds. *Infant Behavior and Development, 9,* 133–150.

Desage, M., Schaal, B., Defaux, O., Cohen, H., & Brazier, J.L. (1996). *Instrumental GC-MS demonstration of the transfer of food aromas into the amniotic fluid in humans.* Unpublished manuscript.

Desage, M., Schaal, B., Orgeur, P., Soubeyran, J., & Brazier, J.L. (1996). Gas chromatographic-mass spectrometric method to characterise the transfer of dietary odorous compounds into plasma and milk. *Journal of Chromatography, B. Biomedical Applications, 678,* 205–211.

Dougherty, R.W., Shipe, W.F., Gudnason, G.V., Ledford, R.A., Peterson, R.D., & Scarpellino, R. (1962). Physiological mechanisms involved in the transmission of flavors and odors to milk I. Contribution of eructed gases to milk flavor. *Journal of Dairy Science, 45,* 472–476.

Duffy, L. (1997). Breastfeeding after strenuous aerobic exercise: A case report. *Journal of Human Lactation, 13,* 145–146.

Dukas, R. (1998). Constraints on information processing and their effects on behavior. In R. Dukas (Ed.), *Cognitive ecology: The evolutionary ecology of information processing and decision making* (pp. 89–128). Chicago: Chicago University Press.

Engen, T., & Lipsitt, L.P. (1965). Decrement and recovery of responses to olfactory stimuli in the human neonate. *Journal of Comparative Physiology and Psychology, 59,* 312–316.

Evans-Pritchard, E.E. (1937). *The Nuer.* Oxford, England: Clarendon Press.

Faas, A.E., Sponton, E.D., Moya, P.R., & Molina, J.C. (2000). Differential responsiveness to alcohol odor in human neonates. Effects of maternal consumption during gestation. *Alcohol, 22,* 7–17.

Farah, M.J., Rabinowitz, C., Quinn, G.E., & Liu, G.T. (2000). Early commitment of neural substrates for face recognition. *Cognitive Neuropsychology, 17,* 117–123.

Farroni, T., Csibra, G., Simion, F., & Johnson, M.H. (2002). Eye contact detection in humans from birth. *Proceedings of the National Academy of Sciences, USA, 99,* 9602–9605.

Fifer, W.P., & Moon, C.M. (1995). The effects of fetal experience with sounds. In J.P. Lecanuet, W.P. Fifer, N.A. Krasnegor, & W.P. Smotherman (Eds.), *Fetal development: A psychobiological perspective* (pp. 351–366). Hillsdale, NJ: Erlbaum.

Font, L. (1990). "Incidental" maternal dietary intake and infant refusal to nurse. *Journal of Human Lactation, 6,* 9.

Galef, B.G., & Henderson, P.W. (1972). Mother's milk: A determinant of the feeding preferences of weaning rat pups. *Journal of Comparative Physiology and Psychology, 78,* 213–219.

Georgiades, J., Gelder, F., & Inglot, A.D. (1996). Isolation and preliminary characterization of a new cytokine present in human colostrum: Its similarity to ovine colostrinin. *European Cytokines Network, 7,* 511.

Gillin, F.D., Reiner, D.S., & Wang, C.S. (1983). Human milk kills parasitic intestinal protozoa. *Science, 221,* 1290–1292.

Grmek, M.D. (1997). *The cauldron of "Médée."* Le Plessis-Robinson: Synthélabo.

Hall, W.G. (1979). The ontogeny of feeding in rats: I. Ingestion and behavioral responses to oral infusions. *Journal of Comparative Physiology and Psychology, 93,* 977–1000.

Hall, W.G., & Rosenblatt, J.S. (1977). Suckling behavior and intake control in the developing rat pup. *Journal of Comparative Physiology and Psychology, 91,* 1232–1247.

Hauser, G.J., Chitayat, D., Berns, L., Braver, D., & Muhlhauser, B. (1985). Peculiar odors in newborns and maternal prenatal ingestion of spicy foods. *European Journal of Pediatrics, 144,* 403.

Hazum, E., Sabatka, J.J., Chang, K.J., Brent, D.A., Findlay, J., & Cuatrecasas, P. (1981). Morphin in cow and human milk: Could dietary morphin constitute a ligand for specific (MU) receptors? *Science, 213,* 1010–1012.

Hepper, P.G. (1987). The amniotic fluid: An important priming role in kin recognition. *Animal Behaviour, 35,* 1343–1346.

Hepper, P.G. (1988a). Fetal "soap" addiction. *Lancet, 1,* 1147–1148.

Hepper, P.G. (1988b). Adaptive fetal learning: Prenatal exposure to garlic affects postnatal preferences. *Animal Behaviour, 36,* 935–936.

Hepper, P.G. (1991). Transiet hypoxic episodes: A mechanism to support associative fetal learning. *Animal Behaviour, 41,* 477–480.

Hepper, P.G. (1995). Human fetal "olfactory" learning. *International Journal of Prenatal, Perinatal and Psychological Medicine, 7,* 147–151.

Hofer, M.A. (1981). *The roots of human behavior.* San Francisco: Freeman.

Hofer, M.A., Shair, H., & Singh, P.J. (1976). Evidence that maternal ventral skin substance promote suckling in infant rats. *Physiology & Behavior, 17,* 131–136.

Hoffman, D.I., Abboud, T.K., Haase, H.R., Hung, T.T., & Goebelsmann, U. (1984). Plasma β-endorphin concentration prior to and during pregnancy, in labor, and after delivery. *American Journal of Obstetrics and Gynecology, 150,* 492–495.

Horowitz, L.F., Montmayeur, J.P., Echelard, Y., & Buck, L.B. (1999). A genetic approach to trace neural circuits. *Proceedings of the National Academy of Sciences, USA, 96,* 3194–3199.

Hudson, R., & Distel, H. (1983). Nipple location by newborn rabbits: Evidence for pheromonal guidance. *Behaviour, 82,* 260–275.

Hudson, R., Labra-Cardero, D., & Mendoza-Soylovna, A. (2002). Sucking, not milk, is important for the rapid learning of nipple-search odors in newborn rabbits. *Developmental Psychobiology, 41,* 226–235.

Hudson, R., Schaal, B., & Bilko, A. (1999). Transmission of olfactory information from mother to young in the European rabbit. In H.O. Box & K.R. Gibson (Eds.), *Mammalian social learning: Comparative and ecological perspectives* (pp. 141–157). Cambridge, UK: Cambridge University Press.

Janusz, M., & Lisowski, J. (1993). Proline-rich polypeptide (PRP): An immunomodulatory peptide from ovine colostrum. *Archives of Immunology, Therapia Experimentalis, 41,* 275–279.

Jeliffe, D.B., & Jeliffe, E.F. (1978). *Human milk in the modern world: Psychosocial, nutritional and economic significance.* Oxford, England: Oxford University Press.

Jirowetz, L., Jäger, W., Buchbauer, G., Nikiforov, A., & Raverdino, V. (1991). Investigation of animal blood samples after fragrance drug inhalation by GC/MS with chemical ionisation and selected ion monitoring. *Biology and Mass Spectrometry, 20,* 801–803.

Johanson, I.B., & Hall, W.G. (1979). Appetitive learning in 1-day-old rat pups. *Science, 205,* 419–421.

Johnson, M.H., Dziurawiec, S., Ellis, H., & Morton, J. (1991). Newborns' preferential tracking of face-like stimuli and its subsequent decline. *Cognition, 40,* 1–19.

Johnson, P., & Salisbury, D.M. (1977). Preliminary studies on feeding and breathing in the newborn. In J.M. Weiffenbach (Ed.), *Taste and development: The genesis of sweet preference.* Bethesda, MD: National Institutes of Health.

Karmowski, A., Sobiech, K.A., Dobek, D., Terpilowski, L., Palczynski, B., & Mis-Michalek, M. (1998). The concentration of cotidine in urine, colostrum and amniotic fluid within the system mother-baby. *Ginekolgia Polska, 69,* 115–122.

Keil, W., von Stralendorff, F., & Hudson, R. (1990). A behavioral bioassay for analysis of rabbit nipple-search pheromone. *Physiology & Behavior, 47,* 525–529.

Kenny, J.T., & Blass, E.M. (1977). Suckling as incentive to instrumental learning in preweaning rats. *Science, 196,* 898–899.

Kodama, N. (1990). *Preference for amniotic fluid in newborn mice.* Paper presented at the annual meeting of the International Society for Developmental Psychobiology, Cambridge, UK.

Kodama, N. (2002). Effects of odor and taste of amniotic fluid and mother's milk on body movements in newborn mice. *Developmental Psychobiology, 41,* 310.

Kodama, N., & Smotherman, W.P. (1997). Effects of amniotic fluid on head movement in cesarean delivered rat pups. *Developmental Psychobiology, 30*, 255.

Koffmann, D.J., Petrov, E., Varlinskaya, E.I., & Smotherman, W.P. (1998). Thermal olfactory and tactile stimuli increase oral grasping of an artificial nipple by newborn rat. *Developmental Psychobiology, 33*, 317–326.

Korman, S.H., Cohen, E., & Preminger, A. (2001). Pseudo-mapple urine disease due to maternal prenatal ingestion of fenugreek. *Journal of Paediatrics and Child Health, 37*, 403–404.

Korthank, A.J., & Robinson, S.R. (1998). Effects of amniotic fluid on opioid activity and fetal responses to chemosensory stimuli. *Developmental Psychobiology, 33*, 235–248.

Kruzel, M.L., Janusz, M., Lisowski, J., Fishleigh, R.V., & Georgiades, J.A. (2001). Towards understanding of biological role of colostrinin peptides. *Journal of Moleclular Neuroscience, 17*, 379–389.

Kubota, T., Tsuzuki, H., & Saito, M. (1989). Determination of prolactin, growth hormone, β-endorphin, and cortisol in both maternal plasma and amniotic fluid during human gestation. *Acta Endocrinologica, 121*, 297–303.

Kuhl, P.K. (1985). Methods in the study of infant speech perception. In G. Gottlieb & N.A. Krasnegor (Eds.), *Measurement of audition and vision in the first year of postnatal life: A methodological overview* (pp. 223–251). Norwood, NJ: Ablex.

Kurata, T., & Nakamura, K. (1994). A basic study of the initial development of food preferences: Feeding experiments with diet containing capsaicin. In K. Kurihara, N. Suzuki, & H. Ogawa (Eds.), *Olfaction and Taste XI* (p. 316). Tokyo: Springer.

Lagercrantz, H. (1996). Stress, arousal, and gene activation at birth. *News in Physiological Sciences, 11*, 214–218.

Lagercrantz, H., & Herlenius, E. (2002). Neurotransmitters and neuro-modulators. In H. Lagercrantz, M. Hanson, P. Evrard, & C. Rodeck (Eds.), *The newborn brain: Neuroscience and clinical applications* (pp. 139–163). Cambridge, UK: Cambridge University Press.

Lagercrantz, H., & Slotkin, T.A. (1986). The "stress" of being born. *Scientific American, 254*, 92–102.

Lambers, D.S., & Clark, K.E. (1996). The maternal and fetal physiologic effects of nicotine. *Seminars in Perinatolology, 20*, 115–126.

Lasiter, P.S., & Diaz, J. (1992). Artificial rearing alters development of the nucleus of the solitary tract. *Brain Research Bulletin, 29*, 407–410.

Le Magnen, J., & Tallon, S. (1968). Préférence alimentaire du jeune rat induite par l'allaitement maternel [Food preference of the young rat induced by maternal breast feeding]. *Comptes Rendus des Séances de la Société de Biologie, 162*, 387–390.

Lichtenberger, L.M., Gardner, J.W., Baretto, J.C., & Morris, F.H. (1991). Evidence for a role of volatile amines in the development of neonatal hypergastrinemia. *Journal of Pediatric Gastroenterology and Nutrition, 13,* 342–346.

Liebl, B., Mayer, R., Ommer, S., Sonnichsen, C., & Koletzko, B. (2000). Transition of notro musks and polycyclic musks into human milk. *Advances in Experimental Medicine and Biology, 478,* 289–305.

London, R.M., Snowdon, C.T., & Smithana, J.M. (1979). Early experience with sour and bitter solutions increases subsequent ingestion. *Physiology & Behavior, 22,* 1149–1155.

Macfarlane, A. (1975). Olfaction in the development of social preferences in the human neonate. *Ciba Foundation Symposium, 33,* 103–113.

Mainardi, M., Poli, M., & Valsecchi, P. (1989). Ontogeny of dietary selection in weanling mice: Effects of early experience and mother's milk. *Biology of Behaviour, 14,* 185–194.

Marchini, G., Lagercrantz, H., Feuerberg, Y., Winberg, J., & Uvnäs-Moberg, K. (1987). The effect of non-nutritive sucking on plasma insulin, gastrin, and somatostatin levels in infants. *Acta Paediatrica Scandinavica, 76,* 573–578.

Marlier, L., & Schaal, B. (1997). Familiarity and discrimination in the newborn: Differential influence of the mode of diet. *Enfance, 1,* 47–61.

Marlier, L., & Schaal, B. (2001). Evidence for inborn olfactory preferences in human neonates: The case of conspecific milk. *Chemical Senses, 26,* 778–779.

Marlier, L., Schaal, B., & Soussignan, R. (1994). Neonatal responsiveness to odors extracted from the prenatal environment [Abstract]. *Infant Behavior and Development, International Conference on Infant Studies Issue,* 807.

Marlier, L., Schaal, B., & Soussignan, R. (1997). Orientation responses to biological odors in the human newborn. Initial pattern and postnatal plasticity. *Comptes Rendu de l'Académie des Sciences, Paris, Life Sciences, 320,* 999–1005.

Marlier, L., Schaal, B., & Soussignan, R. (1998a). Neonatal responsiveness to the odor of amniotic and lacteal fluids: A test of perinatal chemosensory continuity. *Child Development, 69,* 611–623.

Marlier, L., Schaal, B., & Soussignan, R. (1998b). Bottle-fed neonates prefer an odor experienced *in utero* to an odor experienced in the feeding context. *Developmental Psychobiology, 33,* 133–145.

Mennella, J.A., & Beauchamp, G.K. (1991a). Maternal diet alters the sensory qualities of human milk and the nursling's behavior. *Pediatrics, 88,* 737–744.

Mennella, J.A., & Beauchamp, G.K. (1991b). The transfer of alcohol to human milk: Effects on flavor and the infant's behavior. *New England Journal of Medicine, 325,* 981–985.

Mennella, J.A., & Beauchamp, G.K. (1996). The human infants' responses to vanilla flavors in human milk and formula. *Infant Behavior and Development, 19,* 13–19.

Mennella, J.A., & Beauchamp, G.K. (1998). Smoking and the flavor of milk. *New England Journal of Medicine, 339*, 1559–1560.

Mennella, J.A., & Beauchamp, G.K. (1999). Experience with a flavor in mother's milk modifies the infant's acceptance of flavored cereal. *Chemical Senses, 35*, 197–203.

Mennella, J.A., & Beauchamp, G.K. (2002). Flavor experiences during formula feeding are related to preferences during childhood. *Early Human Development, 68*, 71–82.

Mennella, J.A., Jagnow, C.P., & Beauchamp, G.K. (2001). Prenatal and postnatal flavor learning by human infants. *Pediatrics, 107*, 1–6.

Mennella, J.A., Johnson, A., & Beauchamp, G.K. (1995). Garlic ingestion by pregnant women alters the odor of amniotic fluid. *Chemical Senses, 20*, 207–209.

Mickley, A.M., Remmers-Roeber, D.R., Crouse, C., Walker, C., & Dengler, C. (2000). Detection of novelty by perinatal rats. *Physiology & Behavior, 70*, 217–225.

Miller, J.L., Sonies, B.C., & Macedonia, C. (2003). Emergence of oropharyngeal, laryngeal and swallowing activity in the developing fetal upper aerodigestive tract: An ultrasound evaluation. *Early Human Development, 71*, 61–87.

Moio, L., Rillo, L., Ledda, A., & Addeo, F. (1996). Odorous constituents of ovine milk in relationship with diet. *Journal of Dairy Science, 79*, 1322–1331.

Molina, J.C., & Chotro, M.G. (1991). Association between chemosensory stimuli and cesarean delivery in rat fetuses: Neonatal presentation of similar stimuli increases motor activity. *Behavioral and Neural Biology, 55*, 42–60.

Molina, J.C., Chotro, M.G., & Domingez, H.D. (1995). Fetal alcohol learning resulting from alcohol contamination of the prenatal environment. In J.-P. Lecanuet, W.P. Fifer, N.E. Krasnegor, & W.P. Smotherman (Eds.), *Fetal development. A psychobiological perspective*. Hillsdale, NJ: Erlbaum.

Moncomble, A.S., Schaal, B., Quennedey, B., Quennedey, A., Coureaud, G., Brossut, R., et al. (2002). *In search of the exocrin origin(s) of the rabbit mammary pheromone*. Paper presented at the 15th Biennial Congress of the European Chemoreception Research Organisation, Erlangen, Germany.

Morton, J., & Johnson, M.H. (1991). CONSPEC and CONLERN: A two-process theory of infant face recognition. *Psychological Review, 98*, 164–181.

Neville, M.C. (1995). Lactogenesis in women: A cascade of events revealed by milk composition. In R.G. Jensen (Ed.), *Handbook of milk composition* (pp. 87–98). San Diego, CA: Academic Press.

Ng, K.J., Fresen, B.D., & Bianchine, J.R. (1982). Capillary gas chromatographic-mass spectrometric profiles of trimethylsilyl derivates of organic acids from amniotic fluids from different gestational ages. *Journal of Chromatography, 228*, 43–50.

Nichols, T.M., Hähnel, R., & Wilkinson, S.P. (1978). Organic acids in amniotic fluid. *Clinica Chimica Acta, 84,* 11–17.

Nijhuis, J.G., Staisch, K.J.H., Martin, C.B., & Prechtl, H.F.R. (1984). A sinusoid-like fetal heart-rate pattern in association with fetal sucking. *European Journal of Obstetrics, Gynecology and Reproductive Biology, 16,* 353–358.

Nolte, D.L., & Mason, J.R. (1995). Maternal ingestion of orthoamino-acetophenone during gestation affects intake by offspring. *Physiology & Behavior, 58,* 925–928.

Nolte, D.L., Provenza, F.D., Callan, R., & Panter, K.E. (1995). Garlic in the ovine fetal environment. *Physiology & Behavior, 52,* 1091–1093.

Owen, P.R. (1980). *Olfactory correlates of affect.* Unpublished doctoral dissertation, North Texas State University, Denton.

Parfet, K.A.R., & Gonyou, H.W. (1991). Attraction of newborn piglets to auditory, visual, olfactory and tactile stimuli. *Journal of Animal Science, 69,* 125–133.

Patton, S., Huston, G.E., Montgomery, P.A., & Josephson, R. (1986). Approaches to the study of colostrum: The onset of lactation. In M. Hamosh & A.S. Goldman (Eds.), *Human lactation 2. Maternal and environmental factors* (pp. 231–239). New York: Plenum.

Pedersen, P.A., & Blass, E.M. (1981). Olfactory control over suckling in albino rats. In R.N. Aslin, J.R. Alberts, & M.R. Petersen (Eds.), *Development of perception. Psychobiological perspectives: Audition somatic perception and the chemical senses* (Vol. 1, pp. 359–381). New York: Academic Press.

Pedersen, P.A., & Blass, E.M. (1982). Prenatal and postnatal determinants of the first suckling episode in albino rats. *Developmental Psychobiology, 15,* 349–355.

Popik, P., Bobula, B., Janusz, M., Lisowski, J., & Vetuleni, V. (1999). Colostrinin, a polypetide isolated from early milk, facilitates learning and memory in rats. *Pharmacology, Biochemistry and Behavior, 64,* 183–189.

Rangel, S., & Leon, M. (1995). Early odor preference training increases olfactory bulb norepinephrin. *Brain Research, Developmental Brain Research, 85,* 187–191.

Rao, M., Blass, E.M., Brignol, M.M., Marino, L., & Glass, L. (1997). Reduced heat loss following sucrose ingestion in premature and normal newborns. *Early Human Development, 48,* 85–93.

Rimkus, G.G., & Wolf, M. (1996). Polycyclic musk fragrance in human adipose tissue and human milk. *Chemosphere, 33,* 2033–2043.

Robinson, S.R., & Gjerde, K.K. (1998). *Self-exposure to amniotic fluid alters behavior in the rat and sheep fetus.* Paper presented at the annual meeting of the International Society for the Study of Behavioral Development, Orléans, France.

Robinson, S.R., & Smotherman, W.P. (1995). Habituation and classical conditioning in the rat fetus: Opioid involvements. In J.-P. Lecanuet,

W.P. Fifer, N.A. Krasnegor., & W.P. Smotherman (Eds.), *Fetal development: A psychobiological perspective* (pp. 295–314). Hillsdale, NJ: Erlbaum.

Robinson, S.R., Wong, C., Robertson, S.S., Natanielsz, P.W., & Smotherman, W.P. (1995). Behavioral responses of the chronically instrumented sheep fetus to chemosensory stimuli presented *in utero. Behavioral Neuroscience, 109*, 551–562.

Rognon, C., & Chastrette, M. (1992). Analyse des composés volatils du liquide amniotique: premières données chez le brebis et la femme. In B. Schaal (Ed.), *Déterminants prénatals des préférences chimiosensorielles néonatales [Prenatal determinants of newborn chemosensory preferences]* (pp. 11–29). Paris: Ministry of Research and Technology.

Ronca, A.E., Abel, R.A., & Alberts, J.R. (1996). Perinatal stimulation and adaptation of the neonate. *Acta Paediatica, 416*(Suppl), 8–15.

Ronca, A.E., & Alberts, J.R. (1995). Maternal contributions to fetal experience and the transition from prenatal to postnatal life. In J.-P. Lecanuet, W.P. Fifer, N.A. Krasnegor, & W.P. Smotherman (Eds.), *Fetal development: A psychobiological perspective* (pp. 331–350). Hillsdale, NJ: Erlbaum.

Rosenblatt, J.S. (1983). Olfaction mediates developmental transition in the altricial newborn of selected species of mammals. *Developmental Psychobiology, 16*, 347–375.

Roth, L., & Rosenblatt, J.S. (1966). Changes in self-licking during pregnancy in the rat. *Journal of Comparative Physiology and Psychology, 63*, 397–400.

Russell, M.J. (1976). Human olfactory communication. *Nature, 260*, 520–522.

Salk, J. (1962). Mother's heartbeat as an imprinting stimulus. *Transactions of the New York Academy of Science, 24*, 753–754.

Scafidi, F., Field, T., Schanberg, S., Bauer, C., Roberts, J., Morrow, C., et al. (1990). Massage stimulates growth in preterm infants: A replication. *Infant Behavior and Development, 13*, 167–188.

Schaal, B. (1988a). Discontinuité natale et continuité chimiosensorielle: Modèles animaux et hypothèses pour l'homme [Birth discontinuity and chemosensory continuity: Animal models and human hypotheses]. *L'Année Biologique, 27*, 1–41.

Schaal, B. (1988b). Olfaction in infants and children: Developmental and functional perspectives. *Chemical Senses, 13*, 145–190.

Schaal, B., Coureaud, G., Langlois, D., Giniès, C., Sémon, E., & Perrier, G. (2003). Chemical and behavioral characterization of the mammary pheromone of the rabbit. *Nature, 424*, 68–72.

Schaal, B., & Marlier, L. (1998). Maternal and paternal perception of individual odor signatures in human amniotic fluid: Potential role in early bonding. *Biology of the Neonate, 74*, 266–273.

Schaal, B., Marlier, L., & Soussignan, R. (1995a). Responsiveness to the odor of amniotic fluid in the human neonate. *Biology of the Neonate, 67*, 397–406.

Schaal, B., Marlier, L., & Soussignan, R. (1995b). Olfactory preferences in newborn lambs: Possible influence of prenatal experience. *Behaviour, 132*, 351–365.

Schaal, B., Marlier, L., & Soussignan, R. (1998). Olfactory function in the human fetus: Evidence from selective neonatal responsiveness to the odor of amniotic fluid. *Behavioral Neuroscience, 112*, 1438–1449.

Schaal, B., Marlier, L., & Soussignan, R. (2000). Human fetuses learn odors from their pregnant mother's diet. *Chemical Senses, 25*, 729–737.

Schaal, B., Montagner, H., Hertling, E., Bolzoni, D., Moyse, A., & Quichon, R. (1980). Les stimulations olfactives dans les relations entre l'enfant et la mère [Odor stimulations in mother-infant relationships]. *Reproduction, Nutrition, Development, 20*, 843–858.

Schaal, B., & Orgeur, P. (1992). Olfaction *in utero*: Can the rodent model be generalized? *Quarterly Journal of Experimental Psychology, 44B*, 245–278.

Schaal, B., Orgeur, P., Desage, M., & Brazier, J.L. (1994). Transfer of the aromas of pregnant and lactating mother's diet to the fetal and neonatal environments in the sheep. *Chemical Senses, 20*, 93–94.

Schaal, B., Orgeur, P., & Marlier, L. (1994). Amniotic fluid odor in neonatal adaptation: A summary of recent research in mammals. *Advances in the Biosciences, 93*, 239–245.

Schaal, B., Orgeur, P., & Rognon, C. (1995). Odor sensing in the human fetus: Anatomical, functional and chemo-ecological bases. In J.-P. Lecanuet, W.P. Fifer, N.A. Krasnegor, & W.P. Smotherman (Eds.), *Prenatal development: A psychobiological perspective* (pp. 205–237). Hillsdale, NJ: Erlbaum.

Schaal, B., & Porter, R.H. (1991). Microsmotic humans revisited: The generation and perception of chemical signals. *Advances in the Study of Behavior, 20*, 135–200.

Schneirla, T.C. (1965). Aspects of stimulation and organization in approach/ withdrawal processes underlying vertebrate behavioral development. *Advances in the Study of Behavior, 1*, 1–74.

Semke, E., Distel, H., & Hudson, R. (1995). Specific enhancement of olfactory receptor sensitivity associated with fetal learning of food odors in the rabbit. *Naturwissenschaften, 82*, 148–149.

Shayit, M., Weller, A., Goursaud, A.P., Schaal, B., Uvnäs-Moberg, K., & Nowak, R. (2004) *Development of mother preference by newborn lambs: II. Non-nutritive sucking, plasma cholecystokinin and endogenous opioids.* Manuscript submitted for publication.

Shimoda, M., Yoshimura, T., Ishikawa, H., Hayakawa, I., & Osajima, Y. (2000). Volatile compounds of human milk. *Journal of the Faculty of Agriculture, Kyushu University, 45*, 199–206.

Simion, F., Valenza, E., & Umiltà, C. (1998). Mechanisms underlying face preference at birth. In F. Simion & G. Butterworth (Eds.), *The development of sensory, motor and cognitive capacities in early infancy: From perception to cognition* (pp. 87–101). Hove, UK: Psychology Press.

Smotherman, W.P. (1982a). In utero chemosensory experience alters taste preferences and corticosterone responseveness. *Behavioral and Neural Biology, 36*, 61–68.

Smotherman, W.P. (1982b). Odor aversion learning by rat fetus. *Physiology and Behavior, 29*, 769–771.

Smotherman, W.P., & Robinson, S.R. (1985). The rat fetus in its environment: Behavioral adjustment to novel, familiar, aversive, and conditioned stimuli presented *in utero. Behavioral Neuroscience, 99*, 521–530.

Smotherman, W.P., & Robinson, S.R. (1987). Psychobiology of fetal experience in the rat. In N.E. Krasnegor, E.M. Blass, M.A. Hofer, & W.P. Smotherman (Eds.), *Perinatal development. A psychobiological perspective* (pp. 39–60). Orlando: Academic Press.

Smotherman, W.P., & Robinson, S.R. (1992). Dimethyl disulfide mimics the effect of milk on fetal behavior and responsiveness to cutaneous stimuli. *Physiology & Behavior, 52*, 761–765.

Smotherman, W.P., & Robinson, S.R. (1995). Tracing developmental trajectories into the prenatal period. In J.-P. Lecanuet, W.P. Fifer, N.A. Krasnegor, & W.P. Smotherman (Eds.), *Fetal development: A psychobiological perspective* (pp. 15–32). Hillsdale, NJ: Erlbaum.

Smotherman, W.P., & Robinson, S.R. (1996). The development of behavior before birth. *Developmental Psychology, 32*, 425–434.

Smotherman, W.P., Robinson, S.R., LaValle, P.A., & Hennessy, M.B. (1987). Influences of the early olfactory environment on the survival, behavior, and pituitary-adrenal activity of caesarean delivered preterm rat pups. *Developmental Psychobiology, 20*, 415–423.

Snell, S. (1973). Garlic on the baby's breath. *Lancet, 2*, 43.

Soussignan, R., Schaal, B., & Marlier, L. (1999). Olfactory alliesthesia in human neonates: Prandial state and stimulus familiarity modulate facial and autonomic responses to milk odors. *Developmental Psychobiology, 35*, 3–14.

Soussignan, R., Schaal, B., Marlier, L., & Jiang, T. (1997). Facial and autonomic responses to biological and artificial olfactory stimuli in human neonates: Re-examining early hedonic discrimination of odors. *Physiology and Behavior, 62*, 745–758.

Stafford, M., Horning, M.G., & Zlatkis, A. (1976). Profiles of volatile metabolites in body fluids. *Journal of Chromatography, 126*, 495–502.

Steiner, J.E. (1979). Human facial expressions in response to taste and smell stimulations. *Advances in Child Development, 13*, 257–295.

Steiner, J.E., Glaser, D., Hawilo, M.E., & Berridge, K.C. (2001). Comparative expression of hedonic impact: Affective reactions to taste by human infants and other primates. *Neuroscience and Biobehavioral Review, 25*, 53–74.

Stickrod, G., Kimble, D.P., & Smotherman, W.P. (1982). *In utero* taste-odor aversion conditioning of the rat. *Physiology and Behavior, 28,* 5–7.

Sullivan, R.M., Stackenwald, G., Nasr, F., Lemon, C., & Wilson, D.A. (2000). Association of an odor with activation of olfactory bulb noradrenergic beta-receptors or locus coeruleus stimulation is sufficient to produce learned approach responses to that odor in neonatal rats. *Behavioral Neuroscience, 114,* 957–962.

Sullivan, R.M., & Toubas, P. (1998). Clinical usefulness of maternal odors in newborns: Soothing and feeding preparatory movements. *Biology of the Neonate, 74,* 402–408.

Svensson, C.K. (1997). Clinical pharmacokinetics of nicotine. *Clinical Pharmacokinetics, 12,* 30–40.

Tam, P.P.L., & Chan, S.T. (1977). Changes in the composition of maternal plasma, fetal plasma, and fetal extraembryonic fluid during gestation in the rat. *Journal of Reproduction and Fertility, 51,* 41–51.

Teicher, M.H., & Blass, E.M. (1976). Suckling in the newborn rat: Eliminated by nipple lavage, reinstated by pup saliva. *Science, 193,* 422–425.

Teicher, M.H., & Blass, E.M. (1977). First suckling response in the newborn albino rat: The roles of olfaction and amniotic fluid. *Science, 198,* 635–636.

Terry, L.M., & Johanson, I.B. (1987). Olfactory influences on the ingestive behavior of infant rats. *Developmental Psychobiology, 20,* 313–332.

Teschemacher, H., & Koch, G. (1991). Opioids in the milk. *Endocrine Regulations, 25,* 147–150.

Teschemacher, H., Koch, G., & Brantl, V. (1997). Milk-protein-derived opioid receptor ligands. *Biopolymers, 43,* 99–117.

Turkewitz, G. (1994). *Developmental precedence and intersensory influence.* Paper presented at the 19th International Conference on Infant Studies, Paris.

Turkewitz, G., & Kenny, P. (1982). Limitations on input as a basis for neural organization and perceptual development: A preliminary theoretical statement. *Developmental Psychobiology, 15,* 357–368.

Turkewitz, G., Lewkowicz, D.J., & Gardner, J.M. (1983). Determinants of infant perception. *Advances in the Study of Behavior, 13,* 39–62.

van Woerden, H.P., van Geijn, H.P., Caron, A.W., van der Walk, A.W., Swartjes, J.M., & Arts, N.F. (1988). Fetal mouth movements during behavioral states 1F and 2F. *European Journal of Obstetrics, Gynecology and Reproductive Biology, 29,* 97–105.

Varendi, H., Christenson, K., Porter, R.H., & Winberg, J. (1998). Soothing effect of amniotic fluid smell in newborn infants. *Early Human Development, 51,* 47–55.

Varendi, H., Porter, R.H., & Winberg, J. (1996). Attractiveness of amniotic odor: Evidence for prenatal olfactory learning? *Acta Paediatrica, 85,* 1223–1227.

Vijande, M., Brime, J.I., Lopez-Sela, P., Costales, M., & Argüelles, J. (1996). Increased salt preference in adult offspring raised by mother rats consuming excessive amounts of salt and water. *Regulatory Peptides, 66,* 105–108.

Vince, M.A., & Billing, A.E. (1986). Infancy in the sheep: The parts played by sensory stimulation in bonding between the ewe and lamb. In L.P. Lipsitt & C. Rovee-Collier (Eds.), *Advances in Infancy Research* (Vol. 4, pp. 2–37). Norwood, NJ: Ablex.

Wallace, J.P., Inbar, G., & Ernsthausen, K. (1992). Infant acceptance of post-exercise breast milk. *Pediatrics, 89,* 1245–1247.

Wallace, J.P., & Rabin, J. (1991). The concentration of lactic acid in breast milk following maximal exercise. *International Journal of Sports Medicine, 3,* 328–331.

Wilson, D.A., & Sullivan, R.M. (1994). Neurobiology of associative learning in the neonate: Early olfactory learning. *Behavioral and Neural Biology, 61,* 1–18.

Wuensch, K.L. (1975). Exposure to onion taste in mother's milk leads to enhanced preference for onion diet among weanling rats. *Journal General Psychology, 99,* 163–167.

Yamazaki, K., Curran, M., & Beauchamp, G.K. (2000, July). *Development and modification of behavioral responses to MHC-determined odor types.* Paper presented at the 9th Conference on Chemical Signals in Vertebrates, Krakow, Poland.

Zimmer, E.Z., Chao, C.R., Guy, C., Marks, F., & Fifer, W.P. (1993). Vibroaccoustic stimulation evokes human fetal micturition. *Obstetrics and Gynecology, 31,* 178–180.

Zou, Z., Horowitz, L.F., Montmayeur, J.P., Snapper, S., & Buck, L.M. (2001). Genetic tracing reveals a stereotyped sensory map in the olfactory cortex. *Nature, 414,* 173–179.

FURTHER READING

Bateson, P., & Gomendio, M. (1992). *Behavioral mechanisms in evolutionary perspective.* Madrid, Spain: Instituto Juan March.

Elman, J.L., Bates, E.A., Johnson, M.H., Karmiloff-Smith, A., Parisi, D., & Plunkett, K. (1996). *Rethinking innateness: A connectionist perspective on development.* Cambridge, MA: MIT Press.

Gottlieb, G., Wahlsten, D., & Lickliter, R. (1997). The significance of biology for human development: A developmental psychobiological systems view. In R.M. Lerner (Ed.), *Handbook of Child Psychology: Theory* (Vol. 1). New York: Wiley.

Granott, N., & Parziale, J. (Eds.). (2002). *Microdevelopment: Transition processes in development and learning.* Cambridge, UK: Cambridge University Press.

Hinde, R.A., & Bateson, P. (1984). Discontinuities versus continuities in behavioral development and the neglect of process. *International Journal of Behavioral Development, 7,* 129–143.

Johnson, M.H., & Bolhuis, J.J. (2001). Predispositions in perceptual and cognitive development. In J.J. Bolhuis (Ed.), *Brain, perception, memory: Advances in cognitive neurosciences* (pp. 69–84). Oxford, England: Oxford University Press.

Oyama, S. (1985). *The ontogeny of information.* Cambridge, UK: Cambridge University Press.

Schaal, B., Hummel, T., & Soussignan, R. (2004). Olfaction in the fetal and premature infant: Functional status and clinical implications. *Clinics in Perinatology, 31,* 261–258.

Schaal, B., Lecanuet, J.-P., & Granier-Deferre, C. (1999). Sensory and integrative development in the human fetus and perinate: The usefulness of animal models. In M. Haug & R.E. Whalen (Eds.), *Animal models of human cognition and emotion* (pp. 119–142). Washington, DC: American Psychological Association.

Smotherman, W.P., & Robinson, S.R. (1988). The uterus as environment: The ecology of fetal experience. In E.M. Blass (Ed.), *Handbook of behavioral neurobiology: Vol. 9. Developmental psychobiology and behavioral ecology* (pp. 97–106). New York: Plenum Press.

CHAPTER 4

Prenatal Preparation for Early Postnatal Olfactory Learning

Richard H. Porter, Jan Winberg, and Heili Varendi

ABSTRACT

Neonates' preferences or aversions for particular odors may be innate, or the result of prenatal and/or postnatal experience. Within the first one to two hours after birth, babies are alert and highly sensitive to stimulation. This aroused state presumably reflects a massive release of catecholamines (including NE) and activation of the locus ceruleus triggered by labor contractions. NE and locus coeruleus activation have both been implicated in olfactory learning by rodent pups, and a recent experiment suggests that these same processes might play a similar role in human neonates. Neonates delivered by cesarean section were exposed briefly to an odorant shortly after birth. Several days later, babies who had experienced labor contractions before the c-section was performed displayed a preference for the exposure odor, whereas those delivered without preceding labor showed no evidence of olfactory learning. Babies who responded preferentially towards the exposure odor also had higher plasma levels of NE. Neurophysiological events that occur naturally during the final stages of gestation and delivery may prepare the infant to rapidly become familiar with salient features of its postnatal environment. Olfactory learning may be particularly efficient during a brief period postpartum when NE levels remain high and the locus coeruleus is activated.

INTRODUCTION

The olfactory system of newborn human infants, as in other mammalian young, appears to be at least as sensitive as that of adults of the species (Beauchamp, Cowart, & Schmidt, 1991; Porter & Schaal, 2003; Rovee, 1969). Overt reactions by neonates to a wide range of odorants have been observed within the first several days postpartum; however, the precise nature of the response varies across odor stimuli. For example, maternal breast odors elicit positive hedonic responses, including facial orientation and physical movement toward the odor source (Macfarlane, 1975; Schaal et al., 1980; Varendi, Porter & Winberg, 1994; Varendi & Porter, 2001). In contrast, babies more frequently displayed negative facial expressions (presumed to reflect rejection or "disgust") when butyric acid or shrimp flavor, rather than other olfactory stimuli, were presented close to their nostrils (Soussignan, Schaal, Marlier, & Jiang, 1997; Steiner, 1977), while other odorants appear to be hedonically neutral (Engen, 1988). In this chapter, we consider the underlying developmental processes that mediate early discriminative responses to odors, with a primary focus on the neurochemical events associated with labor and delivery that may prepare the newborn baby for rapid, efficient learning. Alternative mechanisms implicated in early hedonic responses to odors—that is, the influence of prenatal learning/exposure and genetically based (innate) responses—will be discussed only briefly.

PRENATAL CHEMOSENSORY LEARNING

Prenatal chemosensory learning is a general phenomenon that has been documented in all five classes of vertebrates (reviewed by Sneddon, 2002): mammals (Hepper, 1988; Smotherman, 1982), birds (Porter & Picard, 1998; Sneddon, Hadden, & Hepper, 1998), fish (Courtenay, 1989; Sneddon, 2002), amphibians (Hepper & Waldman, 1992), and reptiles (Sneddon, 2002). In these experiments, young animals' postnatal responses to odors were affected by prior mere exposure to those same stimuli in the earlier fetal/embryonic environment, or by pairing the odorant with a noxious stimulus prenatally.

The discriminative reactions to *amniotic fluid* odor shown by newborn human infants suggest that fetal chemosensory learning may also occur in our species. Full-term, healthy babies that are placed on their mother's bare chest immediately after birth are capable of locating a nipple and initiating effective sucking without assistance (Widstrom et al., 1987). In this natural testing situation, babies demonstrated a significant preference for a breast moistened with a small amount of amniotic fluid for their initial feeding bout (Varendi, Porter, & Winberg, 1996). The babies' choice was presumably based upon olfactory cues, since they sucked from the first nipple with which they had mouth contact. That is, they appeared to select the nipple before achieving physical contact with it, thereby excluding taste cues. The odor of *amniotic fluid* also has a soothing effect on infants, as indicated by a significant reduction in the amount of time spent crying when they are exposed to that scent shortly after birth (Varendi, Christensson, Porter, & Winberg, 1998). Such positive reactions to *amniotic fluid* odor are believed to reflect *prenatal experience* and subsequent postnatal memory of those familiar cues. The babies that participated in each of the latter two experiments were bathed and dried immediately after delivery, and testing began several minutes later. Accordingly, they had little opportunity to become familiar with amniotic fluid odor postnatally (Varendi, Porter, & Winberg, 1997). An additional series of studies considered two–day old babies' head orientation when they were presented simultaneously with two stimulus odor pads (Marlier, Schaal, & Soussignan, 1998; Schaal, Marlier, & Soussignan, 1995). There was a marked preference to turn toward a pad treated with *amniotic fluid* when paired with an odorless control pad. Moreover, at three days of age, infants responded more positively to their own (familiar) *amniotic fluid* than to a pad moistened with alien *amniotic fluid*.

More convincing evidence of *fetal olfactory learning* in humans comes from an experiment involving the odors of highly flavored substances that mothers ate while pregnant. One day after birth, infants whose mothers had routinely used garlic in their meals displayed a greater attraction to *garlic* odor than did babies born of mothers who never consumed that plant (Hepper, 1995). There was a strong avoidance of garlic odor by babies in the latter condition, whereas those exposed to garlic flavor prenatally displayed a slight preference for that scent. It is improbable that the odor of garlic was rapidly learned postnatally. Mothers in the garlic condition did not consume garlic after their subject infant was born, and all of the babies were bottle-fed, thereby eliminating possible transfer of garlic flavor via *breast milk*. On the other hand, related research found a detectable odor of garlic in samples of *amniotic fluid* collected from pregnant women who ingested essential oil of garlic (Mennella, Johnson, & Beauchamp, 1995). Therefore, fetuses would presumably be exposed to garlic flavor after their mother eats a meal containing that substance. These original results were subsequently corroborated by a methodologically similar experiment with infants born of mothers who consumed anise flavor during pregnancy (Schaal, Marlier, & Soussignan, 2000).

It appears that prenatal exposure to flavors found in the mother's diet may also influence infants' acceptance of similar food after they are weaned. Mennella and colleagues (Mennella, Jagnow, & Beauchamp, 2001) recently reported that infants (approximately six months old) born of mothers who consumed carrot juice during the final trimester of pregnancy displayed fewer negative facial expressions when they were fed cereal flavored with carrot juice for the first time, compared to their responses to untreated cereal. In contrast, such discriminative facial expressions were not exhibited by control infants with no pre-test experience with carrot flavor. In addition, the mothers who drank carrot juice while pregnant (but not the control mothers) rated their infants' enjoyment of carrot-flavored cereal higher than that of the plain cereal. The results of this study suggest that the development of long-term dietary preferences may be biased at least to some extent by *in utero* chemosensory familiarization. (Further discussion of prenatal chemosensory learning can be found in chapter 3 by Schaal.)

INNATE RESPONSES TO ODORS?

In theory, discriminative behavioral/physiological responses to particular odors when they are presented for the first time after birth could either be the result of prenatal experience and learning (as discussed in the preceding section), or be genetically mediated (i.e., innate). One would expect that genetically encoded reactions to specific odors should most likely be high when there is a high probability that those scents will be encountered postnatally (but not *in utero*), and the animal's continued well-being, or survival—hence, its ultimate reproductive success—depends upon appropriate responses to them. The strongest evidence of *innate responsiveness* to olfactory stimuli involves animals reared under strictly controlled conditions, as illustrated by the defensive reactions and elevated blood pressure shown by laboratory rats when exposed to the scent of a cat (see Dielenberg & McGregor, 2001, for a recent review). The observed responses are immediate and appear to be specific to cat odor *per se*; novel odors or scents from mammals that are not natural predators of rats do not have the same effect. In a similar manner, water voles that had no prior contact with mink avoided cages smelling of that predatory mustelid (Barreto & Macdonald, 1999). Such defensive behavior by prey species, when they initially come into contact with cues emitted by predators, would have obvious survival value, and individuals behaving in this manner would therefore gain a selective advantage. A recent genetic tracing study provides further support for the hypothesis that responses to biologically meaningful odors may be genetically "hardwired" (Zou, Horowitz, Montmayeur, Snapper, & Buck, 2001; see also Barinaga, 2001). Particular nasal olfactory receptors in *mice* were found to form orderly links with discrete clusters of neurons in the olfactory cortex, resulting in "a stereotyped sensory map." Moreover, across individual animals, cortical sites receiving projections from a given receptor "have similar or identical locations," which could be a basis for innate species-typical responses to odorants.

Returning to *human neonates*, the relatively high rate of negative facial expressions elicited by chemosensory cues such as *shrimp* flavor and *butyric acid* (Soussignan et al., 1997; Steiner, 1977) cannot be explained readily by pre- or postnatal exposure/learning, and might therefore represent *innate biases*. On the other hand, negative responses to these volatile cues could reflect irritating trigeminal stimulation rather than inborn hedonic responses to specific odorants. For example, a majority of anosmic adult subjects (i.e., lacking functional olfactory nerves but with intact trigeminal nerve function) reported "intranasal sensation" when they inhaled vapors of high concentrations of butyric acid (Doty et al., 1978; see also Doty, 1975). In an attempt to further clarify this issue, Soussignan et al. (1997) analyzed a range of behavioral and autonomic responses by three-day-old neonates to odorants that were presented in dilute concentrations, and therefore presumably had little detectable input to the trigeminal system (see also Doty, 1995). A higher proportion of the babies displayed facial expressions indicative of "disgust" when exposed to the odor of butyric acid than to the odor of *vanillin* (the intensities of the two odorants were judged as equivalent by a panel of adult raters). These results support the authors' tentative conclusion that there may be inherent differences in the hedonic classification of some odors.

In a similar manner, existing data do not provide a clear understanding of the developmental processes mediating newborn infants' preferential responsiveness to odors emanating from the breasts of lactating females. When babies were placed on their mother's chest within minutes after birth, a significantly greater number spontaneously selected the naturally smelling breast for their first sucking bout, rather than the alternative breast that had been thoroughly washed to eliminate its olfactory cues (Varendi et al., 1994). Perhaps the most plausible interpretation of these results is that babies' are innately attracted to *maternal breast odors.* However, the possible influence of prenatal learning cannot be entirely excluded in this context. That is, there is some overlap in the chemical components of *breast milk* and *amniotic fluid,* including flavors from the mother's diet that are transferred into both substances (Hauser, Chitayat, Berns, Braver, & Muhlbauer, 1985; Hepper, 1995; Mennella & Beauchamp, 1991; Mennella et al., 1995; Schaal et al., 2000; Stafford, Horning, & Zlatkis, 1976). In addition, the pregnant mother's genetically determined odortype may be imparted to her fetus (Beauchamp et al., 1995). Thus, chemical stimuli to which the fetus was exposed *in utero* may also be associated with the mother's breasts and recognized by the newborn infant. In this manner, prenatal familiarization with some of the constituent odors found in their mother's milk (or on the surface of her breasts) may have a positive effect on babies' acceptance of the maternal breasts. However, even if amniotic fluid and breast secretions share some common chemical elements, neonates discriminate between the odors of those substances. During tests conducted within the first two hours following delivery, babies that were exposed to the odor of their amniotic fluid cried significantly less than babies in a control condition; exposure to the mother's *breast odor* had the opposite effect (i.e. elicted heightened crying) (Varendi et al., 1998). In another experiment (discussed earlier), when one of their mother's breasts was moistened with *amniotic fluid* before the first feeding attempt, and the other retained its natural odor, babies preferentially sucked from the breast treated with amniotic fluid (Varendi et al., 1996). Because neonates readily distinguish between the odors of *amniotic fluid* versus *maternal breasts,* it seems unreasonable to conclude that the observed attraction to maternal breast odors is primarily the result of prenatal learning of shared components of those distinctive scents.

Further insights into this issue come from experiments demonstrating that even exclusively bottle-fed infants are attracted to *breast odors* produced by lactating women. At two weeks of age, formula-fed infants oriented preferentially toward a breast pad that had been worn by an unfamiliar nursing mother when paired with either that same woman's axillary pad or a breast pad from a non-parturient female (Makin & Porter, 1989). Since the diets of the mothers of the infants and those of the stimulus lactating women were probably quite different, the odor of the babies' *amniotic fluid* and the scent of the (unfamiliar mothers') breasts should have been less similar than in the previously discussed experiment (Varendi et al., 1998), where babies were tested with their own mother's breast odor. This further argues against a strong influence of prenatal learning on the observed breast-odor preference.

In a related study, two-week old *bottle-fed infants* displayed a relative preference for a lactating female's *breast odor* over the scent of their own familiar formula (Porter, Makin, Davis, & Christensen, 1991). It is noteworthy that the response to the unfamiliar *breast odor* was more attractive than an odor that the infants had been repeatedly exposed to while feeding, and which thereby should have acquired a positive hedonic value. Neonates' attraction to lactating females' *breast odors* is clearly adaptive. Throughout the evolutionary history of our species, there were no adequate substitutes for maternal *breast milk*—at least that was the case until recently. Newborn infants are active participants in the breast-feeding process (i.e., to feed effectively, they must grasp and suck from their mother's nipple or that of another the lactating woman). Positive responsiveness to odors that are associated reliably with nursing mothers' nipples/breasts would facilitate colostrum and milk ingestion and thus be favored by natural selection.

Behavioral genetic analyses provide more direct evidence of the contribution of genotype to human chemosensory perception (Segal & Topolski, 1995). Higher correlations for the performance of *monozygotic* (MZ) *twins* as compared to *dizygotic twins* (DZ) on odor identification and detection tests have been reported, indicating a *genetic influence on olfactory acuity* (Segal, Topolski, Wilson, Brown, & Araki, 1995; Wysocki & Beauchamp, 1984). Further research is warranted, however, since clear differences between DZ versus MZ twins on various olfaction tasks are not always found (Segal & Topolski, 1995). According to the results of a recently published experiment, hedonic responses to odors may also be genetically influenced (Jacob, McClintock, Zelano, & Ober, 2002). Women's preferences for the odors of male donors varied according to the donors' genotype; more specifically, alleles in the *major histocompatibility complex* (MHC). Their odor choices reflected alleles that they had inherited from their father, and that were shared by the odor donors. In contrast, *MHC* alleles inherited from the mother were not related to odor choices. Because the subjects would have been exposed to both the father's and mother's MHC-determined odors throughout their lifetimes, the differential responses to those cues do not appear to be the result of differences in familiarity. *MHC*-correlated odors have been implicated in *social recognition* and mating preferences in nonhuman species (Boyse, Beauchamp, Yamazaki, & Bard, 1991; Eggert, Muller-Ruchholtz, & Ferstl, 1999; Penn & Potts, 1999), and they may likewise play a role in human social interactions (Ober et al., 1997; Wedekind, Seebeck, Bettens, & Paepke, 1995). The possible influence of such cues on the behavior of neonates has yet to be investigated, however.

EARLY POSTNATAL OLFACTORY LEARNING

There is an extensive amount of research literature concerning *olfactory learning* in young animals, particularly newborn mammals, which includes numerous examples of olfactory preferences resulting from experience with particular scents in the early rearing environment (Fillion & Blass, 1986; Kaplan, Cubicciotti, & Redican, 1979; Mainardi, Marsan, & Pasquali, 1965; Muller-Schwarze & Muller-Schwarze, 1971). In some instances, brief periods of odor exposure were sufficient for the development of discriminative responsiveness to those stimuli. Spiny *mouse pups* that had been exposed to the odor of *cinnamon* or *cumin* for sixty minutes on the day of birth were attracted to the familiar training odor during subsequent choice tests (Porter & Etscorn, 1974). Likewise, ten-day-old rat pups displayed a preference for an odorant to which they had been exposed for only three minutes on the previous day (Caza & Spear, 1984), while one-day-old pups learned to respond discriminatively to an odor cue associated with a reinforcer (Johanson & Hall, 1979).

Beginning shortly after they are born, human infants are also capable of learning both artificial and natural biologically meaningful odors. Several experiments have demonstrated that neonates respond preferentially to their own mother's odor (collected from either the breast or axillae), thereby indicating that they recognize her unique olfactory signature (Cernoch & Porter, 1985; Macfarlane, 1975; Russell, 1976; Schaal et al., 1980; Sullivan & Toubas, 1998). Recognition of the characteristic *maternal odor* appears to be based on postnatal exposure and conditioning. One-week-old babies became familiar with the perfume that was applied to their mothers' breast before each nursing bout, and they are more often oriented toward that scent rather than toward a control odor (Schleidt & Genzel, 1990). A similar process of familiarization could account for two-week-old *breast-fed neonates' olfactory recognition* of their mother, since they had recurring periods of contact with her bare flesh and *odor signature* while sucking at her breasts. In contrast, *bottle-fed infants* of the same age, who would have less opportunity to become familiar with their *mother's individual odor*, showed no evidence of recognizing that scent (Cernoch & Porter, 1985). Insufficient pre-test exposure could likewise account for breast-fed infants' indiscriminate responses to odor samples from their father as against an unfamiliar adult male (Cernoch & Porter, 1985).

As discussed above, during tests conducted immediately after birth, more babies spontaneously chose to suck from a breast bearing the odor of *amniotic fluid* than an untreated, naturally smelling breast (Varendi et al., 1996). Several days later, however, this odor preference was reversed: babies more frequently grasped and sucked from the untreated breast (Varendi, Porter & Winberg, 1997; see also Marlier et al., 1998). Thus, the babies modified their responsiveness to biologically salient odors as a function of previous exposure and experience with those stimuli. Whereas the odor of *amniotic fluid* disappeared shortly after birth, there would have been continuing intermittent exposure to *breast odors* associated with food intake and physical contact with the mother. It will also be recalled that babies are attracted to *maternal breast odors* within the first hour after birth, even though they show a relative preference for amnniotic fluid at that time. Accordingly, the initial positive responsiveness to maternal breast odors appeared to be augmented by *postnatal learning*.

To further assess the effects of mere stimulus exposure on the development of *olfactory learning* and memory, odorants were introduced into babies' cots on the day of birth (Balogh & Porter, 1986; Davis & Porter, 1991). The odor remained in the cot for approximately twenty-four hours, but babies were not exposed continuously to those scents for this entire period due to the fact that they were occasionally removed by their mother or nursery staff. Although the exposure odors were not associated with any identifiable reinforcer, they elicited greater directional *head orientation* than did control odors during tests conducted up to two weeks after the training session. Mere exposure to an odor beginning on the first day postpartum is therefore sufficient for babies to become familiar with that scent and retain a memory trace of it over an interval of two weeks.

Rapid *olfactory classical conditioning* of newborns has also been reported (Sullivan et al., 1991). On the day of birth, a group of neonates received ten training trials, in which an artificial odor was paired with positive tactile stimulation (gentle stroking) for thirty seconds. The next day, the babies treated in this manner exhibited a head-turning preference for the conditioned odor stimulus, but such discriminative orientation was not found for control infants who had been exposed only to the odor or stroking, or experienced stroking followed by presentation of the odorant.

Up to this point, prenatal and early postnatal learning have been presented as distinctly separate phenomena. In some instances, however, a young animal's reaction to particular odors may reflect an interaction between fetal exposure and postnatal experience. This possibility was illustrated in an experiment in which rat pups were exposed to the scent of lemons either during the last two days of gestation or for a one-hour period shortly after birth, while an additional group received both pre- and postnatal *lemon* exposure (Pedersen & Blass, 1982). When tested with an anesthetized lactating female, only those pups in the latter condition attached preferentially to nipples scented with lemon rather than untreated nipples. There was thus an additive effect of the pre- and postnatal odor exposure, but neither of those treatments alone was sufficient to induce the development of an olfactory preference. In a similar manner, fetal experience with the mother's characteristic *odor signature* might facilitate or reinforce early *postnatal learning* of that cue by human infants (discussed earlier), even though prenatal exposure alone does not appear sufficient for the establishment of an enduring memory trace (Cernoch & Porter, 1985).

DO PHYSIOLOGICAL EVENTS ASSOCIATED WITH LABOR AND DELIVERY CONTRIBUTE TO EFFICIENT POSTNATAL LEARNING?

The rhythmic *uterine contractions* that characterize the onset of *labor* continue—usually at an accelerating rate—until the birth process is completed (Trevathan, 1987). Aside from their role in forcing the fetus through the birth canal, *labor contractions* have additional consequences that help prepare the fetus to respond adaptively to the external postnatal environment. Immediately after birth, *vaginally delivered human infants* are typically awake, appear alert, and are highly responsive to stimulation (Lagercrantz, 1996; Otamiri, Berg, Ledin, Leijon, & Lagercrantz, 1991). In comparison, infants delivered via *cesarean section* before the onset of *labor* tend to be less active, spend more time sleeping, and cry less frequently. Similar behavioral differences between the two modes of delivery have been reported for rhesus monkey neonates (Meier, 1964). In the latter study, vaginally delivered neonates also perfomed better than c-section young onan avoidance conditioning task. Because c-sections were performed under local anesthesia restricted to the site of the incision, the possible effects of maternal medication on the newborn in that group could be ruled out.

The effects of the mechanical stimulation that the fetus experiences during *labor* and delivery have been investigated experimentally by exposing *fetal rats* to treatments designed to mimic *uterine contractions*. On the final day of gestation, the uterine horns of pregnant rats were externalized, allowing direct access to the fetuses (Ronca & Alberts, 1995). Fetuses that were subjected to repeated periods of mechanical compression at that time subsequently displayed increased rates of respiration relative to control fetuses, or those that were cooled or had experienced umbilical cord occlusion. During the first hour following the treatment, the breathing pattern of pups in the simulated labor condition did not differ from that of vaginally delivered pups. It therefore appears that the stimulation provided by *labor contractions* may be important for the onset and maintenance of normal respiration. In a subsequent study by the same research team, simulated uterine contractions were also found to facilitate nipple attachment by newborn c-section pups (Abel, Ronca, & Alberts, 1998).

Neuroendocrine Processes Triggered by Labor

Uterine *labor contractions* trigger a nexus of neural and endocrine processes in the fetus, which in turn are believed to contribute substantially to the behavioral/physiological differences between vaginally delivered and c-section neonates. As discussed by Lagercrantz and his colleagues (Lagercrantz, 1996; Lagercrantz & Slotkin, 1986; Marchini, Lagercrantz, Winberg, & Uvnas-Moberg, 1988), there is an enormous surge in fetal stress hormones during the initial stage of labor. Plasma levels of *norepinephrine* (NE) and other catecholamines remain elevated until *vaginal delivery* is completed, and for a short period postnatally, then decline to resting levels approximately two hours after birth. It is likely that uterine contractions induce brief periods of *fetal hypoxia* and head compression that mediate the peripheral release of catecholamines (from the adrenal medulla and paraganglia), some of which cross the blood–brain barrier. In contrast with the dramatic *NE surge* observed in vaginally born neonates, NE concentrations in blood samples from infants delivered by elective *cesarean section* tend to be relatively low (Hagnevik et al., 1984;

Irestedt, Lagercrantz, Hjemdahl, Hagnevik, & Belfrage, 1982; Jones & Greiss, 1982; Jouppila, Puolakka, Kauppila, & Vuori, 1984). Moreover, *c-section* babies delivered after the onset of labor had higher levels of plasma catecholamines than did c-section newborns who had not experienced *labor contractions* (Wang, Zhang, & Zhao, 1999).

Aside from triggering a massive peripheral output of *NE, labor contractions* may also activate the *locus coeruleus,* a brain structure containing a dense population of noradrenergic cells that project widely throughout the CNS (Lagercrantz, 1996; Svensson, 1987). Shortly after birth, there is a marked increase in *NE turnover* in the brain of rat pups, which most likely reflects *locus coerulus* activity (Lagercrantz, 1996; Lagercrantz, Pequignot, Pequignot, & Peyrin, 1992). Pharmacological and electrophysiological studies suggest that the *locus coeruleus* functions as a general center for brain arousal (Jacobs, 1990; Svensson, 1987). For example, the pattern of EEG activity of the forebrain following stimulation of the locus coerulus resembles that normally associated with an alert state (Foote, Berridge, Adams, & Pineda, 1991). In a similar manner, *locus coerulus activation* may contribute to the high state of arousal displayed by human neonates within the first one to two hours after birth, as well as their sensitivity to stimulus input at that time (Lagercrantz, 1996).

Role of NE and Locus Coeruleus in Early Olfactory Learning in Rats

Survival and normal development of newborn rodents are dependent upon adaptive responses to salient biological odors. Neonates rely on olfactory cues to locate and attach to the nipples (Blass & Teicher, 1980; Teicher & Blass, 1977), and attractive maternal odors function to prevent newly mobile pups from wandering away from the vicinity of their mother and nest area (Leon, 1974; Porter, 1983). Because maternal odors do not remain constant and may change as a function of dietary factors (Doane & Porter, 1978; Leon, 1975), pups must be capable of rapid *olfactory learning* in order to continue to respond effectively to cues emanating from their mother.

NE and activation of the *locus coeruleus* have been directly implicated in neonatal *olfactory learning* in rat pups (for reviews see Gervais, Holley, & Keverne, 1988; Leon, 1992; Nelson & Panksepp, 1998; Sullivan & Wilson, 1994; Wilson & Sullivan, 1994). Sullivan and her collaborators (Sullivan, Wilson, & Leon, 1989) reported that exposure to an artifical odorant paired with an NE receptor agonist

(isoproterenol) is sufficient for the development of a learned preference for the training odor. Moreover, infusion of an NE receptor
antagonist (propranolol) into the olfactory bulbs blocked such *olfactory learning* by five-day-old pups (Sullivan, Zyzak, Skierkowski, &
Wilson, 1992). In related experiments, *rat pups* were exposed to an
odor stimulus associated with pharmacological treatments that presumably stimulate the *locus coeruleus* (Sullivan, Stackenwalt, Nasr,
Lemon, & Wilson, 2000). On the following day, pups that had been
subjected to these procedures oriented preferentially to the training
odor in a two-choice test. In contrast, the same pharmacological treatments did not result in odor-learning in a group of pups that had been
injected with an *NE antagonist* prior to the training session. These
data are particularly interesting in the present context because *locus
coeruleus* neurons in rats are noradrenergic, and a large proportion of
these NE neurons project to the olfactory bulb (Shipley, Halloran, &
de la Torre, 1985).

Influence of Labor on Olfactory Learning in Human Neonates

Given the involvement of *NE* and the *locus coeruleus* in early olfactory learning by rat pups, as well as the surge of catecholamines and
(presumed) locus coeruleus activation triggered by uterine *labor contractions* in humans, we hypothesized that *olfactory learning* should be
more efficient in babies that experience labor contractions during the
final stages of prenatal development, compared to neonates delivered
without preceding labor. In a recent attempt to evaluate this hypothesis (Varendi, Porter, & Winberg, 2002), we compared the performance of fifteen babies that were delivered by c-section after the onset
of uterine contractions (mean length of labor preceding c-section is
6.5 hours), and sixteen neonates born of mothers who had no labor
contractions before elective c-section was performed. Several minutes
after birth, each baby was exposed to the odor of *cherry* or *passion fruit.*
A gauze pad treated with the odorant was placed five centimeters
from the baby's nose and remained there for the thirty-minutes exposure session (see Fig. 4.1). The babies were swaddled in a blanket at
that time and therefore unable to move. The odor stimulus was removed at the end of the exposure session and a two-choice olfactory
preference test was conducted one to five days later.

Across the entire sample of thirty-one babies, significantly more
time was spent oriented toward a stimulus pad treated with the

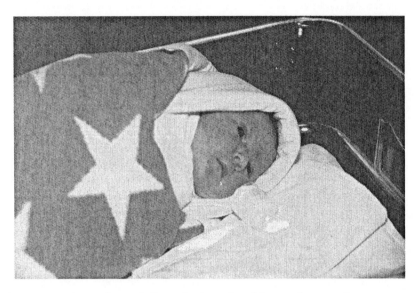

Figure 4.1. A newborn infant during the thirty-minute odor exposure period. A gauze pad treated with the exposure odorant is contained in the cup near the infant's nose.

exposure odor than in the direction of a simultaneously present novel odor (test situation depicted in Fig. 4.2). However, the patterns of responses were not consistent between the two subgroups: babies that were delivered after the onset of labor displayed a significant preference for the exposure odor (Fig. 4.3), and neonates who had not experienced preoperative *uterine contractions* oriented indiscriminately to the two stimulus odors (Fig. 4.4). Thus, there was behavioral evidence of *olfactory learning* and memory only for babies in the labor condition. Analysis of blood samples collected from the umbilical artery immediately after birth revealed a significant positive correlation between *NE* level and duration of pre-delivery labor. Moreover, the level of *NE* in the blood of babies who oriented preferentially to the exposure odor, suggesting learned familiarity with that scent, was reliably higher than that of babies who did not show an exposure-odor preference (median pmol NE/ml = 12.6 and 7.2, respectively).

These data indicate that a brief period of mere exposure to an odorant immediately after birth is sufficient for the development of a learned preference for that stimulus—provided that the fetus had been subjected to uterine *labor contractions*. Therefore, it appears that neurophysiological processes occurring naturally during the final stages of pregnancy prepare the fetus to become rapidly familiar with

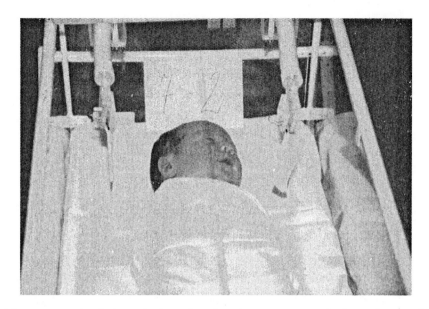

Figure 4.2. An infant during the simultaneous two-choice odor preference test. Odorized stimulus pads are suspended along either side of the infant's face.

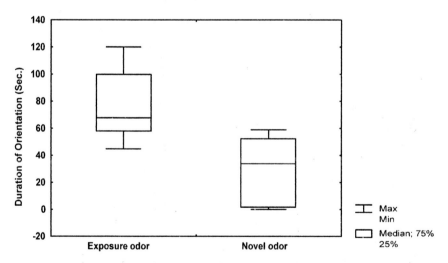

Figure 4.3. Boxplot of the amount of time (sec.) spent oriented toward the exposure odor and a novel odor during the simultaneous two-choice test by babies who had experienced uterine labor contractions (labor condition) before being delivered via c-section (n = 15). The horizontal line within each box represents the median duration of orientation to that odor. (Copyright © 2002 by the American Psychological Association. Adapted with permission.)

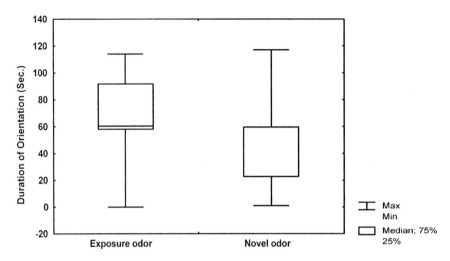

Figure 4.4. Boxplot of the amount of time (sec.) spent oriented toward the exposure odor and a novel odor during the simultaneous two-choice test by babies who were delivered via c-section without preceding labor (no labor condition, n = 16). The horizontal line within each box represents the median duration of orientation to that odor. (Copyright © 2002 by the American Psychological Association. Adapted with permission.)

odors that are present after it emerges into the external environment. Thus, efficient *postnatal olfactory learning* may be facilitated by prenatal events. Because the level of *NE* remains elevated for only a short time after *vaginal birth* with a rapid decline two hours later, and hence a concomitant decline in *locus coeruleus* activation (Lagercrantz, 1996; Lagercrantz & Slotkin, 1986), the neonate may be particularly sensitive to environmental stimuli during a brief, immediate postpartum interval. Up to the present time, there have been no studies that specifically address this *sensitive period* hypotheses.

Influence of Labor/Delivery on Maternal Behavior?

It should be noted that the adaptive consequences of the physical stimulation accompanying labor and delivery are not restricted to the effects discussed above on the neonate. As the fetus proceeds through the birth canal, the mother is subjected to uterine, cervical, and vaginal distension, which in turn may influence her initial responsiveness to her newborn offspring and its associated odors. The positive effects of *genital stimulation* on *maternal behavior* have been demonstrated clearly in domestic sheep (reviewed by Lévy, Porter, Kendrick, Keverne, & Romeyer, 1996; Poindron, Lévy, & Krehbiel, 1988). Although ewes typically avoid the odor of *amniotic fluid*, that scent becomes highly attractive at parturition, and therefore heightens *maternal responsiveness* to the newborn offspring (Lévy & Poindron, 1987; Lévy, Poindron, & Le Neindre, 1983). As the mother licks the *amniotic fluid*, she becomes familiar with her lamb's unique individual odor and subsequently relies on that olfactory signature to recognize her offspring.

This attraction to *amniotic fluid* rapidly declines postpartum, but it can be reinstated by artificial *vaginocervical stimulation* (Poindron, Lévy, & Krehbiel, 1988; Rubianes, 1992). Thus, the hedonic value of *amniotic fluid odor* is modified by a procedure that to some extent mimics the stimulation of the birth canal associated with *vaginal delivery*. Likewise, ewes that have developed a selective bond with their newborn lamb show increased acceptance of alien young immediately after being subjected to a period of vaginocervical stimulation (Keverne, Lévy, Poindron, & Lindsay, 1983). In contrast, maternal behavior was disrupted in ewes that were injected with a local peridural anesthetic at the beginning of labor to block afferent stimulation from the birth canal (Krehbiel, Poindron, Lévy, & Prud'homme, 1987). *Vaginocervical stimulation* also contributes to neuroendocrine activity in the olfactory bulbs (including the release of NE) that is implicated in parturient ewes' rapid learning of their lamb's *individual odor signature* (Kendrick, Lévy, & Keverne, 1992; Lévy et al., 1996). Overall, these experiments indicate that prenatal biological processes prepare the mother ewe to respond in a species-typical manner to her newly emerged young. In effect, the *fetal lamb* contributes to its own postnatal well-being by serving as a source of mechanical stimulation that triggers complex neuroendocrine events. These events foster the expression of appropriate *maternal care* and the establishment of olfactory-based *offspring recognition*.

BIOLOGICAL SIGNIFICANCE OF EARLY OLFACTORY LEARNING?

There is no basis for assuming that there are fundamental qualitative differences in the neural processes involved in learning by the fetus and the newborn infant. Nonetheless, the efficiency of learning might vary between these two developmental stages. As discussed earlier, immediately following *vaginal delivery* neonates tend to be awake and highly aroused, reflecting *locus coeruleus* activation and sharply elevated levels of catecholamines. At that time, they appear to be "supersensitive" to various sensory stimuli (Lagercrantz, 1996). In striking contrast, prior to birth the fetus has relatively low blood pressure and metabolism and usually appears to be sleeping. Because of these differences in arousal and susceptibility to stimulus input, learning may occur more readily during the immediate postpartum period than *in utero*. Furthermore, if heightened *NE* levels and locus coeruleus activation indeed facilitate memory acquisition, the first hours after birth could be a particularly *sensitive period* for the development of familiarization with meaningful features of the environment or other forms of learning/conditioning.

The range and nature of potentially perceptible extraneous stimuli also differ for the fetus versus neonate. Visual stimuli would be of little or no relevance in the dark intrauterine environment, and sounds might be attenuated (depending on their frequencies) or masked by background noises, such as those associated with maternal respiration, digestive processes, or heartbeat (Fifer & Moon, 1988). Although the *amniotic fluid* contains numerous chemical compounds that might stimulate fetal receptors, they are limited to by-products of maternal and fetal metabolism, plus flavorful and odorous substances inhaled or ingested by the mother. This situation changes abruptly at birth when the baby is exposed to an array of visual, auditory, and chemical stimuli. Of course, memory of specific stimuli resulting from prenatal experience would have little utility for the neonate if those same cues are unlikely to be encountered postnatally. For the fetus, as well as the newborn infant, stimuli provided by the mother may be particularly salient. Thus, the mother's voice (which is relatively undistorted *in utero*) and odor may be prominent features of both the pre- and postnatal environments.

Familiarization with the mother's distinctive phenotypic traits (i.e., the development of individual *maternal recognition*) is perhaps the example of rapid early learning that has the most obvious biological significance for the neonate (Hepper, 1996; Porter, 1991). Neonates' discriminative responses to their mother's *odor signature* have been observed as early as the first two to three days postpartum (Porter, 1991; Sullivan & Toubas, 1998) and appear to be mediated by *postnatal learning*, possibly interacting with fetal exposure (as previously noted). *Breast feeding*, which often begins within the first hour postpartum (Righard & Alade, 1990; Trevathan, 1987; Varendi et al., 1994; Widstrom et al., 1987), assures that neonates will have recurring periods of exposure to the characteristic maternal odor. Moreover, anthropological data (Konner & Worthman, 1980) and comparative studies of feeding behavior and milk composition (Ben Shaul, 1962; Blurton-Jones, 1972; Wolff, 1968) suggest that the evolutionary adapted pattern of human mother-infant interactions involves constant bodily contact and frequent sucking bouts throughout the day and night. During *breast feeding*, the mother's scent will also be associated with a combination of reinforcing stimuli (food, warmth, physical contact) that should further strengthen learning of that cue.

Recognition of the mother is important for the newborn, since it is a necessary preliminary step in the *attachment* process. That is, the unique reciprocal relationship that typically exists between an infant and its mother can only begin to develop if those partners can be distinguished from other individuals as social attachment/bonding implies *individual recognition*. Mothers are quite sensitive to various signals produced by their newborn baby (Fleming & Corter, 1988; Klaus & Kennell, 1982; Porter, 1991; Trevathan, 1987). By responding discriminatively to their mother, babies convey the impression that she can be recognized, which in turn can have a positive effect on the parent's continuing relationship with her offspring (Robson & Moss, 1970). Olfactory-based early recognition of the mother has several advantages over *individual discrimination* via other sensory channels. Although recognition of the mother's voice also occurs at a very early age (DeCasper & Fifer, 1980), auditory discrimination is only possible when the mother is speaking. Visual recognition of the mother's face has likewise been documented in two-day-old babies (Bushnell, Sai, & Mullin, 1989), but potential access to salient facial features requires an adequate level of illumination and appropriate orientation of the mother and infant. In contrast with maternal facial/visual and vocal cues, the mother's *odor signature* is continually present at the skin surface. Therefore, olfactory-based recognition is possible regardless of the lighting conditions and the mother's behavioral state, assuming that the infant is in sufficiently close contact.

Due to the precocial development of sensory mechanisms and the availability of stable individually distinctive phenotypic signatures (beginning prenatally), olfaction is an ideal modality for the mediation of early *maternal recognition*. Infants might actually become familiar with their mother's characteristic scent earlier than two days of age, but existing tests may not be sufficiently sensitive to demonstrate that such learning has occurred before that time. In the light of its role in the establishment of the baby's initial discriminative interactions, *olfactory learning* would appear to be a major factor contributing to the social development of human infants.

REFERENCES

Abel, R.A., Ronca, A.E., & Alberts, J.R. (1998). Perinatal stimulation facilitates suckling onset in newborn rats. *Developmental Psychobiology, 32*, 91–99.

Balogh, R.D., & Porter, R.H. (1986). Olfactory preferences resulting from mere exposure in human neonates. *Infant Behavior and Development, 9*, 395–401.

Barinaga, M. (2001). Smell's course is predetermined. *Science, 294*, 1269–1271.

Barreto, G.R., & Macdonald, D.W. (1999). The response of water voles, *Arvicola terrestris*, to the odours of predators. *Animal Behaviour, 57*, 1107–1112.

Beauchamp, G.K., Cowart, B.J., & Schmidt, H.J. (1991). Development of chemosensory sensitivity and preference. In T.V. Getchell, R.L. Doty, L.M. Bartoshuk, & J.B. Snow, Jr. (Eds.), *Smell and taste in health and disease* (pp. 405–416). New York: Raven Press.

Beauchamp, G.K., Katahira, K., Yamazaki, K., Mennella, J.A., Bard, J., & Boyse, E.A. (1995). Evidence suggesting that the odortypes of pregnant women are a compound of maternal and fetal odortypes. *Proceedings of the National Academy of Science, USA, 92*, 2617–2621.

Ben Shaul, D.M. (1962). The composition of the milk of wild animals. *International Zoo Year Book, 4*, 333–342.

Blass, E.M., & Teicher, M.H. (1980). Suckling. *Science, 210*, 15–22.

Blurton-Jones, N. (1972). Comparative aspects of mother-child contact. In N. Blurton-Jones (Ed.), *Ethological studies of child behaviour* (pp. 305–328). Cambridge, UK: Cambridge University Press.

Boyse, E.A., Beauchamp, G.K., Yamazaki, K., & Bard, J. (1991). Genetic components of kin recognition in mammals. In P.G. Hepper (Ed.), *Kin recognition* (pp. 148–161). Cambridge, UK: Cambridge University Press.

Bushnell, I.W.R., Sai, F., & Mullin, J.T. (1989). Neonatal recognition of the mother's face. *British Journal of Developmental Psychology, 7*, 3–15.

Caza, P.A., & Spear, N.E. (1984). Short-term exposure to an odor increases its subsequent preference in preweanling rats: A descriptive profile of the phenomenon. *Developmental Psychobiology, 17*, 407–422.

Cernoch, J.M., & Porter, R.H. (1985). Recognition of maternal axillary odors by infants. *Child Development, 56*, 1593–1598.

Courtenay, S.C. (1989). *Learning and memory of chemosensory stimuli by underyearling coho salmon* (Oncorhynchus kisutch). Unpublished doctoral thesis, University of British Columbia, Canada.

Davis, L.B., & Porter, R.H. (1991). Persistent effects of early odor exposure on human neonates. *Chemical Senses, 16*, 169–174.

DeCasper, A.J., & Fifer, W.P. (1980). Of human bonding: newborns prefer their mothers' voice. *Science, 208*, 1174–1176.

Dielenberg, R.A., & McGregor, I.S. (2001). Defensive behavior in rats towards predatory odors: A review. *Neuroscience and Biobehavioral Reviews*, 25, 597–609.

Doane, H.M., & Porter, R.H. (1978). The role of diet in mother-infant reciprocity in the spiny mouse. *Developmental Psychobiology*, 11, 271–277.

Doty, R.L. (1975). Intranasal trigeminal detection of chemical vapors by humans. *Physiology and Behavior*, 14, 855–859.

Doty, R.L. (1995). Intranasal trigeminal chemoreception: Anatomy, physiology, and psychophysics. In R.L. Doty (Ed.), *Handbook of olfaction and gustation* (pp. 821–833). New York: Marcel Dekker.

Doty, R.L., Brugger, W.E., Jurs, P.C., Orndorff, M.A., Snyder, P.J., & Lowry, L.D. (1978). Intranasal trigeminal stimulation from odorous volatiles: Psychometric responses from anosmic and normal humans. *Physiology and Behavior*, 20, 175–185.

Eggert, F., Muller-Ruchholtz, W., & Ferstl, R. (1999). Olfactory cues associated with the major histocompatibility complex. *Genetica*, 104, 191–197.

Engen, T. (1988). The acquisition of odour hedonics. In S. Van Toller & G.H. Dodd (Eds.), *Perfumery: The psychology and biology of fragrance* (pp. 79–90). London: Chapman and Hall.

Fifer, W.P., & Moon, C. (1988). Auditory experience in the fetus. In W.P. Smotherman & S.R. Robinson (Eds.), *Behavior of the fetus* (pp. 175–188). Caldwell, NJ: Telford Press.

Fillion, T.J., & Blass, E.M. (1986). Infantile experience with suckling odors determines adult sexual behavior in male rats. *Science*, 231, 729–731.

Fleming, A.S., & Corter, C. (1988). Factors influencing maternal responsiveness in humans: Usefulness of an animal model. *Psychoneuroendocrinology*, 13, 189–212.

Foote, S.L., Berridge, C.W., Adams, L.M., & Pineda, J.A. (1991). Electrophysiological evidence for the involvement of the locus coeruleus in alerting, orienting, and attending. *Progress in Brain Research*, 88, 521–532.

Gervais, R., Holley, A., & Keverne, B. (1988). The importance of central noradrenergic influences on the olfactory bulb in the processing of learned olfactory cues. *Chemical Senses*, 13, 3–12.

Hagnevik, K., Faxelius, G., Irestedt, L., Lagercrantz, H., Lundell, B., & Persson, B. (1984). Catecholamine surge and metabolic adaptation in the newborn after vaginal delivery and caesarean section. *Acta Paediatrica Scandinavica*, 73, 602–609.

Hauser, G.J., Chitayat, D., Berns, L., Braver, D., & Muhlbauer, B. (1985). Peculiar odours in newborns and maternal prenatal ingestion of spicy foods. *European Journal of Pediatrics*, 144, 403.

Hepper, P.G. (1988). Adaptive fetal learning: Prenatal exposure to garlic affects postnatal preferences. *Animal Behaviour*, 36, 935–936.

Hepper, P.G. (1995). Human fetal "olfactory" learning. *International Journal of Prenatal and Perinatal Psychology and Medicine, 7,* 147–151.

Hepper, P.G. (1996). Fetal memory: Does it exist? What does it do? *Acta Paediatrica, 416* (Suppl.), 16–20.

Hepper, P.G., & Waldman, B. (1992). Embryonic olfactory learning in frogs. *Quarterly Journal of Experimental Psychology, 44B,* 179–197.

Irestedt, L., Lagercrantz, H., Hjemdahl, P., Hagnevik, K., & Belfrage, P. (1982). Fetal and maternal plasma catecholamine levels at elective cesarean section under general or epidural anesthesia versus vaginal delivery. *American Journal of Obstetrics and Gynecology, 142,* 1004–1010.

Jacob, S., McClintock, M.K., Zelano, B., & Ober, C. (2002). Paternally inherited HLA alleles are associated with women's choice of male odor. *Nature Genetics, 30,* 175–179.

Jacobs, B. (1990). Locus coeruleus neuronal activity in behaving animals. In D.J. Heal & C.A. Marsden (Eds.), *The pharmacology of noradrenaline in the central nervous system* (pp. 248–264). Oxford, England: Oxford University Press.

Johanson, I.B., & Hall, W.G. (1979). Appetitive learning in 1-day-old rats pups. *Science, 205,* 419–421.

Jones, C.M., & Greiss, F.C. (1982). The effect of labor on maternal and fetal circulating catecholamines. *American Journal of Obstetrics and Gynecology, 144,* 149–153.

Jouppila, R., Puolakka, J., Kauppila, A., & Vuori, J. (1984). Maternal and umbilical cord plasma noradrenaline concentrations during labour with and without segmental extradural analgesia, and during caesarean section. *British Journal of Anaesthetics, 56,* 251–255.

Kaplan, J.N., Cubicciotti, D.D., & Redican, W.K. (1979). Olfactory and visual differentiation of synthetically scented surrogates by infant squirrel monkeys. *Developmental Psychobiology, 12,* 1–10.

Kendrick, K.M., Lévy, F., & Keverne, E.B. (1992). Changes in the sensory processing of olfactory signals induced by birth in sheep. *Science, 256,* 833–836.

Keverne, E.B., Lévy, F., Poindron, P., & Lindsay, D.R. (1983). Vaginal stimulation: An important determinant of maternal bonding in sheep. *Science, 219,* 81–83.

Klaus, M.H., & Kennell, J.H. (1982). *Parent-infant bonding.* St. Louis, MO: Mosby.

Konner, M., & Worthman, C. (1980). Nursing frequency, gonadal function, and birth spacing among !Kung hunter-gatherers. *Science, 207,* 788–791.

Krehbiel, D., Poindron, P., Lévy, F., & Prud'homme, M.J. (1987). Peridural anesthesia disturbs maternal behavior in primiparous and multiparous parturient ewes. *Physiology & Behavior, 40,* 463–472.

Lagercrantz, H. (1996). Stress, arousal, and gene activation at birth. *News in Physiological Sciences, 11,* 214–218.

Lagercrantz, H., Pequignot, J., Pequignot, J.M., & Peyrin, L. (1992). The first breaths of air stimulate noradrenaline turnover in the brain of the newborn rat. *Acta Physiologica Scandinavica, 144*, 433–438.

Lagercrantz, H., & Slotkin, T.A. (1986). The "stress" of being born. *Scientific American, 254*, 92–102.

Leon, M. (1974). Maternal pheromone. *Physiology and Behavior, 13*, 441–453.

Leon, M. (1975). Dietary control of maternal pheromone in the lactating rat. *Physiology and Behavior, 14*, 311–319.

Leon, M. (1992). Neuroethology of olfactory preference development. *Journal of Neurobiology, 23*, 1557–1573.

Lévy, F., & Poindron, P. (1987). The importance of amniotic fluids for the establishment of maternal behaviour in experienced and inexperienced ewes. *Animal Behaviour, 35*, 1188–1192.

Lévy, F., Poindron, P., & Le Neindre, P. (1983). Attraction and repulsion by amniotic fluid and their olfactory control in the ewe around parturition. *Physiology and Behavior, 31*, 687–692.

Lévy, F., Porter, R.H., Kendrick, K.M., Keverne, E.B., & Romeyer, A. (1996). Physiological, sensory, and experiential factors of parental care in sheep. *Advances if the Study of Behavior, 25*, 385–422.

Macfarlane, A. (1975). Olfaction in the development of social preferences in the human neonate. In R. Porter & M. O'Connor (Eds.), *Parent-infant interaction* (pp. 103–113). New York: Elsevier.

Mainardi, D., Marsan, M., & Pasquali, A. (1965). Causation of sexual preferences of the house mouse. The behaviour of mice reared by parents whose odour was artificially altered. *Atti della Societáa Italiana di Scienze Naturali e del Museo Civico di Storia Naturale di Milano, 104*, 325–338.

Makin, J.W., & Porter, R.H. (1989). Attractiveness of lactating females' breast odors to neonates. *Child Development, 60*, 803–810.

Marchini, G., Lagercrantz, H., Winberg, J., & Uvnas-Moberg, K. (1988). Fetal and maternal plasma levels of gastrin, somatostatin and oxytocin after vaginal delivery and elective cesarean section. *Early Human Development, 18*, 73–78.

Marlier, L., Schaal, B., & Soussignan, R. (1998). Neonatal responsiveness to the odor of amniotic and lacteal fluids: A test of perinatal chemosensory continuity. *Child Development, 69*, 611–623.

Meier, G.W. (1964). Behavior of infant monkeys: Differences attributable to mode of birth. *Science, 143*, 968–970.

Mennella, J.A., & Beauchamp, G.K. (1991). Maternal diet alters the sensory qualities of human milk and the nursling's behavior. *Pediatrics, 88*, 737–744.

Mennella, J.A., Jagnow, C.P., & Beauchamp, G.K. (2001). Prenatal and postnatal flavor learning by human infants. *Pediatrics, 107*, e88.

Mennella, J.A., Johnson, A., & Beauchamp, G.K. (1995). Garlic ingestion by pregnant women alters the odor of amniotic fluid. *Chemical Senses, 20*, 207–209.

Muller-Schwarze, D., & Muller-Schwarze, C. (1971). Olfactory imprinting in a precocial mammal. *Nature, 229,* 55–56.

Nelson, E.E., & Panksepp, J. (1998). Brain substrates of infant-mother attachment: Contributions of opiods, oxytocin, and norepinephrine. *Neuroscience and Biobehavioral Reviews, 22,* 437–452.

Ober, C., Weitkamp, L.R., Cox, N., Dytch, H., Kostyu, D., & Elias, S. (1997). HLA and mate choice in humans. *American Journal of Human Genetics, 61,* 497–504.

Otamiri, G., Berg, G., Ledin, T., Leijon, I., & Lagercrantz, H. (1991). Delayed neurological adaptation in infants delivered by elective cesarean section and the relation to catecholamine levels. *Early Human Development, 26,* 51–60.

Pedersen, P.A., & Blass, E.M. (1982). Prenatal and postnatal determinants of the first suckling episode in albino rats. *Developmental Psychobiology, 15,* 349–355.

Penn, D.J., & Potts, W.K. (1999). The evolution of mating preferences and major histocompatibility complex genes. *American Naturalist, 153,* 145–164.

Poindron, P., Lévy, F., & Krehbiel, D. (1988). Genital, olfactory, and endocrine interactions in the development of maternal behaviour in the parturient ewe. *Psychoneuroendocrinology, 13,* 99–125.

Porter, R.H. (1983). Communication in rodents: Adults to infants. In R.W. Elwood (Ed.), *Parental behaviour of rodents* (pp. 95–125). Chichester, UK: Wiley.

Porter, R.H. (1991). Mutual mother-infant recognition in humans. In P.G. Hepper (Ed.), *Kin recognition* (pp. 413–432). Cambridge, UK: Cambridge University Press.

Porter, R.H., & Etscorn, F. (1974). Olfactory imprinting resulting from brief exposure in *Acomys cahirinus. Nature, 250,* 732–733.

Porter, R.H., Makin, J.W., Davis, L.B., & Christensen, K.M. (1991). An assessment of the salient olfactory environment of formula-fed infants. *Physiology & Behavior, 50,* 907–911.

Porter, R.H., & Picard, M. (1998). Effects of early odor exposure in domestic chicks. *Reproduction Nutrition Development, 38,* 441–448.

Porter, R.H., & Schaal, B. (2003). Olfaction and the development of social behavior in neonatal mammals. In R. Doty (Ed.), *Handbook of olfaction and gustation* (2nd ed., pp. 309–327). Monticello, NY: Marcel Dekker.

Righard, L., & Alade, M.O. (1990). Effect of delivery room routines on success of first breast-feed. *Lancet, 336,* 1105–1107.

Robson, K.S., & Moss, H.A. (1970). Patterns and determinants of maternal attachment. *Journal of Pediatrics, 77,* 976–985.

Ronca, A.E., & Alberts, J.R. (1995). Simulated uterine contractions facilitate fetal and newborn respiratory behavior in rats. *Physiology & Behavior, 58,* 1035–1041.

Rovee, C.K. (1969). Psychophysical scaling of olfactory response to the aliphatic alcohols in human neonates. *Journal of Experimental Child Psychology, 7*, 245–254.

Rubianes, E. (1992). Genital stimulation modifies behavior towards amniotic fluid in estrous ewes. *Applied Animal Behaviour Science, 35*, 35–40.

Russell, M.J. (1976). Human olfactory communication. *Nature, 260*, 520–522.

Schaal, B., Marlier, L., & Soussignan, R. (1995). Responsiveness to the odour of amniotic fluid in the human neonate. *Biology of the Neonate, 67*, 397–406.

Schaal, B., Marlier, L., & Soussignan, R. (2000). Human foetuses learn odours from their pregnant mother's diet. *Chemical Senses, 25*, 729–737.

Schaal, B., Montagner, H., Hertling, E., Bolzoni, D., Moyse, A., & Quichon, R. (1980). Les stimulations olfactives dans les relations entre l'enfant et la mère [Olfactory stimulations in the relations between child and mother]. *Reproduction Nutrition Development, 20*, 843–858.

Schleidt, M., & Genzel, C. (1990). The significance of mother's perfume for infants in the first weeks of their life. *Ethology and Sociobioogy, 11*, 145–154.

Segal, N.L., & Topolski, T.D. (1995). The genetics of olfactory perception. In R.L. Doty (Ed.), *Handbook of olfaction and gustation* (pp. 323–343). Monticello, NY: Marcel Dekker.

Segal, N.L., Topolski, T.D., Wilson, S.M., Brown, K.W., & Araki, L. (1995). Twin analysis of odor identification and perception. *Physiology and Behavior, 57*, 605–609.

Shipley, M.T., Halloran, F.J., & de la Torre, J. (1985). Surprisingly rich projection from locus coeruleus to the olfactory bulb in the rat. *Brain Research, 329*, 294–299.

Smotherman, W.P. (1982). Odor aversion learning by the rat fetus. *Physiology and Behavior, 29*, 769–771.

Sneddon, H. (2002). *The effects of embryonic chemosensation in vertebrates: A comparative study.* Unpublished doctoral thesis, Queen's University, Belfast, Ireland.

Sneddon, H., Hadden, R., & Hepper, P.G. (1998). Chemosensory learning in the chicken embryo. *Physiology & Behavior, 64*, 133–139.

Soussignan, R., Schaal, B., Marlier, L., & Jiang, T. (1997). Facial and autonomic responses to biological and artificial olfactory stimuli in human neonates: Re-examining early hedonic discrimination of odors. *Physiology and Behavior, 62*, 745–758.

Stafford, M., Horning, M.G., & Zlatkis, A. (1976). Profiles of volatile metabolites in body fluids. *Journal of Chromatography, 126*, 495–502.

Steiner, J.E. (1977). Facial expressions of the neonate infant indicating the hedonics of food-related chemical stimuli. In J.M.Weiffenbach (Ed.), *Taste and development. The genesis of sweet preference* (pp. 173–188). Bethesda, MD: Department of Health, Education, and Welfare.

Sullivan, R.M., Stackenwalt, G., Nasr, F., Lemon, C., & Wilson, D.A. (2000). Association of an odor with activation of olfactory bulb noradrenergic β-receptors or locus coeruleus stimulation is sufficient to produce learned approach responses to that odor in neonatal rats. *Behavioral Neuroscience, 114,* 957–962.

Sullivan, R.M., Taborsky-Barba, S., Mendoza, R., Itano, A., Leon, M., Cotman, C.W., et al. (1991). Olfactory classical conditioning in neonates. *Pediatrics, 87,* 511–518.

Sullivan, R.M., & Toubas, P. (1998). Clinical usefulness of maternal odor in newborns: Soothing and feeding preparatory movements. *Biology of the Neonate, 74,* 402–408.

Sullivan, R.M., & Wilson, D.A. (1994). The locus coeruleus, norepionephrine, and memory in newborns. *Brain Research Bulletin, 35,* 467–472.

Sullivan, R.M., Wilson, D.A., & Leon, M. (1989). Norepinephrine and learning-induced plasticity in infant rat olfactory system. *Journal of Neuroscience, 9,* 3998–4006.

Sullivan, R.M., Zyzak, D.R., Skierkowski, P., & Wilson, D.A. (1992). The role of olfactory bulb norepinephrine in early olfactory learning. *Developmental Brain Research, 70,* 279–282.

Svensson, T.H. (1987). Peripheral, autonomic regulation of locus coeruleus noradrenergic neurons in the brain. Putative implications for psychiatry and psychopharmacology. *Psychopharmacology, 92,* 1–7.

Teicher, M.H., & Blass, E.M. (1977). First suckling response of the newborn albino rat: The roles of olfaction and amniotic fluid. *Science, 198,* 635–636.

Trevathan, W.R. (1987). *Human birth: An evolutionary perspective.* New York: Aldine de Gruyter.

Varendi, H., Christensson, K., Porter, R.H., & Winberg, J. (1998). Soothing effect of amniotic fluid smell in newborn infants. *Early Human Development, 51,* 47–55.

Varendi, H., & Porter, R.H. (2001). Breast odour as the only maternal stimulus elicits crawling towards the odour source. *Acta Paediatrica, 90,* 372–375.

Varendi, H., Porter, R.H., & Winberg, J. (1994). Does the newborn baby find the nipple by smell? *Lancet, 344,* 989–990.

Varendi, H., Porter, R.H., & Winberg, J. (1996). Attractiveness of amniotic fluid odor: Evidence of prenatal olfactory learning? *Acta Paediatrica, 85,* 1223–1227.

Varendi, H., Porter, R.H., & Winberg, J. (1997). Natural odour preferences of newborn infants change over time. *Acta Paediatrica, 86,* 985–990.

Varendi, H., Porter, R.H., & Winberg, J. (2002). The effect of labor on olfactory exposure learning within the first postnatal hour. *Behavioral Neuroscience, 116,* 206–211.

Wang, L., Zhang, W., & Zhao, Y. (1999). The study of maternal and fetal plasma catecholamine levels during pregnancy and delivery. *Journal of Perinatal Medicine, 27,* 195–198.

Wedekind, C., Seebeck, T., Bettens, F., & Paepke, A.J. (1995). MHC-dependent mate preferences in humans. *Proceedings for Royal Society London B, 260,* 245–249.

Widstrom, A.M., Ransjo-Arvidson, A.B., Christensson, K., Matthiesen, A.S., Winberg, J., & Uvnas-Moberg, K. (1987). Gastric suction in healthy newborn infants. *Acta Paediatrica Scandinavia, 76,* 566–572.

Wilson, D.A., & Sullivan, R.M. (1994). Neurobiology of associative learning in the neonate: Early olfactory learning. *Behavioral and Neural Biology, 61,* 1–18.

Wolff, P.H. (1968). Sucking patters of infant mammals. *Brain, Behavior and Evolution, 1,* 354–367.

Wysocki, C.J., & Beauchamp, G.K. (1984). Ability to smell androstenone is genetically determined. *Proceedings of the National Academy of Science, USA, 81,* 4899–4902.

Zou, Z., Horowitz, L.F., Montmayeur, J.P., Snapper, S., & Buck, L.B. (2001). Genetic tracing reveals a stereotyped sensory map in the olfactory cortex. *Nature, 414,* 173–179.

FURTHER READING

Brennan, P., Kaba, H., & Keverne, E.B. (1990). Olfactory recognition: A simple memory system. *Science, 250,* 1223–1226.

Chuah, M.I., & Farbman, A.I. (1995). Developmental anatomy of the olfactory system. In R.L. Doty (Ed.), *Handbook of olfaction and gustation* (pp. 147–171). Monticello, NY: Marcel Dekker.

Hepper, P.G. (1997). Memory in utero? *Developmental Medicine and Child Neurology, 39,* 343–346.

Lagercrantz, H. (1994). Excitation of the sympathoadrenal system at birth. In C. Amiel-Tisson & A. Steward (Eds.), *The newborn infant: One brain for life* (pp. 57–66). Paris: INSERM.

Porter, R.H., & Winberg, J. (1999). Unique salience of maternal breast odors for newborn infants. *Neuroscience and Biobehavioral Reviews, 23,* 439–449.

Rovee-Collier, C. (1996). Shifting the focus from what to why. *Infant Behavior and Development, 19,* 385–400.

Schaal, B., & Porter, R.H. (1991). "Microsmatic humans" revisited: The generation and perception of chemical signals. *Advances in the Study of Behavior, 20,* 135–199.

Stoddart, D.M. (1990). *The scented ape.* Cambridge, UK: Cambridge University Press.

Winberg, J., & Porter, R.H. (1998). Olfaction and human neonatal behaviour: Clinical implications. *Acta Paediatrica, 87,* 6–10.

CHAPTER 5

LEARNING TO MOVE BEFORE BIRTH

*Scott R. Robinson and Gale A. Kleven**

ABSTRACT

The fetus can express coordinated movement during spontaneous and evoked action patterns *in utero*. Prenatal motor coordination, however, occurs in the context of a rapidly changing physical body as well as an immature nervous system, and such coordination is both variable and plastic. Historic and recent research in developmental neuroscience has tended to emphasize dedicated pattern-generating circuits within the central nervous system to explain fetal motility, downplaying the potential importance of experience in prenatal neurobehavioral development. However, new methods for studying perinatal motor plasticity and learning suggest that kinesthetic feedback arising from motor performance may contribute to early motor development. To directly assess the potential for motor experience, our laboratory and others have developed a motor learning paradigm that can be applied to fetal and neonatal subjects. An interlimb yoke is used to create a physical linkage between two limbs.

*Research on fetal motor development reported in this paper was supported by NIH grant HD33862 to SRR. The authors also wish to thank Michele R. Brumley for her helpful comments during preparation of the manuscript. Correspondence should be directed to SRR, and may be sent by electronic mail to: scott-r-robinson@uiowa.edu.

Exposure to the yoke results in greater coordination between the limbs, which increases gradually during training and persists after the yoke is removed. These findings, together with other experimental perturbations of motor coordination, suggest that fetuses are responsive to proprioceptive feedback and can alter the frequency, patterning, and coordination of movement in response to early motor experience.

INTRODUCTION

In the course of communicating the findings of our program of research on prenatal behavioral development to professional and lay audiences alike, few things have sparked greater interest than the image of an active, living fetus. All too often, developmental psychologists take for granted the accessibility of their research subjects. We all have seen children and babies, and many of us have actually raised them. But fetal researchers have been relegated to drawing inferences about behavior from physiological measures (e.g., heart rate) from imprecise measures of activity such as maternal report or strain gauges placed around the mother's abdomen, or from indirect experimental methods, such as manipulating a pregnant animal and evaluating the outcomes for the offspring after birth. Even high technologies, such as *real-time ultrasound*, have until very recently yielded indistinct images that are as difficult to interpret by the uninitiated as X-ray photographs.

In the absence of direct experience, we have turned to the media as a principal source of images of fetal development. The widely recognized photographs of Lennart Nilsson (1977), or dramatic film footage broadcast on public television and other documentary networks, have reinforced the romantic view of the fetus as dwelling in a peaceful and isolated world. It is small wonder, then, given our limited ability to visualize the fetus, that the dominant view of prenatal development continues to be one of a passive organism within a protected environment, buffered from the barrage of stimuli in the outside world. Although ultrasound scans and the mother's own experience confirms that the fetus is active (occasionally exhibiting random jerks, twitches, or rolling movements), such motor activity seems radically different than the behavior we associate with the postnatal world. Apart from the occasional twitch or kick, the fetus seems to merely reside within its watery isolation chamber, awaiting the time of birth.

FETAL ACTION PATTERNS

Recent work conducted in our laboratory paints a somewhat different image of the fetus. Rather than relying on indirect measures of fetal behavior, or the delayed effects of prenatal manipulations on postnatal outcomes, much of our research has applied *direct observational techniques* to understand the organization and development of fetal behavior. Experimental access to rodent fetuses—principally the domestic *Norway rat (Rattus norvegicus)*—is provided through surgical procedures that produce spinal anesthesia in the pregnant rat and permit the uterus and constituent fetuses to be externalized from the mother's abdomen into a supportive fluid medium containing buffered isotonic saline, which is maintained at the mother's body temperature (37.5°C) (Smotherman & Robinson, 1991). Under these experimental conditions, individual fetal subjects can be viewed through the semi-transparent wall of the uterus or after the fetus within its embryonic membranes is delivered into the bath environment. The fetus can be seen clearly through the chorion and amnion that envelop it, although in most studies these embryonic membranes are stripped away, permitting the fetus to float gently within the saline bath. Throughout these procedures, the fetus remains connected via its umbilical cord to the placenta, which is attached to the inner lining of the uterus. In this way, the life-support system of the fetus is preserved, enabling observation and experimental manipulation of healthy, living fetuses for sessions lasting up to several hours.

In the course of early investigations of the associative learning capacities of the *rat fetus*, William Smotherman and I noticed that fetal rats, prepared for behavioral observation by these techniques, typically express a coordinated motor response to certain forms of *chemosensory stimulation* (Smotherman & Robinson, 1987). For instance, if a small volume (20 µl) of a novel odor solution, such as mint or lemon extract, is infused through a fine cannula into the mouth of the fetal rat, it reliably elicits a *facial wiping* response (Fig. 5.1, left). To any casual observer, the *facial wiping* response appears well-coordinated, as it involves coordination between the forelimbs and coordination between each paw and the head. Largely because of this apparent *motor coordination, facial wiping* and comparable *action patterns* of the fetus stand in stark contrast to the random twitches and jerks that usually characterize *fetal motor activity*.

Our initial report that fetuses can express coordinated motor responses (Smotherman & Robinson, 1987) was not new, however.

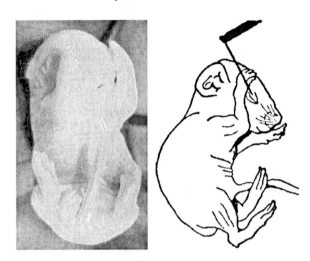

Figure 5.1. *Left*: An E20 rat fetus performing a facial wiping response. Facial wiping involves placement of one or both paws in contact with the side of the face in the vicinity of the ears. The paws are typically supinated. The palms turned toward the face during contact. The paws are then drawn downward, with paw contact sliding over the eyes and along the side of the face, toward the nose. A single infusion of lemon extract may elicit a wiping response consisting of as few as one or as many as fifteen paw-face strokes. *Right*: Illustration of a facial wiping response to a cutaneous stimulus in a fifty-one-day-old guinea pig fetus. (*Source*: From Carmichael & Smith, 1939, reprinted with permission of Heldref Publications.)

Leonard Carmichael observed *facial wiping* responses to a tactile stimulus applied to the perioral area in fetal guinea pigs in 1939 (Fig. 5.1, right). Apart from more recent descriptions of fetal action patterns, such as *nipple attachment* and *stretch responses* to milk (Robinson et al., 1992; Robinson & Smotherman, 1992a), other examples of coordinated motor behavior have also been reported in the classic literature. Graham Brown reported coordinated leg movements resembling "progression" in cat fetuses in 1915, and even Wilhelm Preyer, the earliest observer of embryonic behavior, noticed *stepping*-like movements by fetuses removed from the womb as early as 1885.

SPONTANEOUS MOTOR ACTIVITY

These early attempts to investigate behavior in fetuses spawned a new field of behavioral embryology from 1925 to 1940 in the laboratories of George Coghill (Angulo y Gonzalez, 1932; Coghill 1929), William Windle (Windle & Griffin, 1931; Windle, Minear, Austin, & Orr, 1935; Windle, O'Donnell, & Glasshagle, 1933), Leonard Carmichael (Carmichael, 1934; Coronios, 1933), Joseph Barcroft (Barcroft & Barron, 1939; Barcroft, Barron, & Windle, 1936), and Zing-Yang Kuo (1932, 1967). With the exception of Kuo, who was very interested in the role of natural stimulation in shaping embryonic motor behavior, much of the research from this "Golden Age" of *behavioral embryology* was stimulated by the then-prevailing view of *reflexes* as the foundation stones of more complex behavior. Influential researchers such as Charles Sherrington and Ivan Pavlov actively promoted a central role for *reflexes* in *motor control* (Gallistel, 1980).

In the laboratories of Coghill, Windle, Carmichael, and others, behavior was viewed as a tool by which the development of reflexes could be measured. The primary focus of investigation was evoked responses, in which a discrete stimulus (usually tactile) was applied to the embryo to elicit a discrete, localized reflex reaction. (Thus, even Carmichael's original description of *facial wiping* was reported as a localized reflex action and not as a coordinated *action pattern.*) Systematic extension of such techniques to various regions of the embryo's body (at different prenatal ages) was used to reconstruct progressive stages of *reflex development.* In turn, simple reflexes were thought to be linked together as *chain reflexes,* providing a lawful developmental path to more complex motor behavior. Although strongly criticized by proponents of the alternative view of centrally generated movement (e.g., Graham Brown and Eric von Holst), defenders of the chain reflex theory gathered an impressive body of evidence that seemed to suggest that coordinated motor behavior consists largely of a collection of simple reflexes, in which each reflex response serves as the triggering stimulus for the next reflex in the chain (Gallistel, 1980).

Although nearly all of the classic researchers appreciated that embryos and fetuses move in the absence of stimulation, the importance of spontaneous *motor activity* was largely overlooked until the 1960s, when Viktor Hamburger applied the techniques of experimental embryology to understand the development of movement in the chick embryo. Over a span of just ten years, Hamburger and his students provided compelling evidence that the movements of chick embryos—and by extrapolation, all vertebrate embryos—are generated spontaneously by dedicated elements in the central nervous system (CNS). In one experiment, segments of embryonic spinal cord that were surgically isolated from the brain—with all afferent information in the dorsal roots eliminated—continued to exhibit spontaneous motility (Hamburger, Wenger, & Oppenheim, 1966). This experiment confirmed that at least some embryonic movements are non-reflexogenic. Moreover, the patterning of *spontaneous activity* in the spinal cord mirrored differences in the overt movement of various parts of the body (Provine, 1971). Findings such as these had a revolutionary impact on theories of *prenatal motor development* by emphasizing how the developing nervous system could generate coordinated activity in the absence of sensory experience or *reflexive* stimulation (Hamburger, 1973; Landmesser & O'Donovan, 1984). Now it is widely recognized that the majority of motor activity expressed by embryos and fetuses is associated with *spontaneous activity* within the central nervous system. Spontaneous motor activity therefore provides the neurodevelopmental context for the majority of prenatal behavioral development.

ROLE OF SENSORY FEEDBACK: SPECIFIC VERSUS NONSPECIFIC EXPERIENCE

In Non-Mammalian Embryos

Because motility can be expressed in the absence of proprioceptive feedback, it has been argued that sensory feedback about the frequency, form, or consequences of embryonic movement is of little importance in neurobehavioral development before birth (Haverkamp & Oppenheim, 1986). Data obtained from non-mammalian embryos are divided in their implications for the importance of experience in prenatal motor development. For instance, classic experiments in which amphibian larvae were raised in a solution containing an immobilizing drug seemed to indicate no lasting impairment in swimming behavior when the larvae were removed from the solution and placed in fresh water (Matthews & Detwiler, 1926). These findings were disputed when larval behavior was quantified more carefully (Fromme, 1941), but they recently have been corroborated by exposing frog (*Xenopus laevis*) embryos to alpha-bungarotoxin, lidocaine, or chloretone. After brief recovery from the immobilizing drugs, embryos exhibited normal-looking swimming locomotion with little apparent effect on motor coordination (Haverkamp & Oppenheim, 1986).

Experiments conducted with avian embryos are equally divided in their implications for prenatal motor experience. Chronic blockade

of neural signals to chick hindlimb muscles from E5–E10 with
d-tubocurarine did not prevent the normal development of alternating burst patterns in motoneuron pools projecting to flexor and extensor muscles (Landmesser & Szente, 1986). But *motor development of
chick embryos* nonetheless appears to be influenced by normal changes
in environmental conditions that perturb the biomechanical context of
movement. The alternating pattern of activation of hindlimb flexors
and extensors that is characteristic of chicks on E9 breaks down over
the next four days of incubation, coincident with the emergence of
physical constraint caused by growth of the chick within the egg, then
returns to higher levels of coordination by E17 (Bekoff, 1976). Kinematic analysis of hindlimb coordination has revealed that this disruption does not represent an actual reduction in movement amplitude or
loss of coordination in general, but it specifically entails a decoupling
of movements of the ankle from those of the hip and knee. This finding
suggests that older chick embryos can modulate patterns of *intralimb
coordination* to compensate for biomechanical constraints of movement
that result from the loss of free space within the egg (Sharp, Ma, &
Bekoff, 1999). Similar examples of the responsiveness of chick embryos
to the experimental reduction of buoyant support or ankle restraint
have been reported (Bradley, 1997; Bradley & Sebelski, 2000; see following discussion), suggesting that *sensory feedback* can modulate basic
patterns of motor coordination in avian embryos.

In the Rat Fetus

Despite the experimental findings that suggested sensory feedback
about motor performance was not necessary for prenatal motor
development, our studies of species-typical action patterns in the
rat fetus provided several clues that fetal motor behavior was more
sensitive to experience and environmental context than had generally
been appreciated (Robinson & Smotherman, 1992b; Smotherman &
Robinson, 1989). One such clue emerged from close inspection of the
timing of limb movements during facial wiping responses in the fetal
rat on embryonic day twenty (E20) of gestation. In a typical wiping
response, intra-oral infusion of 20 µl of lemon extract (the odor extract,
not citric acid) elicits an increase in overall motor activity, which
involves a selective activation of the forelimbs and suppression of
hindlimb activity. During the initial phase of the response, both forelimbs are tightly flexed against the chest. Then the forelimbs are

extended in a rostral direction, where one or both establish contact with the side of the head. Over the next several seconds, a flurry of wiping strokes occurs, involving a cycle of downward strokes with the paw in contact with the face, followed by upward strokes without contact. The video frame in which paw–face contact was established was used to define the beginning of each down–up cycle, and the relative phase of each cycle could be calculated as the difference in time between left and right contact divided by the duration of the entire down–up cycle. These measures of relative phase ranged from 0%, indicating in-phase or synchronized trajectories of both limbs through the stroke cycle, to 50%, indicating an anti-phase or alternated pattern of interlimb coordination. By parsing the entire bout of facial wiping into three equal segments (comprising strokes from the first, middle, and last thirds of the wiping response), systematic changes in interlimb coordination during the bout of wiping became evident (Fig. 5.2).

Initial wiping strokes exhibited a uniform distribution of relative phase, suggesting that the first few paw–face strokes were not coordinated but were randomly organized in time. During the middle portion of the bout, the distribution of phase relationships became

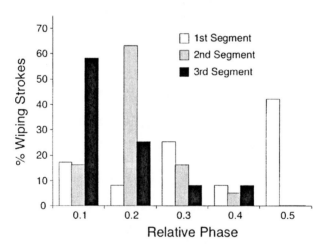

Figure 5.2. Distribution of differences in relative phase between left and right strokes during bouts of facial wiping in the E20 rat fetus. Relative phase, which indicates the pattern of interlimb coordination between forelimbs, is expressed as a percentage of the overall facial wiping cycle (0 = in-phase or synchronized; 0.5 = anti-phase or alternated). Changes in relative phase are evident across three equal time segments (first, middle, and last) of the wiping bout.

skewed toward 0%, indicating a quantitative change in *interlimb co-ordination* away from alternation. Finally, the last strokes in the bout nearly all showed a relative phase of 10% or less, indicating a high degree of synchronization during the stroke cycle. The systematic changes in interlimb phase during a bout of *facial wiping* indicates that interlimb coordination is not manifest at the outset of the response, which might otherwise be expected if it is the product of a centrally organized motor program. Rather, coordination emerged gradually as wiping strokes were performed, suggesting that some form of *kinesthetic feedback* was involved in modulating interlimb coordination during the bout.

Further clues that *sensory feedback* may contribute to *prenatal motor coordination* were provided by striking discontinuities in the development of *facial wiping* responses. Rat fetuses show an abrupt developmental onset of facial wiping. Intra-oral infusion of lemon extract consistently evokes facial wiping responses in nearly 100% of fetal subjects tested on E20 or E21, but in none (0%) of the subjects tested on E19 (Robinson & Smotherman, 1991). These results were obtained by testing fetal subjects under typical experimental conditions (namely, after externalization from the uterus with the embryonic membranes removed). However, E19 fetuses were found to express *facial wiping* if allowed to remain within the amniotic sac during testing. Close inspection of video records indicated that the contribution of the amniotic sac to the coordination of the wiping response was most likely mechanical: the surrounding membranes constrained lateral head movements of the fetus, making it possible for the forepaws to establish contact with the face at the beginning of each wiping stroke. When tested outside the confines of the amniotic sac, however, E19 fetuses showed much more lateral head movement, which interfered with paw–face contact. Only one day later, E20 fetuses showed much greater head stability after lemon infusion when tested outside of the amniotic sac, and paw–face contact was consistently established during the first few forelimb strokes. These findings confirm age differences in the ability of rat fetuses to express facial wiping (namely, that E20 fetuses are better able to coordinate limb movements with head stability). They also emphasize the need to carefully choose and control the conditions of testing, because the testing environment can exert a strong influence on measures of motor capacity, especially in developing animals.

Studies of other action patterns of the rat fetus, such as responses to *suckling* stimuli, further suggested that *sensory feedback* could influence the expression of coordinated responses. These studies were conducted with the original intent of understanding the prenatal development of behavioral capacities that would prove functionally important immediately after birth. In fact, during the last two to three days of gestation, fetal rats exhibit well-defined responses to various stimuli that are absent from the *prenatal environment*, but which are essential components of postnatal suckling behavior. One example is *oral grasping* of an artificial nipple. When the fetus is presented with an artificial nipple fashioned from soft vinyl in the approximate dimensions of a real nipple from a lactating rat, the fetus exhibits immediate orientation toward the tip of the nipple, capture and grasping of the nipple by the mouth, and sucking movements involving both negative and compression pressure while attached to the nipple (Robinson et al., 1992). The triggering stimulus for these responses appears to be simple cutaneous contact with the perioral region. But fetuses can be observed to make corrective movements of the head as the point of contact shifts from one side of the mouth to the other. These corrective movements suggest that the coordination of head movement is modulated by the source of an orienting stimulus.

Rat fetuses also express a coordinated action pattern in response to milk—another important component of the postnatal *suckling* situation. After intra-oral infusion of commercially available light cream (similar in fat and water composition to rat milk), fetuses initially express a reduction in overall activity. Over the ensuing interval of one to five minutes (mean = 180 s), gradual changes occur in the topography of movement, with selective reduction in head and forelimb activity and increases in hindlimb movements. Ultimately, these behavioral changes culminate in expression of the *stretch response*, which entails a coordinated extension of both hindlimbs, often accompanied by dorsiflexion of the back and elevation of the head (Robinson & Smotherman, 1992a). This motor pattern appears isomorphic with the stretch responses of infant rats during *suckling* behavior, although infant rats typically show the stretch within a few seconds of milk letdown (Lau & Henning, 1985). To investigate factors that might contribute to the developmental discontinuity in the latency to stretch, a series of experiments explored the influence of contextual stimuli on the expression of the stretch response. It was found that presentation of other sensory stimuli, delivered sixty seconds after milk infusion, could either disrupt or facilitate expression of the stretch. Application of *cutaneous stimulation* to the perioral region or the back resulted in fewer fetuses stretching. In contrast, cutaneous stimulation of the anogenital region, which produced hindlimb activity, promoted stretch responses in a higher percentage of fetal subjects at shorter latencies than controls. Finally, stretch responses could be best facilitated by physically linking the two hindlimbs together with a piece of thread. In this condition, referred to as *interlimb yoking*, the two limbs were not free to move independently, and fetuses expressed coordinated *stretch responses* on average ninety seconds earlier than untreated subjects (Robinson & Smotherman, 1994). The results of this experiment suggested that alterations in *somatosensory* or *proprioceptive stimulation* after delivery of a milk infusion could significantly alter the expression of a coordinated hindlimb response. It also foreshadowed explicit use of interlimb yoking as a technique for investigating fetal motor experience (see following).

EXPERIENCE DURING PRENATAL MOTOR DEVELOPMENT

Theoretical Foundations

The magnitude of the task faced by the nervous system in generating coordinated motor behavior, ranging from complex adult skills to the simple action patterns of the fetus, was addressed by the Russian motor physiologist Nikolai Bernstein (Bernstein, 1967; Sporns & Edelman, 1993; Whiting, 1984). His formulation of the task of *motor control* drew a distinction between the 3-D space of our real world experience and the multidimensional space that was needed to describe the changes in angle of the various limb joints involved in a movement. Only three values are required to uniquely specify any point in 3-D space using an orthogonal (Cartesian) coordinate system: one each for the X, Y, and Z axes. Therefore, the path described by an object in real space can be described by a series of triplet coordinates detailing a succession of points between a starting position and a terminal or target position.

Multi-joint limbs, however, have many *degrees of freedom* of movement. Some joints, such as the knee, restrict motion to one plane, while other joints, such as the shoulder, permit motion in three independent directions (vertical, horizontal, rotational). Owing to the excess number of degrees of freedom when summed over the length of a single limb, it is possible to fix the position of the hand and shoulder in 3-D space, yet retain some freedom of movement of the wrist and elbow. By applying this analysis to the motion of a limb in 3-D, it is apparent that there are many possible trajectories in joint space that will result in the same trajectory of the hand in real space. More-over, the hand may follow many different paths, with different veloc-ity profiles, to reach the same target. Bernstein's problem, then, is how the nervous system uniquely specifies a motor trajectory when many equivalent options are available.

The Calibration Problem

A predominant tactic in addressing Bernstein's problem has been to identify discrete neural circuits that are capable of generating unique motor trajectories and patterns of coordination. By this view, circuitry located entirely within the CNS is responsible for producing periods of stable oscillation that lead to rhythmic excitation or inhibition of motor neurons and their respective motor units within the limb. By regulating the frequency of tonic stimulation into such circuits, the period of oscillation is made to vary, producing stable cycles of differ-ent duration (Brown, 1914; Stein, Grillner, Selverston, & Stuart, 1997). Similarly, sequential activation of different muscle groups within the limb is coordinated by elements of the oscillating circuit that are active during different portions of the cycle. Postulated circuitry within the CNS that produces such rhythmic activity without afferent feedback are now referred to as *central pattern generators* (*CPG*).

Although the concept of CPG has undergone considerable change over the past twenty-five years, it still is widely viewed as an impor-tant part of a general solution to Bernstein's problem. Basically, this solution entails that the CNS contains predetermined instructions that govern all of the motor elements involved in a coordinated move-ment. By uniquely specifying not only the timing of activity, but also the magnitude of activation of different muscles involved in coordi-nated movement, CPGs would control the torques generated at each joint and thereby govern the patterns of acceleration of limb seg-ments and the ultimate trajectory of a working point, such as a hand or paw, through space.

One of the significant challenges faced by an explanation involving a central motor program is to explain how such a system can con-tinue to function in a developing animal. For a dedicated central pro-gram to specify a movement trajectory without feedback, it must activate dozens of muscles with precise control over the timing and force generated by each muscle. But the timing and force required are not constant, particularly during early development. Young ani-mals undergo continual growth, and often growth is not *allometric*

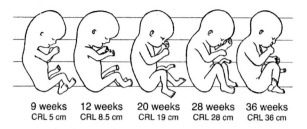

Figure 5.3. Changes in body proportions during prenatal development. Line drawings were adjusted to the same size to emphasize differences in relative proportions of head, trunk, and limbs. Average crown–rump length (CRL) of fetuses at each age is presented.

(Smotherman & Robinson, 1988). Thus, growth leads to changes not merely in absolute body dimensions but in the relative proportions of different parts of the body (Adolph & Avolio, 2000; Carrier, 1996; Thelen, Fisher, & Ridley-Johnson, 1984). At no time do relative body proportions change so dramatically as during prenatal development, as illustrated in Figure 5.3. Because body dimensions, including the length and mass of different limb segments and the size and strength of each muscle, change continually during prenatal development, the timing and magnitude of activation of various muscles must change in order to produce movements of the same kinematic form. For example, in a young fetus the forelimbs must be extended almost completely for the hands to touch the face, but closer to term the forelimbs must be flexed sharply at both shoulders and elbows for the hand to establish contact. What might be seen as the same pattern of behavior—hand-to-face contact—thus requires very different patterns of *motor control* at shoulder and elbow to produce the same end result. In other words, central motor programs must continually be recalibrated to the changing dimensions of the body for coordinated movement to occur in developing animals (or in adult animals under changing posture, load or task demand). And there seems to be no logical alternative but for *sensory feedback* from movement itself to be involved in such a *calibration* function.

Not only is the body undergoing rapid change in physical dimensions, but sensory systems that could provide feedback about movement also undergo continual change during this period of perinatal growth (Adolph, 2002; Carrier, 1996). It is well-documented how *somatosensory fields* and their central representations can be rapidly remodeled in response to injury or altered patterns of activity. For instance, Merzenich severed the median nerve that innervates much of the palmar surface of the hand in adult owl and squirrel monkeys: subsequent recordings from the region of the *somatosensory* cortex that previously had responded to palmar stimulation now responded to stimulation of adjacent regions of the hand (Merzenich et al., 1983). These findings suggested that regions constituting part of an original cortical map could be reassigned to new sources of somatosensory input when original sources were not available. Further experiments confirmed this ability to rapidly reorganize central representations in *somatotopic maps*. Surgical fusion of two middle fingers, for example, resulted in substantial changes in the cortical representations of the two fingers. Originally, when the fingers were capable of independent motion, each was represented in a separate field within the *somatosensory cortex*: after fusion, the two cortical fields representing each finger merged to form a single representation (Clark, Allard, Jenkins, & Merzenich, 1988). Remodeling of central somatotopic maps, therefore, can occur in response to changes in the pattern of *sensory feedback* and not merely to nerve injury. One should expect that this kind of remodeling of central representations of sensory input also must be characteristic in developing animals, in which the relative proportions of the physical body, the size and shape of sensory fields, and their central representations must undergo continual updating and recalibration in response to changes in activity and patterns of use.

Empirical Support

From the arguments presented above, there are ample theoretical reasons to expect experience to be crucial for the control and development of fetal movement. What, then, is the empirical support for *prenatal motor experience*? For experience to provide a significant contribution to *prenatal motor development*, three conditions must be met. First, there must be good evidence of developmental change in *motor control* during the prenatal period. If developmental change in motor coordination is not evident before birth, there is little rationale for searching for mechanisms that may effect such change. Second, there must be evidence that functional *proprioception* develops before birth. If fetuses are unable to detect stimuli arising from their own movement, such information cannot contribute to motor development. Finally, there must be evidence that fetuses can detect and respond to proprioceptive stimuli during spontaneous motor activity, and that *kinesthetic feedback* can be used to alter the quantity or quality of fetal movements.

The third condition may seem less obvious than the first two, because it emphasizes nonspecific experience arising from spontaneous motor activity. However, the *prenatal environment* is, generally speaking, deficient in the kind of task demands that are routinely encountered after birth; and notwithstanding the occasional expression of coordinated action sequences, most fetal movements seem to consist of seemingly purposeless, unoriented, uncoordinated, random activity. If experience plays a significant role in prenatal motor development, we should expect it to derive from what the fetus typically does, and not from what it occasionally can be induced to express.

EXAMPLES OF DEVELOPMENTAL CHANGE DURING PRENATAL MOTOR DEVELOPMENT

Interlimb Synchrony

Although *spontaneous motor activity* expressed by the fetus appears random and unorganized, quantitative analysis of the spatiotemporal organization of *fetal movement* has revealed fundamental forms of *motor coordination* that are expressed early during prenatal development (Robinson, Blumberg, Lane, & Kreber, 2000; Robinson & Smotherman, 1988, 1992c). Fetal movements tend to be brief in duration and can be treated as discrete events for temporal analysis. Using scoring procedures that record every instance of fetal movement and the time of occurrence (± 0.1 s), complete time series of fetal activity can be analyzed for subtle forms of temporal organization. Among the earliest forms of motor organization to be described by this analytic approach is *interlimb synchrony* (Lane & Robinson, 1998). Different limbs can move independently, or movements can occur at nearly the same moment. To measure interlimb movement synchrony, time series for different limbs were combined pair-wise, and the intervals separating successive movements of different limbs were computed. The distribution of intervals provided a quantitative measure of the degree of temporal coupling between limbs during spontaneous *motor activity* (Kleven, Lane, & Robinson, in press; Lane & Robinson, 1998), as shown in Figure 5.4.

While the fetal rat expresses *motor activity* continuously from E16 through term (E22), the number of movements fluctuates with time and involves different regions of the body (Narayanan, Fox, & Hamburger, 1971; Smotherman & Robinson, 1986). To determine whether changes in the occurrence of synchronous movements were

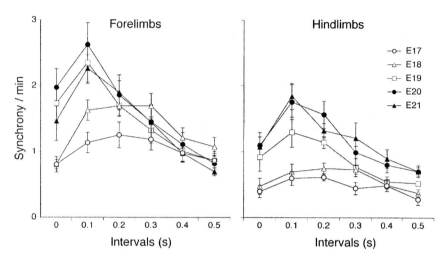

Figure 5.4. Patterns of interlimb movement synchrony from E17 to E21 in fetal rats. Points depict the mean rate of synchronous movement events (± SEM), which are separated by intervals of a given duration, involving both forelimbs (*left*) or both hindlimbs (*right*). At each age, the set of points across the range of intervals from 0.0 to 0.5 s provides a profile that illustrates the degree of temporal coupling between limbs.

the incidental consequence of increasing motor activity, a Monte Carlo randomization technique was used to shuffle and recombine the data sets for each limb pair (Kleven, Lane, & Robinson, in press; Kleven & Robinson, 2000). A comparison of actual versus shuffled time series suggested that *interlimb synchrony* during the first few days after the inception of movement (E16–E17) was no more common than would be expected by chance. Synchronous movements of forelimbs increased above chance levels earlier than other limb pairs (E18), and they continued to increase in frequency and tightness of temporal coupling (evidenced by inter-movement intervals of 0.1 s or less) through E20. Hindlimb synchrony lagged slightly behind, rising above chance levels on E19 and becoming most strongly coupled only by E20. Intersegmental synchrony was also somewhat delayed relative to synchrony within a girdle. Synchronous movements of ipsilateral forelimb-hindlimb pairs were statistically evident on E18, but they did not show strong coupling until E20. The orderly patterns of these synchrony profiles confirm developmental change in a fundamental form of *interlimb coordination* during the prenatal period (see also Provine, 1980; Robinson et al., 2000).

Facial Wiping

Species-typical action patterns expressed by the fetus also undergo substantial developmental change before birth. The abrupt prenatal emergence of *facial wiping*, discussed previously, is representative of the rapidity of change in some of these patterns of behavior. *Oral grasping* of an artificial nipple and *stretch responses* to milk also appear suddenly during prenatal development, on E19 and E20, respectively (Andersen, Robinson, & Smotherman, 1993; Robinson et al., 1992; Robinson & Smotherman, 1992a). Nipple grasping provides a particularly good example of quantitative change in *motor coordination*. Although fetuses were capable of responding to the artificial nipple and grasping it with the mouth from E19–E21, they differed in their effectiveness in seizing the nipple. Grasp attempts could be recognized by abrupt, forward thrusts of the head accompanied by opening of the mouth. Successful grasping, in which the nipple was seized by the mouth, occurred in only 5.4% ± 1.5% (mean ± SEM) on E19, increased to 18.7% ± 4.7% on E20, and peaked at 28.2% ± 5.7% on E21 (Robinson, Hoeltzel, & Smotherman, 1995). Because fetal subjects were tested only at one age, these improvements in grasping success reflected developmental changes in coordination of the head and mouth, and not accruing experience with the nipple. As such, they are comparable to developmental improvement of bill-pecking and begging responses in hatchling birds (Hailman, 1967) and reaching behavior in human infants (Rochat, 1989; Thelen et al., 1993).

Locomotion-Like Movements

A third example of prenatal motor development is provided by *locomotor-like limb activity*. Locomotion by quadrupedal animals (which includes most mammals) is a highly organized postnatal behavior that requires precise control over *interlimb coordination*. Early qualitative reports suggested that alternated limb activity, characteristic of *stepping* during walking locomotion, was occasionally expressed during spontaneous motor activity in the *cat fetus* (Brown, 1915). These subjective descriptions were confirmed by kinematic analysis of selected video sequences in the E20 fetus (Bekoff & Lau, 1980) and neonatal rat (Bekoff & Trainer, 1979). Moreover, alternating locomotor-like bursts of electrical activity in the vental roots of lumbosacral segments have been reported by many laboratories using an *in vitro* preparation of fetal or neonatal rat spinal cord treated with excitatory neurotransmitters (Cazalets, Sqalli-Houssaini, & Clarac,

1992; Cowley & Schmidt, 1994; Kudo & Yamada, 1987). The cate-cholamine precursor *L-DOPA* can also reliably induce coordinated stepping when administered to neonatal and pre-weanling rats, par-ticularly when pups are suspended in a harness, permitting their legs to move freely through the air (McEwen, Van Hartesveldt, & Stehouwer, 1996; Van Hartesveldt, Sickles, Porter, & Stehouwer, 1990). Previous research on *L-DOPA induced air-stepping* has focused on pups five to twenty days of age, when stable locomotor gaits, such as stereotyped stepping, are elicited. The existence of stable gaits at later ages, how-ever, fails to address the more fundamental question of whether orga-nized stepping emerges from a stereotypic or plastic pattern of coordination earlier in development.

To examine the prenatal development of *L-DOPA induced step-ping, rat fetuses* (E20 or E21) or neonates (P0) were positioned in a supine posture to facilitate videotaping and injected with *L-DOPA* (100 mg/kg) (Heberling & Robinson, 1997). At all three ages, subjects began to show rhythmic limb activity within ten to fifteen minutes. Kinematic analysis of limb movement revealed that the typical alter-nating coordination characteristic of stepping was seldom expressed on E20. Over the next two days, however, an increase in both step-ping rate and *interlimb coordination* was apparent (Fig. 5.5, inset).

To quantify *interlimb coordination*, three-second samples of limb activity (comprising 180 video fields) were collected randomly during ten consecutive minutes after the onset of *stepping*. Within each three-second sample, a sixty-field moving correlation was calculated for the spatial position of both forepaws along the rostral-caudal axis of the body. This method yielded 121 correlations for each sample, which ranged from −1.0 (indicative of an alternating or anti-phase pattern of interlimb coordination) to +1.0 (indicative of a synchronized or in-phase pattern). Figure 5.5 presents the distributions of these mov-ing correlations for representative subjects on E21 and P0. Interlimb coordination was fluid and rapidly changing on E21. Some three-second samples showed stable periods of alternated coordination, others were nearly synchronized, and still others showed little evi-dence of any stable pattern. The consequence of this variability was a distribution of moving correlations that occupied the full range from anti-phase to in-phase. One day later, interlimb coordination remained variable but showed evidence of convergence toward a typical pattern of alternation. Indeed, as in the study of *oral grasping* of an artificial nipple, there was evidence of steady improvement in forelimb co-ordination during *L-DOPA induced stepping* across ages. But the

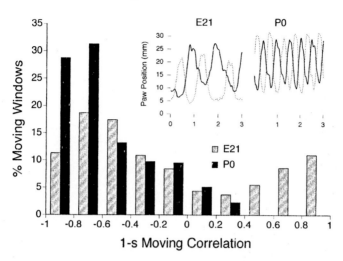

Figure 5.5. Variability of interlimb coordination during L-DOPA in-duced stepping in fetal (E21) and neonatal (P0) rats. Vertical bars depict the percentage of Pearson product–moment correlations of forelimb position within a specified range. Correlations were calculated within a one-second (sixty video fields) moving window across ten three-second samples for each fetal subject. Correlations of –1.0 represent anti-phase or alternated limb activity; correlations of +1.0 indicat in-phase or sychronized limb movement. The inset graphs (*upper right*) depict a three-second sample of alternated stepping expressed by E21 fetuses and P0 pups. The vertical axis presents the absolute position of the right paw (*solid line*) and left paw (*dotted line*) in the rostrocaudal dimension; positive displacements indicate move-ment toward the head.

improvement was quantitative, consisting of a compression of the variance of coordinative patterns.

This gradual improvement in motor performance stands in contrast to many published reports of the underlying pattern generator thought to give rise to basic patterns of alternating coordination, which are stable from E18 to early neonatal ages (Iizuka, Nishimaru, & Kudo, 1998; Nishimaru & Kudo, 2000). This improvement is, however, con-sistent with previous descriptions of high variability in limb coordina-tion during swimming in neonatal rats (Cazalets, Menard, Cremieux, & Clarac, 1990). These findings suggest that the highly stereotypic alternating burst generators from *in vitro* spinal cord preparations (Cazalets, Borde, & Clarac, 1995; Cazalets et al., 1992; Cowley & Schmidt, 1994; Ho & O'Donovan, 1993; Kudo & Yamada, 1987) do not necessarily translate to coordinated motor behavior in the intact fetus; rather, organized *stepping* may require experience to balance intrinsic CNS activity with the demands of a specific biomechanical and environmental context. Such experience may be provided by *spontaneous activity* and need not involve functional locomotion.

FUNCTIONAL PROPRIOCEPTION BEFORE BIRTH

As previously noted, neuroembryological studies of motility in chicken embryos have demonstrated that prenatal movements are not simple reflexive responses to random stimulation, but are the product of *spontaneous activity* in the CNS (Hamburger et al., 1966). Because motility can be expressed in the absence of sensory stimulation, it sometimes has been concluded that *proprioceptive feedback* about the frequency, form, or consequences of embryonic movement is of little importance in prenatal neurobehavioral development (Haverkamp & Oppenheim, 1986). However, critical features of the proprioceptive system develop during the period before birth, and there is growing evidence to support the opposite conclusion about the importance of *spontaneous activity* and *proprioceptive feedback* in early neuromotor development.

Proprioception comprises a number of different sensory receptors and their associated afferent pathways that support kinesthetic (movement) perception. Although unspecialized cutaneous afferents (including touch, pressure, thermal, and even pain receptors) can contribute to proprioception, specialized sensors in muscle, tendons, and joints provide critical information for coordinated *motor control* (Pearson & Gordon, 2000). *Muscle spindles*—which develop from intrafusal muscle fibers in parallel with the force-generating extra-fusal fibers in striatal muscle—provide feedback about muscle length, rate of contraction, and rapid changes in muscle activity, and they are probably crucial for providing information about the relative position and trajectory of limb movement. Moreover, *spindle organs* are inner-vated by *gamma motor neurons*, which permit modulation of the sensi-tivity of the spindles to both static (length) and dynamic (activity) aspects of muscle action. Anatomical evidence from the *soleus muscle* (a hindlimb extensor) in rats suggests that spindles differentiate from primary myotubes during the late fetal period and are likely to be capable of responding to changes in muscle length by E19–E20 of gestation (Kucera, Walro, & Reichler, 1989). Spindles begin to receive innervation from *motor neurons* one to two days later. Direct neural recording from primary afferents in the dorsal root ganglion of fetal rats has corroborated these inferences from anatomy. As early as E17, *sensory neurons* were identified that were responsive to small changes in limb position, but until E19 the responsiveness of these muscle afferents was confounded by high levels of *spontaneous activity* within the afferent neurons (Fitzgerald, 1987). This finding is consistent with anatomical evidence that primary afferents reach target muscles several days before spindles begin to develop (Kucera et al., 1989). It also calls attention to the ubiquitous nature of spontaneous activity during fetal neural development: not only are motor neurons and networks of *interneurons* within the central nervous system spontaneously active, but developing sensory neurons exhibit spontaneous activity as well (Erwin & Miller, 1998; Galli & Maffei, 1988; Shatz, 1990; Wong, Sanes, & Wong, 1998).

Spontaneous activity of motor units (motor neurons and the muscle fibers they innervate) and associated sensory neurons appear to be necessary for the normal processes of *cell death,* synapse *elimination,* and restructuring of neuronal connectivity within the motor system that occur during prenatal and early postnatal development. Reduction or elimination of neuronal activity results in sparing of supernumerary motor neurons, while externally applied stimulation accelerates the rate of cell death (Oppenheim, 1991). Activity in the motor system is also thought to be responsible for the reduction of *polysynaptic innervation of muscle fibers* and establishment of the 1:1 ratio of motor neurons to muscle fibers typical of adult mammals (Navarrete & Vrbova, 1993). Moreover, the amount of neural activity appears to be not as important as the pattern of activity: bursts of electrical stimulation are more effective in promoting selective attrition of synapses than a steady rate of stimulation (Thompson, 1983). *Spontaneous activity in primary afferents* is also important for restructuring neuronal connectivity (Seebach & Ziskind-Conhaim, 1994) and may be necessary for spindle formation in muscles (Zelena, 1976).

Recent studies of *transgenic mice* that lack the gene for the trkC receptor provide further confirmation that *proprioceptive feedback,* and not just efferent activity, is important in early neuromotor development. The trkC receptor binds NT-3, a neurotrophin that promotes survival and neurite outgrowth of *sensory neurons* associated with primary proprioceptive afferents (Hory-Lee, Russell, Linday, & Frank, 1993). The absence of NT-3 binding leads to *cell death.* Furthermore, *muscle spindles* are completely absent in newborn mice lacking the *trkC gene* (Helgren et al., 1997; Kucera, Ernfors, Walro, & Jaenisch, 1995;

Snider, 1994), and such mice show gross motor impairment (Klein et al., 1994). Motor deficits also have been reported in chicks prenatally exposed to pyridoxine, which induces selective loss of proprioceptive neurons (Sharp, Boyle, & Bekoff, 1998). These findings suggest that many of the functional properties of the motor system are shaped by *spontaneous activity* in both efferent and afferent pathways, and by *proprioceptive feedback* arising from patterned motor activity during prenatal development (Thompson, 1983).

PERINATAL RESPONSIVENESS TO PROPRIOCEPTIVE FEEDBACK

Is there evidence to suggest that proprioceptive feedback may contribute to plasticity in the development of organized behavior and not just in the physical components of the motor system? Although earlier studies suggested that avian embryos (and by logical extension mammalian fetuses) are largely unresponsive to *proprioceptive stimulation* (Hamburger et al., 1966; Oppenheim, 1972), more recent experimental work has provided compelling evidence that *spontaneous activity* and species-typical motor patterns are strongly influenced by proprioceptive cues. A dramatic example is provided by *hatching behavior* in the *chick embryo*. Hatching consists of a complex behavioral sequence involving pecking movements by the head coupled with coordinated activity of the legs (Hamburger & Oppenheim, 1967). Hatching is normally expressed just once in life, during the last day before emergence from the egg (E21). But the immediate cue that initiates hatching behavior appears to be a proprioceptive stimulus generated by the posture of the neck (Bekoff & Sabichi, 1987). Embryos that received local anesthetic administered to discrete regions of the neck failed to exhibit hatching behavior. More remarkably, adult chickens that were experimentally placed into glass eggs (suitably scaled to accommodate their larger bodies), and positioned with the head and neck bent to the side and tucked under one wing in the typical embryonic posture, expressed characteristic hatching behavior (Bekoff & Kauer, 1984).

Biomechanical Influences

Chick embryos have also been shown to be responsive to alterations in the *biomechanical context of spontaneous movement.* Withdrawal of a portion of the amniotic fluid that surrounds the E9 embryo reduced buoyant support of the wings and legs, resulting in increased activity but diminished *intralimb coordination* (Bradley, 1997). Experimental restraint at a single joint, by applying a rigid brace to the right ankle, caused comparable changes in movement parameters in the E12 chick embryo. Although ankle restraint disrupted coordination among joints in the same leg, coordination of movement between the leg and wing remained high, suggesting some compensation in *motor control* through *sensory feedback* from the limbs (Bradley & Sebelski, 2000). Because *muscle spindles* in the hindlimbs are poorly developed in the chick earlier than E13 (Maier, 1993), this feedback may have been provided by cutaneous afferents stimulated by body-on-body contact (Bradley & Sebelski, 2000). Similar lasting effects on the organization of EMG activity in hindlimb muscles have been reported in rats, following immobilization of one limb during the first two postnatal weeks (Westerga & Gramsbergen, 1993a, 1993b). Although the young rats eventually developed normal-looking adult locomotion, interference with afferent feedback during development was suggested as the cause of persistent abnormalities in *motor control.*

Proprioception and Human Development

Until very recently, only sparse information has been available about responsiveness of mammalian fetuses to proprioceptive cues. Much of the available evidence comes from classic studies of externalized *human fetuses* (Hooker, 1952; Humphrey, 1969) and *preterm infants,* which retain fetal patterns of neural development despite their early arrival into a postnatal environment (Mouradian, Als, & Coster, 2001). As early as 7.5 weeks of gestation, human fetuses can respond to stimulation that consists of stroking the skin with a fine hair (Hooker, 1952). Generally, this response is limited to the perioral area served by the *trigeminal nerve.* Only two weeks later, proprioceptive *stretch responses* can be elicited from the arms, and by eleven or twelve weeks the fetus begins to exhibit palmar responses, first in the hands and later in the feet. Also at this age, stimulation of the perioral region may bring about either orienting or aversive movements of the head, depending on the strength of the stimulus applied (Humphrey, 1969). These fields of sensitivity to stimulation continue to expand, and the primitive nature of the corresponding reflexes change across development, culminating in their more mature forms seen at term (e.g., Brazelton & Nugent, 1995; Dubowitz, 1999).

Recent ultrasonographic study of fetuses *in utero* has confirmed these overall developmental trends, noting some of the same reflexive movement patterns described by classic observers during spontaneous movement (de Vries, Visser, & Prechtl, 1982). *Preterm infants* also exhibit a similar (primitive to mature) developmental pattern of reflexive response (Dubowitz, 1999; Mandich, Simons, Ritchie, Schmidt, & Mullett, 1994). Even though the environments of the fetus and *preterm infant* are radically different, similarities between fetal and preterm infant reflexive development do not necessarily imply that these changes occur independent of environment. Studies of infants born in breech position during the last two to eight weeks of gestation have revealed abnormal flexing of the hips during walking, often until the infants are twelve to eighteen months old (Sival, Prechtl, Sonder, & Touwen, 1993). Such results, along with the studies of response to stimulation mentioned above, suggest not only that the *human fetus* possesses a functional proprioceptive sense during the last two trimesters of gestation, but also that prenatal experience with proprioceptive stimuli may exert effects that persist long after birth.

Although experimental data from fetuses is lacking, perturbation of *proprioceptive feedback* has been shown to exert pronounced effects on motor behavior in *human infants*. For example, attachment of an external weight to the ankle of *human infants* significantly altered the dynamics of *spontaneous kicking*. At six weeks, the additional load imposed by the weight either produced no effect (Thelen, Skala, & Kelso, 1987) or modest increases (Vaal, van Soest, & Hopkins, 2000) in the frequency and amplitude of motion of the weighted leg. But in both studies, infants showed disproportionate increases in movement rate and amplitude of the unweighted leg. By twelve to sixteen weeks, unilateral weighting exerts effects on the coordination of both legs (Ulrich, Ulrich, Angulo-Kinzler, & Chapman, 1997; Vaal et al., 2000). These findings demonstrate that the developing motor system can compensate, albeit imperfectly, for changes in static load, suggesting that *proprioceptive feedback* can serve as a means of regulating the quantity or quality of movement during spontaneous motor activity.

The ability of infants to alter limb coordination as compensation for an externally applied weight may represent an early form of *motor learning*. Clearer demonstrations of infant motor learning have been provided with the *conjugate reinforcement training paradigm*, developed by Rovee-Collier and colleagues (1991). In this paradigm, one end of

a ribbon is attached to the ankle of an infant lying in a supine position, and the other end is attached to an overhead mobile. Kicking of
the tethered leg results in movement of the mobile, and infants quickly
learn the association to produce increases in the frequency and amplitude of kicking. Thelen (1994) applied this training method to determine whether three-month-old infants also could learn a new pattern
of *interlimb coordination*. An elastic cord was attached by Velcro straps
to the ankles of both legs of the infant, and the ribbon was attached in
the typical fashion. Under these conditions, kicking of just one leg, or
of both legs in the alternated pattern typical of *spontaneous kicking*
(Thelen, 1985), resulted in physical restraint and thus reduced movement amplitude. Infants fitted with the elastic yoke altered their kicking movements by increasing the correlation between movement
trajectories of the two legs. In effect, *yoke training* shifted infant kicking behavior from an alternated to a synchronous, in-phase pattern of
interlimb coordination (Thelen, 1994).

Insights from the Development of Locomotion in Rabbits

A similar approach to motor training approach has demonstrated
plasticity in the development of *locomotion in newborn rabbits*. Shortly
after leaving the nest at around ten days after birth, rabbit neonates
exhibit an alternated quadrupedal walking *locomotion*. The alternating pattern of *interlimb coordination* is evident for both forelimbs and
hindlimbs and is expressed at both a behavioral level and at the level
of neural discharge in ventral roots of the spinal cord (*fictive locomotion*) (Viala, Viala, & Fayein, 1986). Between ten to twenty days after
birth, this alternating *stepping* is replaced by the familiar half-bound
pattern characteristic of *adult rabbits*, in which the forelegs step alternately but the hindlegs exhibit a synchronized hopping pattern. This
transition from anti-phase to *in-phase coordination* of the hindlimbs also
has been noted in other species that exhibit hopping or ricochetal
locomotion as adults (Blumberg-Feldman & Eilam, 1995; Eilam, 1997;
Eilam & Shefer, 1997).

Although the transition in locomotor coordination has typically been
attributed to neural maturation, developmental outcomes can be influenced by early motor experience. In the course of investigating the
development of *locomotion in spinalized rabbits*, Viala et al. (1986) noted
that older rabbits prepared by mid-thoracic spinal transection soon
after birth sometimes retained the alternating pattern of hindlimb
coordination characteristic of infants, but they sometimes showed the

in-phase pattern more typical of juveniles. To explore this apparent plasticity, two-day-old rabbits were prepared with a mid-thoracic spinal transection and then exposed to daily motor training beginning ten days after birth. Training consisted of securing the young rabbit in a harness and attaching both feet to pedals, which allowed either an in-phase pattern of movement, an alternated pattern (rotating like bicycle pedals), or exposure to both patterns. Motor training was repeated in six fifteen-minute sessions each day for twenty days.

The effects of training on hindlimb coordination were evaluated daily by recording the pattern of movement when hindlimbs were allowed to move freely in response to a light tail pinch, and they were evaluated after the end of training by measuring fictive activity in hindlimb nerves. Rabbits that received anti-phase training showed alternated hindlimb activity exclusively by sixteen days (after six days of training). However, about 75% of hindlimb movements by rabbits that received in-phase training were synchronized, not alternated, by the end of training. Because rabbits were able to express independent limb movements outside of training, an additional experimental group was fitted with an *interlimb yoke* between training sessions. In this group, in-phase hindlimb activity was exclusively expressed by twenty days. After training was complete, measurement of *fictive locomotor activity* confirmed that burst patterns in hindlimb nerves conformed to anti-phase or in-phase patterns of coordination, contingent on patterns of motor training. These experimental results provide compelling evidence that infant animals and humans can alter fundamental patterns of *motor coordination* as a consequence of explicit motor training, and that *proprioceptive feedback* from the hindlimbs may have a structuring effect during early development on the neural networks involved in controlling *interlimb coordination* (Thelen, 1994; Viala et al., 1986).

MOTOR LEARNING IN THE RAT FETUS: EVIDENCE FROM YOKE TRAINING

The *yoke training* paradigm just described appears to have been independently developed in at least three laboratories as a method for probing the early plasticity of the motor system (Robinson & Smotherman, 1994; Thelen, 1994; Viala et al., 1986). In our laboratory, yoke training has been used to systematically explore the ability of *rat fetuses* to acquire and express new patterns of *interlimb coordination*. In initial experiments, the interlimb yoke consisted of a length of suture thread attached to both ankles of the fetus; we subsequently have modified this procedure by drawing loops of thread through a length of PE-50 polyethylene tubing, creating a yoke that is resistant to compression, tension, or flexion. In applying this procedure for yoke training, it was expected that active movement by one limb would result in dampened movement of the active limb and passive movement of the other limb, thereby altering *kinesthetic feedback* from both limbs. Fetal subjects are exposed to the interlimb yoke during a thirty-minute training period, after which the yoke is cut and limb activity is monitored for an additional thirty-minute test period. Subjects are usually videotaped during the experimental session, and limb movements are quantified to measure *interlimb coordination* during and after yoke training.

Hindlimb Movements

When exposed to these training and testing procedures, fetal rats exhibit consistent changes in the coordination of the yoked limbs (Robinson, in press). The basic effect of fetal *yoke training* is illustrated in Figure 5.6. In this experiment, three groups of E20 fetuses were prepared: one group had a thread that yoked the two hindlimbs (Yoked group), another group had a thread that was attached and immediately cut (Unyoked group), and the third group had no treatment (NT). Changes in hindlimb coordination were most evident in the expression of *conjugate limb movements.* A conjugate movement is defined as flexion and extension of two limbs that are initiated at the same moment and follow parallel trajectories. Yoked subjects showed a gradual increase in conjugate hindlimb movements during the thirty-minute period of training, whereas such movements were expressed infrequently by either Unyoked or NT control subjects. The magnitude of this increase in conjugate hindlimb activity was pronounced, regardless of whether conjugate activity was expressed as an absolute frequency (Fig. 5.6, left) or as a percentage of all hindlimb movements (Fig. 5.6, right). Furthermore, elevated levels of conjugate movement persisted during the test period, after the yoke was cut. Fetuses in the Yoked group continued to express conjugate hindlimb movements at rates greater than Unyoked and NT controls for fifteen to twenty-five minutes after removal of the physical linkage between the limbs.

Yoke-induced changes in hindlimb coordination have been confirmed by kinematic analysis of hindlimb movements (Robinson,

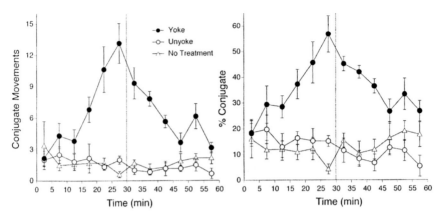

Figure 5.6. Changes in conjugate hindlimb movements during and after yoke training in the E20 rat fetus. Fetuses were assigned to three conditions: Yoked (in which the interlimb yoke was attached during the first thirty minutes of training, then removed during the last thirty minutes), Unyoked (in which the interlimb yoke was attached and immediately removed before training), and No Treatment (in which fetuses received no explicit manipulation). *Left*: Points depict mean (± SEM) number of conjugate movements within five-minute intervals during the sixty-minute experimental session. *Right*: Changes in conjugate movement expressed as a percentage of overall hindlimb activity within each five-minute interval.

Peterson, & Gjerde, 1997). E20 fetuses were positioned in a supine posture within a calibrated space to permit frame-by-frame measurement of hindlimb position before and after thirty minutes of hindlimb *yoke training*. Fetuses were videotaped for five minutes before yoke training and five minutes after the interlimb yoke was removed. Kinematic analysis of hindlimb movements was conducted with a dedicated motion analysis system (Peak Performance MOTUS), which allows reference points on the fetus (e.g., tip of a hindpaw) to be marked with a cursor from two camera views and the 3-D coordinates of the limb positions within the calibrated space to be calculated by direct linear transformation (Scholz & Millford, 1993). Visual scoring indicated that conjugate movements of both hindlimbs occurred rarely before the yoke, increased six-fold during yoke training, and persisted at high levels after the yoke. Frame-by-frame coding permitted calculation of 3-D positions, which were used to reconstruct movement trajectories and velocity profiles of each hindpaw. This kinematic analysis revealed that hindlimb movements were significantly

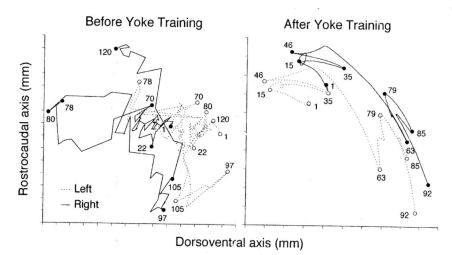

Figure 5.7. Examples of movement trajectories of hindlimbs before and after interlimb yoke training in the E20 rat fetus. Movement paths represent the rostrocaudal and dorsoventral coordinates of hindpaw position, as calculated from 3-D coordinates obtained from frame-by-frame motion analysis. The position of right (*solid line*) and left hindpaws (*dotted line*) at selected points are indicated by field numbers (1 s = 60 video fields). Note how movement paths undergo sudden changes in direction and velocity independently in the two limbs before yoke training (*left*), in contrast to the smooth changes in direction and velocity and parallel trajectories during conjugate hindlimb activity after training (*right*).

more coordinated after yoke training, as exemplified by two plots of one-to-two-second limb trajectories by the same fetal subject (Fig. 5.7). In the left plot (before training), the two limbs are seen to move independently, with little evidence of smooth coordination of path or velocity. In the right plot (after training), a sequence of *conjugate hindlimb movements* is illustrated, with both limbs following parallel paths and velocity profiles.

A moving one-second correlation was used to quantify rapidly changing patterns of coordination between the limbs, as described above in our study of *L-DOPA induced stepping* (see also Thelen, 1994). The moving window analysis yielded a distribution of correlations between limb positions (corresponding to the rostrocaudal, dorsoventral, and mediolateral dimensions) and instantaneous resultant velocity of the hindlimbs (vector sum) for each subject. Conjugate or in-phase limb activity increased in the rostrocaudal and dorsoventral axes after *yoke training*, as did the correlation of limb velocities. The increased correlation of limb position did not occur at the expense of limb activity; hindlimbs showed no decrease in activity after yoke training, and variability in limb position actually increased. However, the average distance between the left and right paws became less variable after yoke training, decreasing from 31.1% ± 1.8% before training to 17.3% ± 2.3% (mean C.V. ± SEM) after training, which suggested that the magnitude of separation between the limbs (in the mediolateral axis) was conserved during *spontaneous activity* even after the yoke was removed. Together, these kinematic measures indicated that fetuses altered *interlimb coordination* in response to yoke training by producing more movements with parallel movement paths and velocities, and by maintaining a more constant separation between the limbs (Robinson et al., 1997).

Interpretation of Findings

Interlimb *yoke training* appears to result in adaptive modification of *motor coordination* in the E20 fetus, and therefore would seem to represent a form of *motor learning*. Alternatively, conjugate hindlimb movements might be attributed to struggling or other reflexive responses to limb restraint. Several aspects of the fetal response to yoke training support a motor learning interpretation. First, conjugate hindlimb movements were not immediately expressed after the yoke was applied; rather, they increased gradually in occurrence during the training period. Second, *conjugate movements* continued to be expressed after the yoke was removed, suggesting that persistent changes in the control of hindlimb movement had occurred. Fetal hindlimb movements did not become more stereotyped in response to the interlimb yoke. In contrast, individual limb position became more variable, but the relative position of both limbs became more highly correlated, and the distance between paws became less variable. Finally, several experiments have confirmed that the effects of yoke training are restricted to the limbs that experience the interlimb yoke. Conjugate movement of forelimbs did not increase when hindlimbs were yoked, although conjugate hindlimb movements showed a pronounced increase (Fig. 5.6). Conversely, *conjugate movement* of hindlimbs did not increase when the forelimbs were yoked, although yoke training resulted in an increase in conjugate forelimb movement. Furthermore, when the yoke was applied to the left forelimb and hindlimb, the limb pair ipsilateral to the yoke showed an increase in conjugate movement, while the limb pair contralateral to the yoke showed no significant change in coordination (Robinson, in press). These behavioral changes provide evidence that the E20 *rat fetus* can (1) detect changes in *proprioceptive feedback* that are induced by the interlimb yoke, (2) modify *interlimb coordination* of the yoked limbs to adjust to the conditions of dynamic restraint, and (3) continue to express changes in *interlimb coordination* for fifteen to thirty minutes after the yoke is removed.

Duration of the Effects of Yoke Training

The ability of the *rat fetus* to modify its *motor coordination* in response to an interlimb yoke has numerous implications for prenatal *motor control* and development. First, it implies that the fetus possesses a functional kinesthetic sense, and that it can use *proprioceptive feedback* to modulate *motor coordination*. Second, the persistence of conjugate limb activity after removal of the yoke suggests that fetal experience with the yoke may have lasting effects on motor performance. After a thirty-minute period of *yoke training*, conjugate limb activity remains elevated in the E20 fetus for fifteen to twenty minutes. However, if the effects of yoke training were truly extinguished after so brief a period, then fetal responses to biomechanical contexts, such as provided by the yoke, may be important only for the immediate control of behavior and may not contribute to long-term motor development.

To evaluate whether the effects of *yoke training* are transient, fetuses were exposed to a second *yoke training* trial after conjugate limb movements had returned to baseline levels (Robinson, in press). The experimental session was divided into three thirty-minute blocks comprising an initial training period, an intervening test period, and a second training period. Control fetuses were exposed to a hindlimb yoke only during the first training period (Y-U-U group) or during the second training period (U-U-Y). Experimental subjects experienced the hindlimb yoke during both training periods (Y-U-Y). As summarized in Figure 5.8, both Y-U-U and Y-U-Y groups showed a gradual increase in *conjugate hindlimb movements* during the first training period that persisted after the yoke was cut, but which gradually declined to baseline levels by the end of the test period. The U-U-Y group also showed a gradual increase in conjugate hindlimb movement during the second training period that was comparable to the increases shown by the other groups in the first training period. However, fetuses that experienced the interlimb yoke for the second

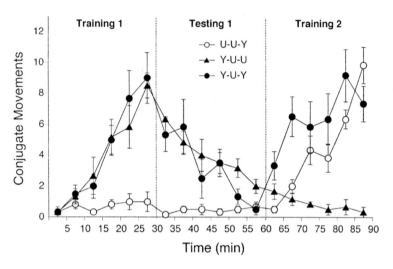

Figure 5.8. Changes in conjugate hindlimb movements in E20 rat fetuses exposed to repeated yoke training. Fetuses were assigned to three training conditions. Yoke training occurred in either the first or last thirty-minute blocks of the ninety-minute session, or both. Y-U-U subjects were exposed to the interlimb yoke only during the first training period; U-U-Y subjects were exposed to the yoke only during the second training period; Y-U-Y subjects received yoke training during both first and second training periods. For all subjects, the interlimb yoke was removed during the middle thirty-minute block (Testing). Points depict mean number of conjugate hindlimb movements in five-minute intervals; vertical lines show SEM.

time (Y-U-Y) showed a more rapid increase in conjugate hindlimb activity during the second training period. The savings that were evident upon repeated *yoke training* indicate that some information about the interlimb yoke was retained from the initial period of training. These results are completely consistent with the interpretation that interlimb yoke training represents a form of *motor learning* that can be expressed by the fetus.

Age-Specificity in Detecting Feedback from Yoke Training

The experiments previously discussed demonstrate that by E20 of gestation—two days before birth—the fetal rat can modify its *motor coordination* in response to an interlimb yoke. Presumably, the ability of the fetus to control the trajectory of each hindlimb must be dependent on afferent information that derives from *muscle spindles* or other

proprioceptors that provide *kinesthetic feedback* about motor performance. Given the evidence that spindles may become functional as late
as E19–E20 (Kucera et al., 1989), it may not be possible for younger
fetuses to detect errors in feedback created by the interlimb yoke during spontaneous movement, and therefore they may be unresponsive
to *yoke training*. To evaluate this hypothesis, rat fetuses were prepared
for training and testing in the yoke motor learning paradigm at ages
ranging from E18–E21 (Robinson & Kleven, 1999). The yoke was
modified to adapt to fetuses of widely varying size. Two loops of 4-0
suture thread were passed through a length of PE-50 tubing: the loops
then could be slipped over the hindfeet of the subject and tightened
to fit the yoke snugly around the ankle. This modification provides
more precise control over the length of the yoke by varying the length
of the connecting tubing (yokes were fabricated in lengths of 3, 5, 8,
and 10 mm for fetuses on E18, E19, E20, and E21, respectively).

Subjects were tested in an initial five-minute baseline period without the yoke attached, followed by a thirty-minute training period
with the yoke intact, and a subsequent thirty-minute test period after
the yoke was cut. E20 fetuses performed as they did in previous
experiments, exhibiting a steady increase in *conjugate hindlimb movements* during training that persisted for fifteen to twenty minutes during the test period (Fig. 5.9). E21 fetuses showed a more rapid
response to the yoke during training and maintained elevated levels
of conjugate movement through the thirty-minute test. Although
E19 fetuses showed much lower levels of response, they did exhibit a
yoke-induced increase in conjugate movement; however, this increase
was not maintained above baseline levels during the test period.
Finally, E18 fetuses failed to respond to the interlimb yoke at all.
These results imply a developmental pattern in the fetal response to
yoke training that is consistent with current understanding of the
emergence of proprioceptive function (Robinson & Kleven, 1999).

CONCLUDING COMMENTS: THE ROLE OF FETAL MOTOR ACTIVITY

The study of motor development has re-emerged in the past decade
as a vibrant area of rich empirical and theoretical interest. Because
motor activity offers distinct advantages for quantitative measurement and experimental manipulation, studies of motor behavior
are providing unique model systems and conceptual approaches to
understanding basic principles of neural organization and behavioral

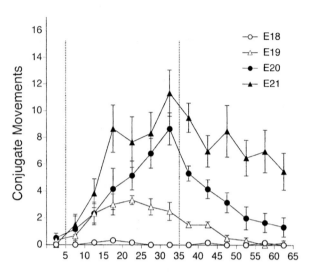

Figure 5.9. Developmental changes in yoke motor learning across the last four days of gestation (E18–E21) in the rat fetus. The sixty-five-minute experimental session was divided into an initial five-minute baseline period (no manipulation), a thirty-minute training period in which the interlimb yoke was attached to both hindlimbs, and a final thirty-minute test period when the yoke was removed. Points depict mean number of conjugate hindlimb movements in five-minute intervals during the session; vertical lines show SEM.

development (Edelman, 1987; Sporns & Edelman, 1993; Thelen, 1989; Thelen & Smith, 1994). The nervous system, after all, exists for the primary purpose of controlling when and how animals move. The motor system provides researchers with more than the *final common path*, by which complex neural functions such as sensation, learning, and cognition can be measured. How the nervous system governs the details of action in time and space has come to be recognized as one of the fundamental problems facing modern neuroscience. Understanding how motor coordination and behavioral organization emerge during early development simply compounds this problem.

Although studies of motor development helped to establish developmental psychology as a distinct field (Gesell & Thompson, 1938; McGraw, 1945), experimental work on sensation and learning during early development in some ways has outpaced basic understanding of motor behavior (Gottlieb, 1997; Lecanuet, Fifer, Krasnegor, & Smotherman, 1995). Yet, understanding the roots of action is fundamentally important. In animal studies, experimenters must infer sensory or learning capacities from motor performance, placing a premium on selection of motor tasks that are appropriate for very young subjects (Smotherman & Robinson, 1998). In human clinical settings, *reflexes*, motor activity, and coordination provide the earliest diagnostic tools for assessing function in the nervous system (Brazelton & Nugent, 1995; Prechtl, 1997). Fetal motor activity is known to exert facilitative effects on the physical development of muscles, bones, joints, skin, and parts of the respiratory, circulatory, and alimentary systems (Moessinger, 1988). *Spontaneous activity* within the CNS in particular has come to be widely recognized as a critical determinant of prenatal neural development (Colman & Lichtman, 1993; Navarrete & Vrbova, 1993).

Ironically, advances in developmental neuroscience have tended to accentuate the distinction between *activity-dependent* and experience-dependent processes in neural development. This distinction is unfortunate because developing motor systems, like immature sensory systems, may be *experience-expectant* accepting information as input from a variety of sources internal and external to the organism. Indeed, Gottlieb (1997) has argued that there is no principled reason to distinguish between neural activity arising spontaneously within the nervous system, derived from *sensory feedback* from spontaneously generated movements, or emanating from sources in the external environment. It is in this sense that motor experience during prenatal development may form a continuum of functions that range from spontaneous neural activity that helps to assemble dedicated, pattern-generating circuitry in the CNS, to critical information available only in *kinesthetic feedback* about the frequency and form of self-generated movements.

One of the central truths to emerge from research in developmental psychobiology is that early neural and behavioral development is the *epigenetic* product of interactions between the developing organism and its immediate environment (Hall & Oppenheim, 1987). Organisms do not develop in a vacuum as a simple unfolding of a preformed structure, nor are they blank slates written upon by an organizing environment. Rather, organization emerges from a process of interaction between the organism, its inherited potential realized as the orchestrated products of multiple, interdependent genes, and unique features of the immediate environment that provoke and constrain change. It has become almost axiomatic that there is no *homunculus* or pre-existing *blueprint* that determines a particular outcome (Oyama, 1985). The challenge of developmental science, then, is to identify the particular interactions between organism and environment that give rise to change, and that guide the path of growth and differentiation to predictable endpoints.

In a few organisms, the seemingly simple distinctions between activity and experience, or between organism and environment, are no more blurred than in the mammalian fetus. The fetus develops in a unique environment created by tissues of both embryonic and maternal origin. It is commonplace to consider the *prenatal environment* as static and unchanging, and the fetus as passive and unresponsive. However, research on fetal behavioral and neural development is replacing this still life with a dynamic portrait of an organism that develops within and in relation to a complex and changing environment in which the fetus is an active participant (Smotherman & Robinson, 1996).

REFERENCES

Adolph, K.E. (2002). Learning to keep balance. *Advances in Child Development and Behavior, 30*, 1–40.

Adolph, K.E., & Avolio, A.M. (2000). Walking infants adapt locomotion to changing body dimensions. *Journal of Experimental Psychology: Human Perception and Performance, 26*, 1148–1166.

Andersen, S.L., Robinson, S.R., & Smotherman, W.P. (1993). Ontogeny of the stretch response in the rat fetus: Kappa opioid involvement. *Behavioral Neuroscience, 107*, 370–376.

Angulo y Gonzalez, A.W. (1932). The prenatal development of behavior in the albino rat. *Journal of Comparative Neurology, 55*, 395–442.

Barcroft, J., & Barron, D.H. (1939). The development of behavior in foetal sheep. *Journal of Comparative Neurology, 70*, 477–502.

Barcroft, J., Barron, D.H., & Windle, W.F. (1936). Some observations on genesis of somatic movements in sheep embryos. *Journal of Physiology, 87*, 73–78.

Bekoff, A. (1976). Ontogeny of leg motor output in the chick embryo: A neural analysis. *Brain Research, 106*, 271–291.

Bekoff, A., & Kauer, J.A. (1984). Neural control of hatching: Fate of the pattern generator for the leg movements of hatching in posthatching chicks. *Journal of Neuroscience, 4*, 2659–2666.

Bekoff, A., & Lau, B. (1980). Interlimb coordination in 20-day-old rat fetuses. *Journal of Experimental Zoology, 214*, 173–175.

Bekoff, A., & Sabichi, A.L. (1987). Sensory control of the initiation of hatching in chicks: Effects of a local anesthetic injected into the neck. *Developmental Psychobiology, 20*, 489–495.

Bekoff, A., & Trainer, W. (1979). The development of interlimb co-ordination during swimming in postnatal rats. *Journal of Experimental Biology, 83,* 1–11.

Bernstein, N.A. (1967). *The co-ordination and regulation of movements.* New York: Pergamon Press.

Blumberg-Feldman, H., & Eilam, D. (1995). Postnatal development of synchronous stepping in the gerbil (*Gerbillus dasyurus*). *Journal of Experimental Biology, 198,* 363–372.

Bradley, N.S. (1997). Reduction in buoyancy alters parameters of motility in E9 chick embryos. *Physiology & Behavior, 62,* 591–595.

Bradley, N.S., & Sebelski, C. (2000). Ankle restraint modifies motility at E12 in chick embryos. *Journal of Neurophysiology, 83,* 431–440.

Brazelton, T.B., & Nugent, J.K. (1995). *Neonatal behavioral assessment scale.* London: MacKeith Press.

Brown, T.G. (1914). On the nature of the fundamental activity of the nervous centres; together with an analysis of the conditioning of rhythmic activity in progression, and a theory of evolution of function in the nervous system. *Journal of Physiology, 48,* 18–46.

Brown, T.G. (1915). On the activities of the central nervous system of the unborn foetus of the cat; with a discussion of the question whether progression (walking, etc.) is a "learnt" complex. *Journal of Physiology, 49,* 208–215.

Carmichael, L. (1934). An experimental study in the prenatal guinea-pig of the origin and development of reflexes and patterns of behavior in relation to the stimulation of specific receptor areas during the period of active fetal life. *Genetic Psychology Monographs, 16,* 337–491.

Carmichael, L., & Smith, M.F. (1939). Quantified pressure stimulation and the specificity and generality of response in fetal life. *Journal of Genetic Psychology, 54,* 425–434.

Carrier, D.R. (1996). Ontogenetic limits on locomotor performance. *Physiological Zoology, 69,* 467–488.

Cazalets, J., Borde, M., & Clarac, F. (1995). Localization and organization of the central pattern generator for hindlimb locomotion in the newborn rat. *Journal of Neuroscience, 15,* 4943–4951.

Cazalets, J.R., Menard, I., Cremieux, J., & Clarac, F. (1990). Variability as a characteristic of immature motor systems: An electromyographic study of swimming in the newborn rat. *Behavioural Brain Research, 40,* 215–225.

Cazalets, J.R., Sqalli-Houssaini, Y., & Clarac, F. (1992). Activation of the central pattern generators for locomotion by serotonin and excitatory amino acids in neonatal rat. *Journal of Physiology, 455,* 187–204.

Clark, S.A., Allard, T., Jenkins, W.M., & Merzenich, M.M. (1988). Receptive fields in the body-surface map in adult cortex defined by temporally correlated inputs. *Nature, 332,* 444–445.

Coghill, G.E. (1929). *Anatomy and the problem of behavior.* Cambridge, UK: Cambridge University Press.

Colman, H., & Lichtman, J.W. (1993). Interactions between nerve and muscle: Synapse elimination at the developing neuromuscular junction. *Developmental Biology, 156,* 1–10.

Coronios, J.D. (1933). Development of behavior in the fetal cat. *Genetic Psychology Monographs, 14,* 283–386.

Cowley, K.C., & Schmidt, B.J. (1994). A comparison of motor patterns induced by N-methyl-D-aspartate, acetylcholine and serotonin in the in vitro neonatal rat spinal cord. *Neuroscience Letters, 171,* 147–150.

de Vries, J.I.P., Visser, G.H.A., & Prechtl, H.F.R. (1982). The emergence of fetal behavior. I. Qualitative aspects. *Early Human Development, 7,* 301–322.

Dubowitz, L. (1999). *Neurological assessment of the preterm and full-term newborn infant.* London: MacKeith Press.

Edelman, G.M. (1987). *Neural Darwinism.* New York: Basic Books.

Eilam, D. (1997). Postnatal development of body architecture and gait in several rodent species. *Journal of Experimental Biology, 200,* 1339–1350.

Eilam, D., & Shefer, G. (1997). The developmental order of bipedal locomotion in the jerboa (*Jaculus orientalis*): Pivoting, creeping, quadrupedalism, and bipedalism. *Developmental Psychobiology, 31,* 137–142.

Erwin, E., & Miller, K.D. (1998). Correlation-based development of ocularly matched orientation and ocular dominance maps: Determination of required input activities. *Journal of Neuroscience, 18,* 9870–9895.

Fitzgerald, M. (1987). Spontaneous and evoked activity of primary afferents in vivo. *Nature, 326,* 603–605.

Fromme, A. (1941). An experimental study of the factors of maturation and practice in the behavioral development of the embryo of the frog *Rana pipiens. Genetic Psychological Monographs, 24,* 219–256.

Galli, L., & Maffei, L. (1988). Spontaneous impulse activity of rat retinal ganglion cells in prenatal life. *Science, 242* (4875), 90–91.

Gallistel, C.R. (1980). *The organization of action: A new synthesis.* Hillsdale, NJ: Erlbaum.

Gesell, A.L., & Thompson, H. (1938). *The psychology of early growth including norms of infant behavior and a method of genetic analysis.* New York: Macmillan.

Gottlieb, G. (1997). *Synthesizing nature-nurture: Prenatal roots of instinctive behavior.* Mahwah, NJ: Erlbaum.

Hailman, J.P. (1967). The ontogeny of an instinct. *Behaviour Supplement, 15,* 1–159.

Hall, W.G., & Oppenheim, R.W. (1987). Developmental psychobiology: Prenatal, perinatal, and early postnatal aspects of behavioral development. *Annual Review of Psychology, 38,* 91–128.

Hamburger, V. (1973). Anatomical and physiological basis of embryonic motility in birds and mammals. In G. Gottlieb (Ed.), *Behavioral embryology* (Vol. 1, pp. 51–76). New York: Academic Press.

Hamburger, V., & Oppenheim, R. (1967). Prehatching motility and hatching behavior in the chick. *Journal of Experimental Zoology, 166,* 171–204.

Hamburger, V., Wenger, E., & Oppenheim, R.W. (1966). Motility in the chick embryo in the absence of sensory input. *Journal of Experimental Zoology, 162,* 133–160.

Haverkamp, L.J., & Oppenheim, R.W. (1986). Behavioral development in the absence of neural activity: Effects of chronic immobilization on amphibian embryos. *Journal of Neuroscience, 6,* 1332–1337.

Heberling, J.L., & Robinson, S.R. (1997). Kinematic analysis of L-DOPA-induced stepping in fetal and newborn rats [Abstract]. *Developmental Psychobiology, 32,* 150.

Helgren, M., Cliffer, K.D., Torrento, K., Cavnor, C., Curtis, R., Di Stefano, P.S., et al. (1997). Neurotrophin-3 administration attenuates deficits of pyridoxine-induced large-fiber sensory neuropathy. *Journal of Neuroscience, 17,* 372–382.

Ho, S., & O'Donovan, M. (1993). Regionalization and intersegmental coordination of rhythm-generating networks in the spinal cord of the chick embryo. *Journal of Neuroscience, 13,* 1354–1371.

Hooker, D. (1952). *The prenatal origin of behavior.* Lawrence, KS: University of Kansas Press.

Hory-Lee, R., Russell, M., Linday, R.M., & Frank, E. (1993). Neurotrophin-3 supports the survival of developing muscle sensory neurons in culture. *Proceedings of the National Academy of Science, USA, 90,* 2613–2617.

Humphrey, T. (1969). Postnatal repetition of human prenatal activity sequences with some suggestions of their neuroanatomical basis. In R.J. Robinson (Ed.), *Brain and early behaviour: Development in the fetus and infant* (pp. 43–84). New York: Academic Press.

Iizuka, M., Nishimaru, H., & Kudo, N. (1998). Development of the spatial pattern of 5-HT-induced locomotor rhythm in the lumbar spinal cord of rat fetuses in vitro. *Neuroscience Research, 31,* 107–111.

Klein, R., Silos-Santiago, I., Smeyne, R.J., Lira, S., Brambilla, R., Bryant, S., et al. (1994). Disruption of the neurotrophin-3 receptor gene trkC eliminates Ia muscle afferents and results in abnormal movements. *Nature, 368,* 249–251.

Kleven, G.A., Lane, M.S., & Robinson, S.R. (in press). Development of intra- and inter-segmental synchrony of limb activity in the rat fetus. *Behavioral Neuroscience.*

Kleven, G.A., & Robinson, S.R. (2000). A comparative study of development of interlimb movement synchrony in altricial and precocial rodent fetuses [Abstract]. *Developmental Psychobiology, 36,* 245.

Kucera, J., Ernfors, P., Walro, J., & Jaenisch, R. (1995). Reduction in the number of spinal neurons in neurotrophin-3-deficient mice. *Neuroscience, 69*, 321–330.

Kucera, J., Walro, J.M., & Reichler, J. (1989). Role of nerve and muscle factors in the development of rat muscle spindles. *American Journal of Anatomy, 186*, 144–160.

Kudo, N., & Yamada, T. (1987). N-methyl-D,L-aspartate-induced locomotor activity in a spinal cord-hindlimb muscles preparation of the newborn rat studied in vitro. *Neuroscience Letters, 75*, 43–48.

Kuo, Z.-Y. (1932). Ontogeny of embryonic behavior in aves: I. The chronology and general nature of the behavior in the chick embryo. *Journal of Experimental Zoology, 61*, 395–430.

Kuo, Z.-Y. (1967). *The dynamics of behavior development.* New York: Random House.

Landmesser, L.T., & O'Donovan, M.J. (1984). Activation patterns of embryonic chick hindlimb muscles recorded in ovo and in an isolated spinal cord preparation. *Journal of Physiology, 347*, 189–204.

Landmesser, L.T., & Szente, M. (1986). Activation patterns of embryonic chick hindlimb muscles following blockade of activity and motoneurone cell death. *Journal of Physiology, 380*, 157–174.

Lane, M.S., & Robinson, S.R. (1998). Interlimb dependencies in the spontaneous motor activity of the rat fetus and neonate and preterm human infant [Abstract]. *Developmental Psychobiology, 33*, 376.

Lau, C., & Henning, S.J. (1985). Investigation of the nature of the "stretch response" in suckling rats. *Physiology & Behavior, 34*, 649–651.

Lecanuet, J.-P., Fifer, W.P., Krasnegor, N.A., & Smotherman, W.P. (Eds.). (1995). *Fetal development: A psychobiological perspective.* Hillsdale, NJ: Erlbaum.

Maier, A. (1993). Development of chicken intrafusal muscle fibers. *Cell Tissue Research, 274*, 383–391.

Mandich, M., Simons, C.J., Ritchie, S., Schmidt, D., & Mullett, M. (1994). Motor development, infantile reactions and postural responses of preterm, at-risk infants. *Developmental Medicine and Child Neurology, 36*, 397–405.

Matthews, S.A., & Detwiler, S.R. (1926). The reaction of Amblystoma embryos following prolonged treatment with chloretone. *Journal of Experimental Zoology, 45*, 279–292.

McEwen, M.L., Van Hartesveldt, C., & Stehouwer, D.J. (1996). A kinematic comparison of L-DOPA-induced air-stepping and swimming in developing rats. *Developmental Psychobiology, 30*, 313–327.

McGraw, M.B. (1945). *The neuromuscular maturation of the human infant.* New York: Columbia University Press.

Merzenich, M.M., Kaas, J.H., Wall, J.T., Sur, M., Nelson, R.J., & Felleman, D.J. (1983). Progression of change following median nerve section in the cortical representation of the hand in areas 3b and 1 in adult owl and squirrel monkeys. *Neuroscience, 10,* 639–665.

Moessinger, A.C. (1988). Morphological consequences of depressed or impaired fetal activity. In W.P. Smotherman & S.R. Robinson (Eds.), *Behavior of the fetus* (pp. 163–173). Caldwell, NJ: Telford Press.

Mouradian, L.E., Als, H., & Coster, W.J. (2001). Neurobehavioral functioning of healthy preterm infants of varying gestational ages. *Journal of Developmental and Behavioral Pediatrics, 21,* 408–416.

Narayanan, C.H., Fox, M.W., & Hamburger, V. (1971). Prenatal development of spontaneous and evoked activity in the rat (*Rattus norvegicus*). *Behaviour, 40,* 100–134.

Navarrete, R., & Vrbova, G. (1993). Activity-dependent interactions between motoneurones and muscles: Their role in the development of the motor unit. *Progress in Neurobiology, 41,* 93–124.

Nilsson, L. (1977). *A child is born.* New York: Delacorte Press.

Nishimaru, H., & Kudo, N. (2000). Formation of the central pattern generator for locomotion in the rat and mouse brain. *Brain Research Bulletin, 53* (5), 661–669.

Oppenheim, R.W. (1972). An experimental investigation of the possible role of tactile and somatosensory in certain aspects of embryonic behavior in the chick. *Developmental Psychobiology, 5,* 71–91.

Oppenheim, R.W. (1991). Cell death during development of the nervous system. *Annual Review of Neuroscience, 14,* 453–501.

Oyama, S. (1985). *The ontogeny of information.* Cambridge, UK: Cambridge University Press.

Pearson, K., & Gordon, J. (2000). Spinal reflexes. In E.R. Kandel, J.H. Schwartz, & T.M. Jessell (Eds.), *Principles of neural science* (4th ed., pp. 713–736). New York: McGraw-Hill.

Prechtl, H. (1997). State of the art of a new functional assessment of the young nervous system: An early predictor of cerebral palsy. *Early Human Development, 50,* 1–11.

Preyer, W.T. (1885). *Spezielle physiologie des embryo: Untersuchungen über die lebensercheinungen vor der geburt* [*Specific physiology of embryos: Studies on manifestations of life prior to birth*]. Leipzig: Grieben.

Provine, R.R. (1971). Embryonic spinal cord: Synchrony and spatial distribution of polyneuronal burst discharges. *Brain Research, 29,* 155–158.

Provine, R.R. (1980). Development of between-limb movement synchronization in the chick embryo. *Developmental Psychobiology, 13,* 151–163.

Robinson, S.R. (in press). Conjugate limb coordination after experience with an interlimb yoke: Evidence for motor learning in the rat fetus. *Developmental Psychobiology.*

Robinson, S.R., Blumberg, M.S., Lane, M.S., & Kreber, L. (2000). Spontaneous motor activity in fetal and infant rats is organized into discrete multi-limb bouts. *Behavioral Neuroscience, 114,* 328–336.

Robinson, S.R., Hoeltzel, T.C.M., Cooke, K.M., Umphress, S.M., Murrish, D.E., & Smotherman, W.P. (1992). Oral capture and grasping of an artificial nipple by rat fetuses. *Developmental Psychobiology, 25,* 543–555.

Robinson, S.R., Hoeltzel, T.C.M., & Smotherman, W.P. (1995). Development of responses to an artificial nipple in the rat fetus: Involvement of mu and kappa opioid systems. *Physiology & Behavior, 57,* 953–957.

Robinson, S.R., & Kleven, G.A. (1999). Developmental changes in inter-limb motor learning in the rat fetus [Abstract]. *Society for Neuroscience Abstracts, 25,* 2178.

Robinson, S.R., Peterson, D.W., & Gjerde, K.K. (1997). Kinematic analysis of hindlimb coordination before and after motor training in the rat fetus [Abstract]. *Society for Neuroscience Abstracts, 25,* 2178.

Robinson, S.R., & Smotherman, W.P. (1988). Chance and chunks in the ontogeny of fetal behavior. In W.P. Smotherman & S.R. Robinson (Eds.), *Behavior of the fetus* (pp. 95–115). Caldwell, NJ: Telford Press.

Robinson, S.R., & Smotherman, W.P. (1991). The amniotic sac as scaffold-ing: Prenatal ontogeny of an action pattern. *Developmental Psychobiology, 24,* 463–485.

Robinson, S.R., & Smotherman, W.P. (1992a). Organization of the stretch response to milk in the rat fetus. *Developmental Psychobiology, 25,* 33–49.

Robinson, S.R., & Smotherman, W.P. (1992b). Fundamental motor patterns of the mammalian fetus. *Journal of Neurobiology, 23,* 1574–1600.

Robinson, S.R., & Smotherman, W.P. (1992c). The emergence of behavioral regulation during fetal development. *Annals of the New York Academy of Sciences, 662,* 53–83.

Robinson, S.R., & Smotherman, W.P. (1994). Behavioral effects of milk in the rat fetus. *Behavioral Neuroscience, 108,* 1139–1149.

Rochat, P. (1989). Object manipulation and exploration in 2- to 5-month-old infants. *Developmental Psychology, 25,* 871–884.

Rovee-Collier, C.K. (1991). The "memory system" of prelinguistic infants. *Annals of the New York Academy of Sciences, 608,* 517–536.

Scholz, J.P., & Millford, J.P. (1993). Accuracy and precision of the Peak Per-formance Technologies motion measurement system. *Journal of Motor Behavior, 25,* 2–7.

Seebach, B.S., & Ziskind-Conhaim, L. (1994). Formation of transient inap-propriate sensorimotor synapses in developing rat spinal cords. *Journal of Neuroscience, 14,* 4520–4528.

Sharp, A.A., Boyle, C.A., & Bekoff, A. (1998). Pyridoxine induced proprio-ceptive neuronal loss during embryogenesis alters both embryonic and posthatching motility [Abstract]. *Society for Neuroscience Abstracts, 24,* 654.2.

Sharp, A.A., Ma, E., & Bekoff, A. (1999). Developmental changes in leg coor-dination in the chick at embryonic days 9, 11, and 13: Uncoupling of ankle movements. *Journal of Neurophysiology, 82,* 2406–2414.

Shatz, C.J. (1990). Impulse activity and the patterning of connections during CNS development. *Neuron, 5,* 745–756.

Sival, D.A., Prechtl, H.F., Sonder, G.H., & Touwen, B.C. (1993). The effect of intra-uterine breech position on postnatal motor functions of the lower limbs. *Early Human Development, 32,* 161–176.

Smotherman, W.P., & Robinson, S.R. (1986). Environmental determinants of behaviour in the rat fetus. *Animal Behaviour, 34,* 1859–1873.

Smotherman, W.P., & Robinson, S.R. (1987). Prenatal expression of species-typical action patterns in the rat fetus (*Rattus norvegicus*). *Journal of Comparative Psychology, 101,* 190–196.

Smotherman, W.P., & Robinson, S.R. (1988). The uterus as environment: The ecology of fetal experience. In E.M. Blass (Ed.), *Handbook of behavioral neurobiology: Vol. 9. Developmental psychobiology and behavioral ecology* (pp. 149–196). New York: Plenum Press.

Smotherman, W.P., & Robinson, S.R. (1989). Cryptopsychobiology: The appearance, disappearance and reappearance of a species-typical action pattern during early development. *Behavioral Neuroscience, 103,* 153–160.

Smotherman, W.P., & Robinson, S.R. (1991). Accessibility of the rat fetus for psychobiological investigation. In H. Shair, G.A. Barr, & M.A. Hofer (Eds.), *Developmental psychobiology: New methods and changing concepts* (pp. 148–166). New York: Oxford University Press.

Smotherman, W.P., & Robinson, S.R. (1996). The development of behavior before birth. *Developmental Psychology, 32,* 425–434.

Smotherman, W.P., & Robinson, S.R. (1998). Prenatal ontogeny of sensory responsiveness and learning. In G. Greenberg & M. Haraway (Eds.), *Comparative psychology: A handbook* (pp. 586–601). New York: Garland.

Snider, W. (1994) Functions of the neurotrophins during nervous system development: What the knockuts are teaching us. *Cell, 77,* 627–638.

Sporns, O., & Edelman, G.M. (1993). Solving Bernstein's problem: A proposal for the development of coordinated movement by selection. *Child Development, 64,* 960–981.

Stein, P.S.G., Grillner, S., Selverston, A.I., & Stuart, D.G. (1997). *Neurons, networks, and motor behavior.* Cambridge, MA: MIT Press.

Thelen, E. (1985). Developmental origins of motor coordination: Leg movements in human infants. *Developmental Psychobiology, 18,* 1–22.

Thelen, E. (1989). The (re)discovery of motor development: Learning new things from an old field. *Developmental Psychology, 25,* 946–949.

Thelen, E. (1994). Three-month-old infants can learn task-specific patterns of interlimb coordination. *Psychological Science, 5,* 280–285.

Thelen, E., Corbetta, D., Kamm, K., Spencer, J.P., Schneider, K., & Zernicke, R.F. (1993). The transition to reaching: Mapping intention and intrinsic dynamics. *Child Development, 64,* 1058–1098.

Thelen, E., Fisher, D.M., & Ridley-Johnson, R. (1984). The relationship between physical growth and a newborn reflex. *Infant Behavior and Development*, 7, 479–493.

Thelen, E., Skala, K.D., & Kelso, J.A. (1987). The dynamic nature of early coordination: Evidence from bilateral leg movements in young infants. *Developmental Psychology*, 23, 179–186.

Thelen, E., & Smith, L.B. (1994). *A dynamic systems approach to the development of cognition and action.* Cambridge: MIT Press.

Thompson, W. (1983). Synapse elimination in neonatal rat muscle is sensitive to pattern of muscle use. *Nature, 302,* 614–616.

Ulrich, B., Ulrich, D., Angulo-Kinzler, R., & Chapman, D. (1997). Sensitivity of infants with and without Down syndrome to intrinsic dynamics. *Research Quarterly for Exercise and Sport, 68,* 10–19.

Vaal, J., van Soest, A.J.K., & Hopkins, B. (2000). Spontaneous kicking behavior in infants: Age-related effects of unilateral weighting. *Developmental Psychobiology, 36,* 111–122.

Van Hartesveldt, C., Sickles, A.E., Porter, J.D., & Stehouwer, D.J. (1990). L-DOPA-induced air-stepping in developing rats. *Developmental Brain Research, 58,* 251–255.

Viala, D., Viala, G., & Fayein, N. (1986). Plasticity of locomotor organization in infant rabbits spinalized shortly after birth. In M.E. Goldberger, A. Gorio, & A. Murray (Eds.), *Development and plasticity of the mammalian spinal cord* (pp. 301–310). New York: Springer.

Westerga, J., & Gramsbergen, A. (1993a). Development of locomotion in the rat: The significance of early movements. *Early Human Development, 34,* 89–100.

Westerga, J., & Gramsbergen, A. (1993b). The effect of early movement restriction: An EMG study in the rat. *Behavioural Brain Research, 59,* 205–209.

Whiting, H.T.A. (Ed.) (1984). *Human motor actions: Bernstein reassessed.* New York: North Holland.

Windle, W.F., & Griffin, A.M. (1931). Observations on embryonic and fetal movements of the cat. *Journal of Comparative Neurology, 52,* 149–188.

Windle, W.F., Minear, W.L., Austin, M.F., & Orr, D.W. (1935). The origin and early development of somatic behavior in the albino rat. *Physiological Zoology, 8,* 156–185.

Windle, W.F., O'Donnell, J.E., & Glasshagle, E.E. (1933). The early development of spontaneous and reflex behavior in cat embryos and fetuses. *Physiological Zoology, 6,* 521–541.

Wong, W.T., Sanes, J.R., & Wong, R.O.L. (1998). Developmentally regulated spontaneous activity in the embryonic chick retina. *Journal of Neuroscience, 18,* 8839–8852.

Zelena, J. (1976). The role of sensory innervation in the development of mechanoreceptors. *Progress in Brain Research, 43,* 49–64.

FURTHER READING

Adolph, K.E. (1997). Learning in the development of infant locomotion. *Monographs of the Society for Research in Child Development, 62* (3, Serial No. 251).

Elman, J.L., Bates, E.A., Johnson, M.H., Karmiloff-Smith, A., Parisi, D., & Plunkett, K. (Eds.). (1996). *Rethinking innateness: A connectionist perspective on development.* Cambridge, MA: MIT Press.

Kelso, J.A.S. (1995). *Dynamic patterns: The self-organization of brain and behavior.* Cambridge, MA: MIT Press.

Michel, G.F., & Moore, C.L. (1995). *Developmental psychobiology: An interdisciplinary science.* Cambridge, MA: MIT Press.

Oyama, S., Griffiths, P.E., & Gray, R.D. (Eds.). (2001). *Cycles of contingency: Developmental systems and evolution.* Cambridge, MA: MIT Press.

Smotherman, W.P., & Robinson, S.R. (Eds.). (1988). *Behavior of the fetus.* Caldwell, NJ: Telford Press.

CHAPTER 6

FETAL MOVEMENTS AND POSTURES: WHAT DO THEY MEAN FOR POSTNATAL DEVELOPMENT?

Johanna I.P. de Vries and Brian Hopkins

ABSTRACT

During the 1960s, the first signs of motility in the chick and rat embryo were revealed to be the products of a spontaneously active nervous system. It was not, however, until the 1970s that the same was generally accepted for the human. This change in opinion was affected by the use of non-invasive, real-time sonography to observe the movements of the human embryo and fetus *in utero*. The neural basis for these endogenously generated movements was ascribed to central pattern generators located at various levels of the spinal cord. After about eight weeks gestational age, motility in the human rapidly differentiates into a number of distinct movement patterns such that the behavioral repertoire seen the full-term newborn is already established by the end of the third trimester of pregnancy. Some of these movements become temporally integrated, leading to the formation of stable behavioral states toward the end of pregnancy. We consider the functional significance of these developments for postnatal life as we do for changes in the positioning and posture of the fetus. Some movements and postures appear to be specific adaptations to life in the womb and for the process of delivery, while others can be interpreted as in some way being "anticipatory" functions required for postnatal development. Two features of human prenatal development stand out: one is that the first movements are generated on the basis of minimal neural and muscle differentiation, and the other that wakefulness really only emerges after birth, with the possible exception of the nonvocal components of crying. We conclude with comments on the import of prenatal motor development for psychological development and parenting after birth.

INTRODUCTION

Sonographic observations have demonstrated that *human embryonic motility* initially consists of stereotyped shifts in the body contours that are discernible at seven weeks of gestation, and which consist of lateral bendings of the head and rump. This specific movement pattern disappears within one week and is followed by a veritable explosion of more variable ones appearing within a period of ten weeks. They remain through birth, either for a few months or as a manifestation of behavior into adulthood. The first recognizable posture consists of the embryo lying on the back near to the uterine wall, with the extremities maintained in close proximity to the body. By eight weeks, the fetus moves freely throughout the amniotic fluid and as a consequence is able to adopt a range of different positions (namely, supine, prone, sideways, upside down, and even sitting), with the limbs assuming a variety of extended and flexed postures. Subsequently, there is a succession of clear-cut preferential postures involving the head and the arms, such that the former becomes increasingly lateralized during the final trimester of a full-term pregnancy.

In what follows, we elaborate further on this developmental scenario. To do so we must discuss a diverse range of topics: the emergence of fetal behavioral states; interrelationships between neuromuscular and behavioral development; and the adaptive significance of movements and postures for life in the womb, the birth process, and for subsequent postnatal development. Before embarking on this topical discussion, we begin with a brief coverage of the historical background of research on the behavioral development of the human fetus.

FETAL RESEARCH: PAST AND PRESENT

In the past, the prenatal development of motility was accounted for in biologically implausible ways, while at the same time age-related changes in posture were all but ignored. Largely through the dominating influence of *reflexology*—a close cousin of *behaviorism* and lasting until the middle of the last century—all embryonic and fetal motility was ascribed to the effects of external stimulation, although their sources *in utero* were often unknown (Hooker, 1952). Movements, rather than postures, were the focus of interest as the former lent themselves more readily to being treated as observable responses (i.e., reflexes) to what constituted nonphysiological forms of elicitation (e.g., the use of horse hair to stimulate skin at various parts of the body). It is important to realize that this ascription was derived from eliciting responses in fetuses that were in a terminal condition and operatively removed from the uterus at various ages. In such a condition, *reflexes* can still be elicited, but the expression of spontaneous movements is severely repressed.

A radical change in our understanding of the nature of human prenatal development came about not through a shift in theoretical opinion, but rather in the first instance due to a technical innovation that enabled non-invasive observations of fetuses in their physiological environment. The innovation, of course, was *real-time, linear array ultrasound* that was incorporated into fetal research during the early 1970s, and which was shown not to induce fetal movements (Hertz, Timor-Tritsch, Dierker, Chick, & Rosen, 1979). Since that time, a wealth of studies have revealed convincing evidence that the movements of the developing fetus are spontaneously generated and appear for the first time at the same ages as those that can be elicited in the exteriorized fetus. Some linked this evidence to *central pattern generators* situated at various levels of the neuroaxis, a theory whose beginnings can be credited to the pioneering work of Brown (1914). In general, the prevailing opinion now is that there is no pre-reflexogenic period during which reflexes are established prior to spontaneous movements.

If *reflexology* is no longer an appropriate paradigm for studying human prenatal development, it would be misplaced to contend that the fetus does not respond to extrauterine forms of stimulation. The only qualification we add is that responses (e.g., increases in motor activity) to particular sorts of stimulation (e.g., auditory, vibro-acoustical) are state-dependent (de Vries & van Geijn, 1994). An overview of this burgeoning area of research can be found in chapter 2 by Lecanuet et al.

Dating from the end of the nineteenth century, and intimated in the theory of recapitulation as expounded by Ernst Haeckel (1839–1919), the concept of *ontogenetic adaptation* has, since the 1980s, re-established itself in the context of trying to understand the nexus between pre- and postnatal development, largely through the writings of Oppenheim (2005). Holding that certain structures and functions are adaptations to life in the egg or womb with no necessary connections to development after birth, it has proved to be a challenging concept in its application to human ontogeny. In short, as we shall see later, it challenges the widely held view of all embracing continuities between fetal and postnatal development. For now, however, we turn to what is known about the emergence and development of discrete movement patterns in the human fetus.

DEVELOPMENT OF SPECIFIC MOVEMENT PATTERNS

Fifteen of the various movements that have so far been identified in the human fetus can be classified into three broad categories: whole body movements, isolated movements of the extremities, and perioral movements. Those that cannot be assigned to one of these categories are considered under "Remaining movements" (Table 6.1). It should be noted with regard to the category "Whole body movements" that startles are initiated in the extremities only and hiccups in the diaphragm. The abrupt character of both movements, however, results in passive displacements of the whole body.

Developmental Origins: First Ages of Appearance

The first recognizable pattern, sideways *head-rump movements* (HRMs), appearing at the end of the embryonic period when the *crown-rump length* (CRL) is slightly more than 2 cm, was previously labeled only as "just discernible movements" due to insufficient imaging resolution at the time (de Vries, Visser, & Prechtl, 1982). With the subsequent use of high resolution imaging by means of transvaginal rather than transabdominal sonography, it became possible to discern that such movements consisted of repetitive displacements of the head and rump. From studies on *chick embryos* (Bradley, 2001) and *rat embryos* (Bekoff, 2001), it is well established that the earliest forms of motility are neurogenic in origin and the product of one or more spinal pattern generators whose output comes to be modulated by sensory feedback. Such may be the case for the frequently occurring HRMs. What is known is that their emergence in the human corresponds to the segmentation of the cranial end of *neuromeres* that are high in mitotic activity and with the formation of *neuromuscular junctions* (Larsen, 2001).

There is one important point to make about the ensuing proliferation of movement types that occurs over the following couple of months or so. All either disappear or undergo qualitative changes in early postnatal life, with the exception of stretches, yawns, and hiccups. These complex movement patterns persist throughout the life

Table 6.1: A Four-Part Classification of Different Types of Movement Patterns Identified in the Healthy Human Fetus

A. Whole Body Movements

Type	First Age	Description	Comments	References
Sideward head and rump movements (HRMs)	7.5–8 w	Small, stereotyped sideways bending of the head and rump occurring for 1–2 seconds about every 2 minutes[a]	They can be found throughout the mammalian order and have been demonstrated, for example, in the mouse embryo[b]	[a] de Vries (1997) [b] Suzue & Shinodo (1999)
Startles	8.5–10 w	An abrupt generalized and stereotyped movement always starting in the limbs and often spreading to the trunk and neck. Mostly occurring as single events lasting about 1 second, they may sometimes follow each other in rapid succession with an interval of a few seconds between them[a]	Seen most frequently up to 9 weeks and decreasing thereafter, they do not induce changes in the upper and lower extremities, but can lift the fetus from the lying surface[b]	[a] de Vries et al. (1982) [b] de Vries et al. (1985)
General movements (GMs)	8.5–9.5 w	Gross movements varying in speed and amplitude involving the whole body, but which lack a particular sequencing of body parts. Performed in an apparently fluent and elegant manner, they give the impression of waxing and waning in intensity with gradual onsets	Perhaps the most thoroughly studied movement pattern, they increase to about 15% of observation time by 15 weeks and remain at this level until the end of pregnancy.[c] Evident until about 4 months after birth, they undergo two main qualitative changes	[a] Hopkins (2003) [b] de Vries et al. (1985) [c] de Vries et al. (1985) [d] Hadders-Algra & Prechtl (1992) [e] Hopkins & Prechtl (1984)

continued

Table 6.1: continued

A. Whole Body Movements

Type	First Age	Description	Comments	References
		and offsets. They may last from a few seconds to 1 minute.[a] During GMs in the first half of pregnancy, and especially when involving alternating leg movements that resemble neonatal stepping, the fetus can undergo radical changes in position, some of which look like backward somersaults. Such changes in position can be completed within about 2 seconds[b]	following preterm GMs typified by excessive variation and complexity as well as many movements of the trunk[d]: "writhing" quality disappearing at 6–8 weeks to be replaced by ones with a "fidgety" appearence[e]	
Hiccups	9–11 w	Abrupt displacements of the diaphragm, chest, and abdomen. Single events last about 1 second, but more frequently occur repetitively at intervals of 2–3 seconds for periods of up to 20 minutes. Like startles, they may lift the fetus from the lying surface[a]	Strictly speaking, they are not the same as the other three generalized movements, as those of the extremities are not generated actively. However, they can be so forceful that the whole fetus is moved passively. They have a high rate of occurrence, the value for 11–17 weeks being about 100 per hour[b]	[a] de Vries et al. (1982) [b] de Vries et al. (1985)
Stretches	10–15 w	Complex, but quite stereotyped, movement carried out slowly with a clear sequence of body parts: head backward, trunk arching, and arms lifting. Only occur singly and lasting for several seconds[a]	Occurs infrequently during pregnancy (e.g., 0–9 times per hour at 10–19 w)[b]	[a] de Vries et al. (1982) [b] de Vries et al. (1985)

B. Isolated Movements of the Extremities

Type	First Age	Description	Comments	References
Isolated arm movements	9–10.5 w	Movement of an arm in the absence of other body parts moving and frequently accompanied by finger extensions, except when the arm moves slowly. They vary in speed and amplitude as well as in direction[a]	Incidence increases rapidly during the first half of pregnancy[b]	[a] de Vries et al. (1982) [b] de Vries et al. (1985)
Isolated leg movements	9–12 w	Leg moved in isolation without accompaniment of other body parts. As with isolated arm movements, they vary in speed and amplitude, but less so in direction[a]	Both isolated arm and leg movements can be performed in a fast and jerky manner either as a single event (twitch) or repeatedly at a rate of about 3–4 per second (clonus). Twitches and cloni occur not only in isolation, but also superimposed on GMs or may precede them[b]	[a] de Vries et al. (1982) [b] de Vries et al. (1985)
Isolated head movements	9.5–12 w	Retroflexion, anteflexion, and rotation are carried out slowly, occur as isolated events and persist for a few seconds up to 1 minute before the head returns to the original position[a]	After 11 weeks, retroflexions occur most frequently and large anteflexions least or sometimes not all during 1-hour recordings.[b] After birth, head anteflexion is constrained by gravity and does not appear again until 9–12 weeks after birth[c]	[a] de Vries et al. (1982) [b] de Vries et al. (1985) [c] Hopkins & Prechtl (1984)

continued

Table 6.1: continued

C. Perioral Movements

Type	First Age	Description	Comments	References
Jaw open-ings	10.5–12.5 w	Occurring as a single or repeated event, each opening lasts less than 1 second to 5 seconds, and can be slow or quick and variable in extent of opening[a]	After 12 weeks, it is a frequently occurring event (median > 20 per hour), and up to 15 weeks a single wide opening is more common than later. After 15 weeks, irregular repeated openings occur more often than before, with durations lasting from 1–5 seconds[b]	[a] de Vries et al. (1982) [b] de Vries et al. (1985)
Yawns	11.5–13.5 w	Like a stretch, a complex movement consisting of a slow and prolonged opening of the jaws, lasting several seconds, followed by quick closure and often accompanied by head retroflexion and elevation of the arms[a]	As with stretches, an infrequently occurring event (e.g., 2–5 times at 12–19 weeks).[b] Phylogenetically, it is an old behavior that has been observed in reptiles, birds, and other mammals[c]	[a] de Vries et al. (1982) [b] de Vries et al. (1985) [c] Argiolis & Melis (1988)
Tongue protrusions	13–14 w	An infrequently occurring movement that accompanies jaw opening[a]	After birth, human newborns match tongue protrusions and jaw openings with those same movements modeled by an adult, thus indicating an ability to imitate behaviors that are part of spontaneous repertoire[b]	[a] Ianniruberto & Tajani (1981) [b] Meltzoff & Moore (1983)

D. Remaining Movements

Type	First Age	Description	Comments	References
Breathing movements	10–16.5 w	Paradoxical and simultaneous movements of the diaphragm (downward), chest (inward), and abdomen (outward). Displacements of the diaphragm can be small or large and less than 1 second, with larger ones resembling a sigh. Sometimes appearing in conjunction with jaw opening, swallowing, and GMs, they can occur as isolated events but more often as repetitive regular or irregular movements. The earliest ones tend to have a regular pattern[a]	No amniotic fluid enters the lungs during these movements and a similar paradoxical pattern is seen in preterm infants as well as during REM sleep in the full-term infant. A frequent pattern throughout pregnancy (e.g., > 100 per hour after 13 weeks), they have age-specific breath-to-breath intervals: 2–3 seconds at 10 weeks, <1 second at 17 weeks,[b] and about 1.3 seconds after 30 weeks.[c] Their rate, unlike any other movement pattern, is related to glucose intake: an increase after maternal food and a delay of 1 week in their appearance with fetuses of diabetic mothers[d]	[a] de Vries et al. (1982) [b] de Vries et al. (1985) [c] Trudinger et al. (1980) [d] Mulder & Visser (1991)
Hand–face contacts	10–12 w	Slow movement of the hand during which the digits extend and flex and 1–5 of them eventuate in contact with the face[a]	Head movements, especially rotations, facilitate contacting the face with the hand. Their median incidence increases from 10–15 weeks and decreases up to 19 weeks,[b] an outcome supported in another study that found them to continue to decrease up to 37 weeks.[c] A report of thumb sucking as early as 10–15 weeks[d]	[a] de Vries et al. (1982) [b] de Vries et al. (1985) [c] Sparling et al. (1999) [d] Hepper et al. (1998) [e] de Vries et al. (2001)

continued

Table 6.1: continued

Type	First Age	Description	Comments	References
			was not found in a subsequent longitudinal study from 12–38 weeks in which it occurred only 4 times[e]	
Sucking & swallowing	12.5–16 w	Rhythmical and regular bursts of jaw opening at the rate of about 1 per second and of varying length, followed by swallowing (displacements of tongue and cheek) indicating that the fetus is ingesting amniotic fluid[a]	Number of bursts increases slowly during the first half of pregnancy.[a] By 14 weeks, the rate of sucking is similar to that of full-term infants during breast feeding. Despite a wide variation, the amount of amniotic fluid ingested increases from about 10–20 ml at 10 weeks to about 800 ml at 24 weeks, increasing only slightly thereafter[b]	[a] de Vries et al. (1982) [b] Brace (1997)
Eye movements	16–23 w	Repetitive movements that are slow (and rolling) or rapid (and nystagmoid-like). They are observed as flicker in the ultrasound echo between the orbit or as changes in the position of the echo of the lens[a]	Slow movements appear first, followed by rapid ones at about 22 weeks[b]	[a] Bots et al. (1981) [b] Birnholz (1981)

The first type of movement pattern (HRM) can be discerned sonographically at the end of the embryonic period, by which time the upper and lower extremities have become distinctive entities relative to the rump. Together with a description of each pattern, the range of their respective first ages of appearance are given in weeks (w). The entries under "Comments" mainly refer to what is known about the subsequent developmental course of each one.

span, but without changing their pattern. The fetal yawn (Fig. 6.1) is immediately recognizable for its adult-like phenotype, and when observers are confronted with a real-time recording of it, they find it difficult to repress a yawn. Although its functions are unknown, it is regulated by the *brain stem* (Sandyk, 1999) and under the control of central *neurotransmitters* and *neuropeptides* (Argiolis & Melis, 1998). With both yawning and stretches being mediated by the release of *dopamine*, it is possible that they are triggered by the dopamine agonist system during pregnancy. Testing this suggestion, in terms of whether they follow changes in *oxytocin* levels, will be difficult given the low rates of occurrence of both movements.

Visible for about two weeks at most, HRMs are replaced by *general movements* (GMs). What happens to GMs and other movement patterns that burst onto the scene in the next couple of months? More specifically, do they abide by particular developmental trends?

Developmental Trends

In dealing with this topic, it is necessary to realize that a fetus grows rapidly between eight and twenty weeks. In fact, there is a seven-fold increase in *crown-rump length* across this age period, culminating in a mean value of 16 cm by twenty weeks. At this length, the fetus is too large for the whole body to be viewed by one ultrasound scanner. Thus, the use of two scanners is required after this age if the same movement patterns are to be observed from twenty weeks onward. In one longitudinal study to adopt this approach, fetal movements were recorded from twenty to thirty-six weeks at one-month intervals (Roodenburg, Wladimiroff, van Es, & Prechtl, 1991). The *quantitative trends* that can be extracted from this study can be compared with those revealed by a previous one (de Vries, Visser, & Prechtl, 1985), as movement patterns were classified in the same way on both occasions. The latter study consisted of serial recordings made with one scanner from eight to nineteen weeks.

Commonalities between both studies amounted to developmental trends for the incidence per hour of seven movement patterns (*startles, hiccups, head rotations, head retroflexions, hand–face contacts, jaw openings, breathing movements*), and for percentage of recording time for an eighth category (GMs). For these movements, trends from eight to thirty-six weeks are depicted in Figure 6.2. Despite a wide range of individual differences across age, most of these movement patterns show an initial increase in incidence (or percentage) followed by a

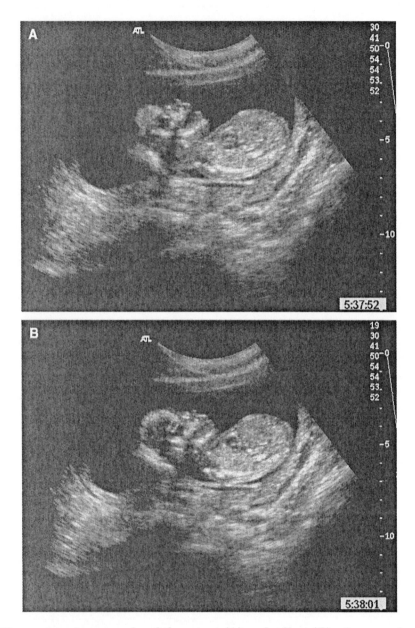

Figure 6.1. An example of the onset (A) and offset (B) of a yawn in a fetus at sixteen weeks of gestational age. The head of the fetus is on the left-hand side of the image.

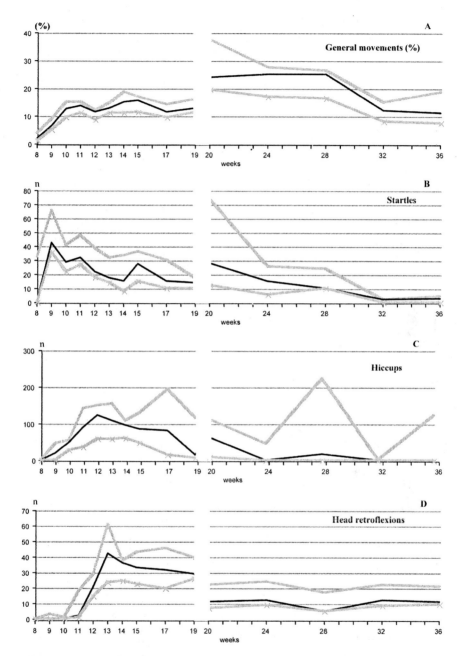

Figure 6.2. Median (*black line*) and interquartile range (*gray lines*) for eight movement patterns from eight to thirty-six weeks of gestational age. (*Source*: Figure adapted from de Vries, Visser, & Prechtl, 1982; Roodenburg et al., 1991.)

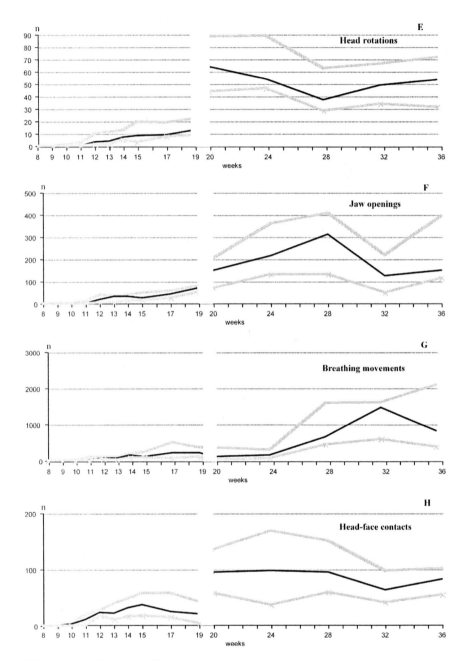

Figure 6.2. (continued).

decrease just before or during the third trimester. The most noticeable exception is breathing movements that continue to increase, especially during the last trimester.

Data for six other movement patterns, which also show substantial individual differences, are only available either from eight to nineteen weeks, or from twenty to thirty-six weeks. In the first instance (Fig. 6.3), *isolated arm movements*, as well as *sucking and swallowing*, reveal a trend of increasing incidence up to twenty weeks. In contrast, *isolated leg movements*, which occur relatively infrequently, gradually increase in number and then decrease just prior to twenty weeks. From twenty weeks onward (Fig. 6.4), the frequency of occurrence per hour of both GMs and *stretches*, but not *eye movements*, continue to decrease up to thirty-six weeks. Stretches, however, have a negligible incidence during the first half of pregnancy (de Vries et al., 1985).

Generally speaking, most movements show a trend that decreases, particularly after twenty weeks, and as such probably reflects the imposition of increasing intrauterine restrictions due to the rapid growth of the fetus from the second trimester onward. This growth is captured by measurements of *crown-rump length* that is 2.3 cm at eight weeks, increasing to 20 cm by twenty-four weeks, and attaining 35 cm by forty weeks. Movement patterns not abiding by this trend (namely, *head rotations, breathing movements, hand–face contacts*) would appear to be unaffected by such restrictions, in terms of a decreasing frequency with which they are expressed. Finally, data are lacking on the quantitative development of isolated limb movements and *sucking and swallowing* after twenty weeks.

Summing the durations of all movement patterns to derive a measure of total activity provides another slant on the development of fetal motility (de Vries, Visser, & Prechtl, 1988). Attaining a median value of 20% of recording time by eleven weeks, total activity increases only marginal thereafter. From this age onward, the fetuses moved more than 85% of the recording time. Until twenty weeks, periods without movements were only short-lasting (median values two to six minutes). Thus, the large amount of *total activity*, together with the short periods of quiescence, accounts for the first sonographers' incorrect conclusion that ultrasound induces fetal motility. Furthermore, the chances of obtaining periods of inactivity sufficiently long enough to examine fetal responses to stimulation is so small that it explains why such studies are overwhelmingly restricted to the second half of pregnancy.

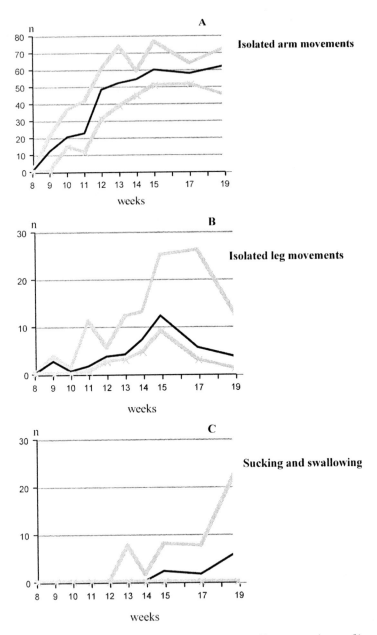

Figure 6.3. Median (*black line*) and interquartile range (*gray lines*) for three movement patterns from eight to nineteen weeks of gestational age. (*Source*: Figure adapted from de Vries et al., 1985.)

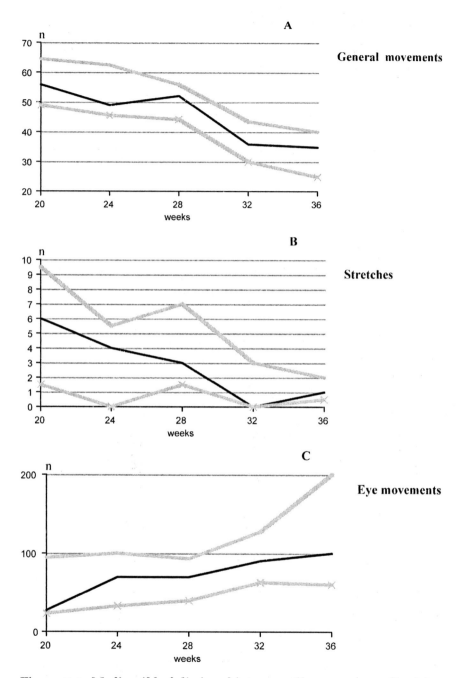

Figure 6.4. Median (*black line*) and interquartile range (*gray lines*) for three movement patterns from twenty to thirty-six weeks of gestational age. (*Source*: Figure adapted from Roodenburg et al., 1991.)

FROM MOVEMENTS TO BEHAVIORAL STATES

With increasing gestational age, the distribution of GMs over an observation period of one to two hours begins to take on a distinct rest-activity cycle. By thirty-six to thirty-eight weeks, the cycle of GMs has assumed a strong association with the absence and presence of *eye movements* on the one hand and certain *heart rate patterns* on the other, giving rise to recognizable and stable *behavioral states* (Nijhuis, Prechtl, Martin, & Bots, 1982), which are summarized in Table 6.2.

While movements of the extremities and eyes constitute necessary state criteria for the fetus, others are treated as being state

Table 6.2: Four Behavioral States Identified in Healthy Human Fetus at Thirty-Eight Weeks Pregnancy Duration

State	Body Movements	Eye Movements	Heart Rate Pattern
1F	None, but quiescence can be interrupted by gross movements that are mostly startles	Absent	FHRP A: small oscillation band within which isolated accelerations can occur related to movements
2F	Frequent and periodic gross movements that are mainly stretches and retroflexions as well as movements of the extremities (i.e., general movements)	Both REMs and SEMs continually present	FHRP B: wider oscillation band than FHRP A, with frequent accelerations during movements
3F	No general or other gross movements present	Continually present	FHRP C: stable, but with wider oscillation bandwidth than FHRP A and no accelerations
4F	Vigorous and continual general movements, including many trunk rotations	When observable, they are continuously present	FHRP D: unstable, with large and sustained accelerations

All of these behavioral states have a close similarity to those in the full-term newborn, but using somewhat different criteria. FHRP: fetal heart pattern of which there are four different types (A, B, C, and D); REM: rapid eye movements; SEM: slow eye movements. *Source*: From Nijhuis et al., 1982.

concomitants during gestational ages of thirty-six to forty weeks. The state-dependent nature of the latter for their expression is most clearly evident for the two *states* 1F and 2F. Thus, for example, the fetal breathing rhythm is more regular in 1F than 2F (Nijhuis et al., 1982). The same is the case for *mouthing movements*, as well as for *sucking and swallowing* (van Woerden et al., 1988).

To complete the picture on findings concerning behavioral states, three comments are in order. First, even though such states are robust enough to maintain their integrity during labor (Griffin, Caron, & van Geijn, 1985), they can become disorganized following a *maternal alcohol intake* of only two glasses of wine (Mulder, Morrsink, van der Schee, & Visser, 1998). Second, coordination among the cyclical patterns of heart rate variation, eye movements, and body movements have been reported as being present before thirty-six weeks (Visser, Poelman-Weesjes, Cohen, & Bekedam, 1987), suggesting a more gradual development of behavioral states than a sudden emergence at this age. Third, all findings to date, including those on the state-dependent effects of external stimulation, have focused on the two sleep states that display incidental (1F) and frequently occurring (2F) movements. Why then has the state with vigorous and continual GMs (4F), thought to be indicative of *fetal wakefulness*, all but been ignored?

FETAL WAKEFULNESS

The question of whether the fetus manifests states of wakefulness remains largely unanswered. One reason is that state 3F occurs too infrequently for reliable observations to be made, and another reason is that the criteria for 4F cannot be properly applied due to a strong association between FHRP D and motility in this state (Nijhuis et al., 1982). A third reason is that *crying*, when treated as including the forceful expression of air from the lungs necessary for vocalizing, cannot be expected in the intrauterine environment. If, however, this criterion is disbanded, then evidence for some measure of fetal crying becomes possible. Such evidence should rest on verifying the suggestion that nonvocal accompaniments of crying are developed before birth, with the transition to the extrauterine environment resulting in the establishment of the vocal component (Hopkins, 2000). What prenatally developed nonvocal behaviors would form part of the act of crying postnatally? Possible candidates include breathing movements, jaw openings, sucking and swallowing, and movements of the face.

Already during the first twenty weeks of pregnancy, fetal *breathing movements* sometimes co-occur with *jaw openings* and *swallowing* (de Vries, Visser, & Prechtl, 1982). Although presently unknown, it is more than likely that such co-occurrences develop in a systematic fashion during the second half of pregnancy. Initially appearing as isolated events, the jaw movements begin to be performed repetitively between twelve and twenty weeks (Table 6.1). As for sucking and swallowing, it involves both tongue movements and displacements of the larynx. Recently, the increasing complexity of lip, jaw, tongue, and laryngeal movements has been elegantly demonstrated by means of 4-D ultrasound (Miller, Sonier, & Macedonia, 2003). Thus, all the necessary movements required for modulating vocalizations after birth are established and subjected to practice in a different functional context before birth. But what about the expressive aspect of crying as conveyed by movements of the face?

Descriptions of the developmental course of *facial movements* in the human fetus are still limited. Nevertheless, it has long been known that the innervation of well-formed *facial muscles* begins at about eight weeks (Crelin, 1969) and is complete by eighteen to twenty-nine weeks of gestation (Gasser, 1967). Moreover, all but one of the discrete *facial actions* seen in adults can be identified in *preterm newborns* shortly after the beginning of what corresponds to the last trimester of pregnancy (Oster, 1978). One such action, detected by 4-D ultrasound in the last trimester fetus, is "scowling" that becomes associated with expressions of anger during postnatal life (Kurjak et al., 2003). As for the expressive gestalt known as the "cry face," examples of it obtained from ultrasound recordings suggest its emergence by the middle of the third trimester (Birnholz & Farrell, 1984).

Before turning to the functional significance of fetal movements raised by the issue of whether crying is established in some respects before birth, we hasten to add a qualification: *crying* probably never assumes the mantle of being credited as a stable state during fetal life, such that it lasts for at least three minutes (Nijhuis et al., 1982). What might be expected is that the act of crying, in terms of its nonvocal components, emerges as a fleeting transition between sleep and other forms of wakefulness in the last trimester. Certainly, it will be fleeting if a study comparing fetal and newborn behavioral states in the same subjects was correct in concluding that only 1%–2% of total prenatal recording time was consistent with postnatal wakefulness (Junge, 1979). Despite these qualifications, the admittedly circumstantial evidence cited leads us to the belief that the developmental origins of crying are rooted in prenatal life, and that the act itself does not appear *de novo* in its entirety only after birth.

FUNCTIONAL SIGNIFICANCE OF FETAL MOVEMENTS

Perhaps the first question to ask is this: why does the fetus moves so much? *Embryonic motility* is a widespread phenomenon in both vertebrates and invertebrates, and thus it must have been selected in evolution to serve some function or functions. Movements, however, expend energy resources that are increasingly drawn upon by a rapidly developing brain in a human fetus. For the human, this conflict for resources is partially resolved by the incursion of distinct periods of activity and rest, together with an equally distinct *diurnal rhythm* in the incidence of fetal movements by around twenty to twenty-two weeks (de Vries, Visser, Mulder, & Prechtl, 1987). It is from this age onward that the cerebral hemispheres start to develop rapidly. What functions then does the movement repertoire of the fetus serve? A number of suggestions, but no definitive answers, can be made in response to this question.

The first suggestion is somewhat pessimistic: fetal motility could just be an epiphenomenon of neural maturation with no particular adaptive function—at least not *in utero*. As such, it reminds us that cells, tissues, and organs mature in advance of their ultimate function, a view encapsulated by Anokhin's (1964) concept of *systemogenesis*. In this way, fetuses born too soon can survive in the extrauterine environment.

Another suggestion is that some fetal movements are necessary precursors of functions after birth, such as *yawns, stretches, breathing movements, eye movements,* and *head rotations*. Such a view fits well with current epigenetic notions about developmental continuities between prenatal and postnatal life. In fact, it consists of two interrelated versions. The first version is that fetal motility represents an indispensable form of practice or use for behaviors that realize their functions postnatally. For example, prenatal *breathing movements* may promote the development of lung tissue and of the diaphragmatic and intercostal muscles. This contention gains support from the observation derived from animal experiments that the abolition of breathing movements, by means of high spinal cord transaction, eventuates in *lung hypoplasia* (Liggins, Vilos, Kitterman, & Lee, 1981). Other examples include the activity-dependent nature of *apoptosis, synapse elimination,* and the change from transient *polyinnervation* to monoinnervation of muscles fibers (Oppenheim, 1981). The second version is that prenatal sensory experiences serve to shape the development of mature behavior, a "continuity" standpoint most closely associated with Kuo (1967) and his followers. More recently, it has become increasingly recognized that movement and sensory experience during prenatal life are not mutually exclusive entities (Smotherman & Robinson, 1988). Rather, certain movement patterns (e.g., swallowing amniotic fluid whose contents are influenced by maternal diet) generate particular (chemo-) sensory experiences (e.g., leading to taste and odor preferences), which in turn promote increasing control over these movements.

A third suggestion stems from the "discontinuity" concept of *ontogenetic adaptations* (Oppenheim, 1981). What this concept stresses is the need to recognize a whole class of ontogenetic events that are important in their own right, and which are not just stepping stones to adulthood. Accordingly, some behaviors may represent transient phenotypes or age-specific adaptations restricted to the intrauterine environment, and thus without consequence for postnatal development. Fetal movements appearing to comply with this class of events are *GMs*, with or without alternating leg movements that can result in changes in position. The same applies to startles and hiccups, which often result in temporarily lifting the fetus from the resting surface. Among other things, such movements may prevent adhesions and local stasis in the circulation of fetal skin. For its part, swallowing may function to regulate the amount of amniotic fluid, thereby countering the risk of *polyhydramnios* that can result in a *preterm birth*. In addition, swallowing *amniotic fluid* can supply the fetus with supplementary nutrients as well as growth-enhancing factors beneficial to the maturation of the *gastrointestinal tract* (Mulvihill, Stone, Debes, & Fonkalrud, 1985). Finally, swallowing can be used to exemplify a fourth interpretation: fetal movements are both a prenatal adaptation and a necessary precursor for their subsequent expression in postnatal life.

There are no clear-cut guidelines for deciding between these various speculations about the functional relevance of the fetal movement repertoire. Wolff (1986) elegantly put his finger on the problem in pointing out that it is difficult to devise critical experiments that would establish whether early functions contribute nothing to later ones, or that all antecedent conditions are preparations for subsequent developmental states, with the former somehow being integrated into the latter. In particular, inconvertible evidence for the existence of *ontogenetic adaptations* in human development has yet to be found, while a "continuity" interpretation based on epigenetic principles will always be easier to find. For example, the various forms of fetal motility might provide the bases for later, seemingly different, behaviors, not necessarily just in terms of facilitating appropriate neuromuscular differentiation, but in the context of *operational principles*, such as serial order control (Lashley, 1952) derived from earlier movements. Wolff (1986) then goes on to suggest that such functional acquisitions could be exported to entirely different movement patterns after birth, while the observed fetal movements are in fact deleted from the repertoire.

Having raised the issue of the adaptive significance of fetal movements for neuromuscular development, we will now move on to consider how changes in both co-develop during human prenatal and early postnatal development.

FETAL MOVEMENTS AND NEUROMUSCULAR DEVELOPMENT

The dividing line between the embryonic and fetal periods in the human is taken to be about seven weeks after conception, which corresponds to the time of closure of the secondary plate (Wilson, 1973). Beyond the embryonic period, there is a lack of information about the neurogenesis of the human fetal nervous system relative to what we know about functional development during the fetal period. In particular, this assertion applies to the neuromaturation of the *spinal cord* in the humans. Nevertheless, the fact that fetal movement patterns remain recognizable during gestation and beyond supports the view that the mediating neural substrates and connectivity are in all probability correctly established from the start (Bekoff, 1981). In addition to neurogenesis and synaptogenesis, we also need to consider myelination and myogenesis, or muscle development.

Neurogenesis and Myogenesis in the Embryonic Period

The wealth of findings from the more abundant literature on *neurogenesis* in the human embryo is restricted to three relevant comments, derived largely from Larsen (2001). First, by three weeks, nerve cells are present and the nervous system begins the process of differentiation. Also, at about the same age, *limb buds* have been formed, with the forelimbs being evident a couple of days before the hindlimbs. Second, two weeks later, neural innervation follows the separation of *myotomes* (from which skeletal muscle develops) in the trunk into a ventral and a dorsal root. Third, by seven to eight weeks, a ventral motor column is clearly formed in the *cervical spinal cord*, consisting of three components: motoneurons, interneurons, and primary afferents. They are not yet connected. Further up-to-date information on both neurogenesis and *myogenesis*, as well as the *musculoskeletal system* (more generally during the embryonic period), can be found in a succinct and readable overview by Parson and Ribchester (2005).

Synaptogenesis

Turning from neurogenesis to *synaptogenesis*, electron microscopical studies of the *human cervical spinal cord* have revealed three phases (Okada & Kojima, 1984). By eight to ten weeks, there is a major progression in synaptogenesis with the emergence of connections between interneurons and sensory fibers, and thus completion of the closure of the spinal *reflex arc*. In addition, *neuromuscular junctions* are beginning to form. It is around this age that an increase in the variety of spontaneous movements can be observed and spinal reflexes reliably elicited, while the synaptic innervation of cervical motoneurons has only just begun. In addition, the upper and lower extremities undergo a ninety-degree torsion in opposite directions, so that the elbows point dorsally and the knees point ventrally (Langman, 1963). This change in so-called growth *movements* (Blechschmidt, 1977) greatly facilitates the task of making distinctions among fetal movement patterns by means of ultrasound recordings.

The next critical phase in synaptogenesis occurs during the eleventh week, when there is about an eight-fold increase in (mainly) excitatory *axodendritic synapses* on *motoneurons*, with a much smaller advance in the number of axosomatic synapses. This phase coincides with the appearance of startles, isolated movements, and a quantitative jump in the presence of *GMs*. The third phase takes place between thirteen and fifteen weeks, with a three-fold increase in the density of *axosomatic synapses* that are chiefly inhibitory in nature. Associated with this increase is a marked decrease in the number of *startles*, but there are no other striking correlates with either quantitative or qualitative changes in movement patterns.

Myelination

Much has been written about the *myelination* of pathways before birth and postnatally (e.g., Gilles, Shankle, & Dooling, 1983)

Myelination of nerve fibers in the spinal cord begins about a week after the third phase of synaptogenesis (Okada & Kojima, 1984). The effect of myelination is to increase conduction velocity and to reduce neuronal discharge fatigue, with the latter having more significance during prenatal life. Thus, one might expect fetal movements or bursts of activity to be sustained for longer than prior to twelve weeks. The only evidence in support of this expectation is that after twelve weeks, and particularly at fourteen weeks, epochs of *GMs* do become more prolonged (de Vries, Visser, & Prechtl, 1982).

Before addressing prenatal muscle development, we ask a question that brings us into an area of some controversy: do supraspinal structures begin to exert an influence on spinal centers during fetal development?

Supraspinal Influences

Almost fifty years ago, light microscopy studies led to the claim that *corticospinal tract* (CST) axons project to the medulla by eight weeks, the lumbar spinal cord by eighteen weeks, and sacral levels by twenty-nine weeks, with decussation beginning before fifteen weeks (Humphrey, 1960). More recently, it has been reported that these axons have attained the *mid-thoracic spinal cord* by seventeen weeks (Okada & Kojima, 1984) and the cervical spinal cord by at least twenty-four weeks (Eyre, Miller, Clowry, Conway, & Watts, 2000). The nub of the controversy is that evidence for CST projections is much more readily obtained than evidence for functional CST connections.

In a pioneering study, using *transcranial magnetic stimulation* and EMG recordings for the biceps muscle, Eyre, Miller, and Ramesh (1991) concluded that functional CST connections have been established by birth, and thus during the last trimester of pregnancy. Using the same approach, a subsequent study could not find evidence of any *EMG responses* before one year, and therefore it questioned the presence of such connections in the newborn (Müller, Homberg, & Lenard, 1991). There was, however, an important difference between the two studies: the first study evoked EMG responses from muscles in a relaxed state, while the other did so when they were active. Thus, the issue of whether functional CST connections are achieved prenatally (or at least by birth) is still not resolved. Certainly, if they are achieved prenatally, then they bear no interpretable relationship to what is known about the development of fetal movements during the third trimester. An alternative interpretation is that the CST may form transient projections or '"pioneering" fibers that lay down the pathways for subsequent functional connections between the motor cortex and the spinal cord to follow, and begin to assume adaptive significance some time later in postnatal life. But what about the muscles they eventually innervate at the various levels of the spinal cord?

Muscle Development

With the onset of movements at about seven to eight weeks, and during their development up to mid-pregnancy, the differentiation of skeletal muscles has hardly begun. Some forty years ago, Dubowitz (1966) divided the prenatal development of human muscle into three phases on the basis of enzyme histochemistry of fibers. In phase 1, from early fetal life to about twenty weeks, there is no obvious differentiation into distinct *muscle fiber types*. During phase 2, from twenty to twenty-six weeks, a clear differentiation takes place into two fiber types corresponding to Type I ("slow-twitch") and Type II ("fast-twitch"), as found in mature muscle. The majority consists of undifferentiated *Type II C fibers*, while the smaller number of Type I are in effect *Wohlfart-B fibers*. Thus, caution is required in comparing these earliest fiber types with mature Types I and II. Phase 3, from about thirty weeks to full term, shows a pattern of differentiation similar to that of mature muscle, with an approximately equal number of Type I and Type II fibers.

Relatively little data exist for muscle development during phase 3. Such information is important for a proper understanding of the effects of late-occurring complications, such as hypoxia and intrauterine growth restriction. One of the few studies to have encompassed this phase indicated that a critical phase in muscle development occurs after thirty weeks, when fibers begin to lose their fetal properties and assume more mature characteristics (Schloon, Schlottmann, Lenard, & Goebel, 1979). After thirty-three weeks, a second population of initially smaller *Type I fibers* suddenly appears, replacing many of the *Wohlfart-B fibers*. By term, they form 40%–50% of the total fiber population, particularly in those trunk muscles innervated by motoneurons in the anteromedial nucleus of the anterior horn (Kumagai et al., 1984). These fibers are responsible for tonic activity in the muscles, and they therefore play an important role in the maintenance of posture. During the newborn period, the remaining Wohlfart-B fibers disappear (Colling-Saltin, 1978). It then takes a further six months before the new Type I fibers have a mean diameter as large as the Wohlfart-B fibers at birth.

Type II fibers also differentiate rapidly during the last weeks of pregnancy (Kumagai et al., 1984): *Type IIC fibers* abruptly disappear in the remaining five weeks, while Types IIA and B make a sudden appearance at thirty-seven weeks. In all instances of muscle fiber transformation from fetal to mature properties, the role of innervation represents another controversial issue. However, histochemical research reveals that *myosins* in human fetal muscle, which together with the protein *actin* triggers muscular contraction, are retained into postnatal life (Thornell et al., 1984). The conversion to adult-like myosin takes place after the first postnatal month, a change that is shortly followed by the two-to-three month transformation in the fetal movement repertoire of the human newborn (Hopkins & Prechtl, 1984).

Having attempted to associate changes at the neuromuscular and behavioral levels during fetal development, we raise a note of caution: changes in neural and muscle development should not be assumed to be a direct structural basis for the functional changes observed in the fetus and young infant. The two sets of changes could be coincidental, with no straightforward cause-and-effect relationship. Nevertheless, neurons, synaptic density, and transmitters are sufficiently developed by eight weeks of gestation to be capable of producing spontaneous (or induced) movements. It seems, therefore, on the basis of minimal neural structure and hardly any muscle differentiation, that recognizable and organized patterns of movement can be generated. This is perhaps the best and safest conclusion we can draw at the present time, and it is supported by the findings of a study on *anencephalic fetuses* between the gestational ages of sixteen to thirty-five weeks (Visser, Laurini, de Vries, Bekedam, & Prechtl, 1985). GMs and *startles*, as well as isolated arm and leg movements, were present in most fetuses, although the quality of expression was decidedly abnormal. Even in a seventeen-week-old fetus with no spinal cord above the lumbar region, these and other movements could be observed, seemingly generated by a few ectopic clusters of motoneurons with a haphazard orientation.

The appearance of well-defined *Type I fibers* in the last trimester of pregnancy intimates that fetal postural preferences should become more evident during this period. To some extent, this supposition is correct, but it turns out to be something of an oversimplification, as we shall see in the next section.

DEVELOPMENT OF POSTURE

In contrast to current knowledge about the prenatal development of motility, there is a paucity of information with regard to that concerning posture. Quite apart from the lack of a descriptive corpus of data, it is unknown as to what degree postures can be ascribed to myogenic or neurogenic influences in the human fetus, or to what extent they are active as opposed to passive in nature. Presumably, neurogenic influences play an increasing role as development proceeds in tandem with changes in the composition of muscles, thus making postural control more of an active process. If this were the case, then one would expect *muscle activation* to become more eccentric or isometric in order that particular postures can be actively maintained. At present, we simply do not have the requisite findings to support such intuitions.

What do we mean by "posture"? Given the dearth of insights into postural mechanisms that may function in the intrauterine environment, we use the term only as a descriptive concept. As such, it refers to the position of the fetus relative to this environment and to the relative disposition of body parts to each other while the fetus is inactive. The latter referral comprises a description of the total body configuration as well as how the position of one body part (e.g., the head) is taken with reference to another segment (e.g., the trunk). Thus, there are at least three descriptors that are considered under the headings of "Orientation *in utero*," "The typical curled fetal posture," and "Head position."

Orientation *In Utero*

Sonographic observations have shown that position relative to the surface on which the fetus is laying changes with age (de Vries et al., 1982). At eight and nine weeks, all fetuses lay supine or on the side, but between eleven and fifteen weeks things begin to change: the supine position is still predominant, but now prone, upright, and even upside-down orientations begin to appear for the first time (Fig. 6.5). By eighteen to nineteen weeks, most fetuses lay on the side, mainly lengthwise rather than transverse or diagonally, relative to the uterus. After thirty-two weeks, the majority of fetuses tend to be in a lengthwise cephalic position with the head nearest to the pelvis (Ververs, de Vries, van Geijn, & Hopkins, 1994a).

The number of positional changes increases rapidly after the emergence of *GMs*, attaining a maximum of twenty-five displacements per

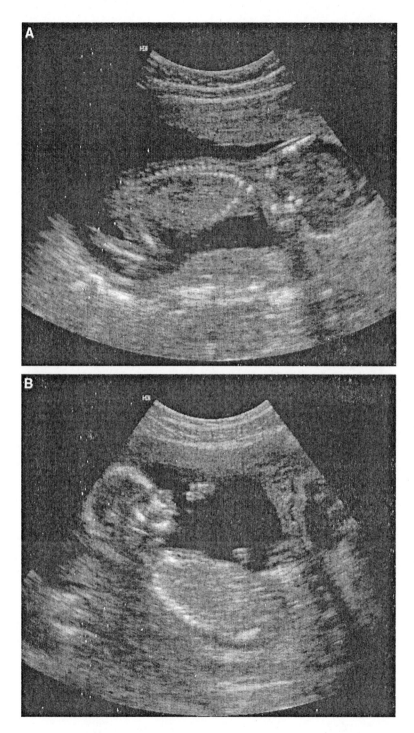

Figure 6.5. Examples of various fetal positions. A: Prone; B: Supine; C: Side; D: Upside down (head down, thorax/ribcage above, and arm in front of thorax and head).

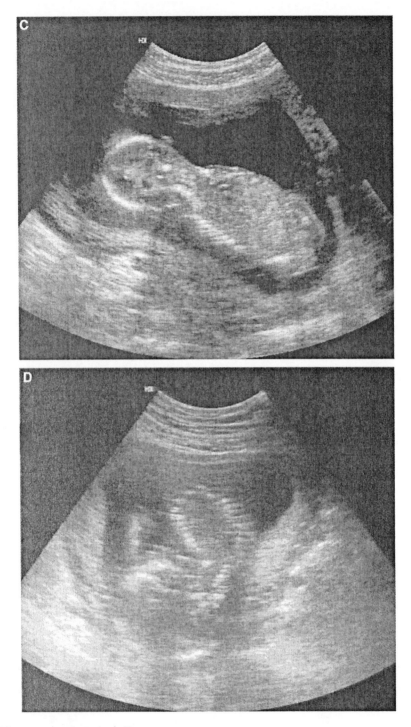

Figure 6.5. (continued).

hour at fifteen weeks (de Vries et al., 1982). Subsequently, and up to twenty weeks, the rate of change diminishes. What can account for this decrease? *Total activity* can be discounted, as it does not show a concomitant decline from fifteen to twenty weeks. The same applies to the amount of *amniotic fluid* surrounding the second trimester fetus. A more probable explanation is that changes in the form of the uterus, together with intrauterine contractions, impose constraints on the growing fetus that make it increasingly difficult for shifts in position to take place. Nevertheless, we have noted that even when a fetus is inactive, small repetitive displacements in position can be induced by *maternal breathing* and less frequently by the heartbeat of the mother's abdominal aorta. We have also observed quick and quite large changes when the mother coughs or laughs.

Parity also has a bearing on the orientation of the fetus *in utero*. Compared to first pregnancies, it is well known that during the second and subsequent gestations the fetus lies longer in the transverse position. This is because the uterus imposes fewer constraints, as it has been stretched during earlier pregnancies. Finally, orientation with respect to gravity reveals that during the first trimester the fetus is laying at the lowest point of the uterus (de Vries et al., 1982). As term approaches, it is essential that the fetus assumes the *vertex position*—with the head in the pelvic inlet—if the risks of mechanical problems at birth are to be avoided.

The Typical Curled Fetal Posture

Sonographically, the total body configuration has not been studied systematically. Our impression, from carrying out many ultrasound observations of healthy pregnancies, is that both flexed and extended postures involving the head, trunk, and extremities can be maintained for relatively long periods of time when the fetus is resting. While the head and trunk are in alignment to begin with, our impression is that this relationship changes near term: now the head is flexed forward in both cephalic and breech positions, and, together with the head facing downward, it represents an adaptation to the exigencies of delivery. Further dedicated ultrasound recordings are needed to confirm this impression.

If a *typically curled* (i.e., *flexed*) *posture* of the whole body cannot be confirmed during the second trimester of pregnancy, this is not the case when individual extremities are considered. For example, it has been found that the *elbows* and *fingers* adopt a flexion preference as early as twelve and sixteen weeks, respectively (Ververs, van Gelder-Hasker, de Vries, Hopkins, & van Geijn, 1998). According to the same study, such a preference is evident in the wrists from twenty-eight weeks onward.

This development of a flexed *arm posture* that is completed by the beginning of the last trimester necessitates two comments. First, its early onset cannot be attributed to spatial limitations within the uterus, given the small size of the fetus at twelve weeks (CRL: 5.6 cm) and sixteen weeks (CRL: 11 cm). Instead, it must be an expression of the developing neuromuscular system, and as such an indication that flexor neurons in the extremities become functionally dominant prior to their extensor counterparts. Second, complete flexion of the arms in front of the trunk denotes yet another adaptation facilitating fetal passage through the *pelvic inlet*. This adaptation is particularly pertinent to the case of *breech deliveries*. During such deliveries, obstetricians strive not to contact the fetus, as doing so can result in an upward movement of the arms, which then have to be manually manipulated back into the pelvis. The hazards associated with this correction procedure led to an internationally randomized trial to evaluate the comparative risks of a *vaginal delivery* as opposed to a *caesarian section* in breech fetuses near term (Hannah, Hannah, Hewson, Saigal, & Willan, 2000). The conclusion reached was that an operative birth should be considered to be the safer option in such instances—an outcome that has had an enormous influence on the practice of obstetrical care in recent years.

Head Position

Does the fetus develop a *lateralized head position preference* relative to the trunk? As such a preference posture is clearly evident immediately after a full-term birth (Hopkins, Lems, Jansen, & Butterworth, 1987), one could expect it to have been established during prenatal life. But when? These questions motivated a longitudinal study from twelve weeks to term involving serial ultrasound recordings of fetuses without any complications of pregnancy (Ververs et al., 1994a; Ververs, de Vries, van Geijn, & Hopkins, 1994b). In short, it was shown that the head position of the fetus is initially midline in the body, but that it becomes increasingly lateralized after thirty weeks, with a predominant right-sided preference by thirty-six weeks. Thus, compared to other postural changes during prenatal development, this particular achievement is a late-occurring event.

A number of models can be referred to in attempting to adjudicate on the reasons for this dextral bias. They range from genetic and brain models to those that address potential sources of lateralized influences *in utero*, and which are epigenetic in their assumptions (Hopkins & Rönnqvist, 1998). Perhaps the most comprehensive and compelling model to date is the *left otolithic-dominance* (LOD) *hypothesis* (Previc, 1991). In a nutshell, this epigenetic model contends that when the head is engaged with the pelvic inlet in the common vertex position (i.e., with the right side of the body facing outward), the hair cells in the two *otoliths* are subjected to unequal shearing when the mother walks forward. This inequality is due to the fact that the deceleration phase of *maternal walking* delivers a sharp inertial force traveling backward, and as a consequence the left otolith is stimulated more than the right one. Impulses from the otoliths terminate on interneurons in the spinal cord via the *vestibulospinal tract*, whose main function is to control ipsilateral extensor muscles. If the left otolith is dominant, then the left *sternocleidomastoid neck muscle* should be preferentially activated, thus giving rise to a right-sided head position preference (Hopkins & Rönnqvist, 1998).

There are a number of challenges that confront this model. One is that the fetal spine is not always to the left side of the mother during the last trimester (Ververs et al., 1994b). Consequently, when the head is turned to the right, it will not consistently face outward; therefore, any differential stimulation of the otoliths will be at best intermittent. The *LOD model* at present does not cater for this possibility. A related challenge is that even when the head is engaged in the pelvic inlet, it does not remain fixed in one direction but rather continues to change position up until term (Ververs et al., 1994a). Next, some fetuses assume other positions than the one with the head down throughout the latter part of pregnancy (namely, lengthwise or transverse orientations). So far, we do not know if such fetuses fail to manifest a posture after birth in which the head is consistently lateralized to one side of the body. Similarly, it is unknown if the offspring of mothers who have to take a protracted period of *bed rest* during the last trimester (e.g., because of complications such as *pre-eclampsia*) also fail to exhibit such consistency after birth. These sorts of challenges do not undermine the predictions of the LOD model, but instead offer ways in which they can be tested more fully.

By way of a last look at the prenatal development of posture, consider the following question: does the developing fetus acquire functional synergies that in some way reveal integration between posture and movement? One way of making this question more empirically tractable is to pose it in more specific terms: does the third trimester fetus make *hand–face contacts* that are ipsilateral to the side on which it is turned, a finding reported for newborns in the first hour after birth (Hopkins et al., 1987)? In short, the answer is no. In one longitudinal study from twelve to thirty-eight weeks designed to address this question, we found that hand contact and head position did not co-develop a *preferred ipsilateral synergy* (de Vries et al., 2001), despite the fact that fetuses of this age have adopted a flexed *arm posture*, thereby making it easier for the hand on the same side as the head to contact the face than the contralateral one. Why the discrepancy between the fetal and newborn findings? One conjecture is that the newborn, but not the fetus, is exposed to the stretch-inducing effects of *gravity* that appear to exert more influence on flexors than on extensor muscles (Schulte, 1970). Here then, we have an example of a fetal behavior that does not show a direct continuity with its performance after birth due to a radical change in environmental circumstances.

DISCUSSION AND CONCLUSIONS

The advent of real-time ultrasound scanning for research purposes in the 1970s reopened a number of fundamental questions about the origins of human behavioral development. We now know that fetal motility is evident by the end of the embryonic period, and that thereafter it differentiates at a rapid pace into distinct and well-organized movement patterns. Its onset and subsequent diversification during the first trimester appear to be based on minimal neural and myogenic structures. Despite the fact that both nervous and muscle tissue show substantial differentiation during the rest of prenatal life, the various movement patterns so far identified remain essentially similar (i.e., recognizable) until some two to three months after birth, leading to the claim that the human newborn resembles an *exterogestate fetus* in terms of many non-vital functions (Prechtl, 1984).

This assertion, not shared by some others (e.g., Finlay, Clancy, & Kingsbury, 2003), should be tempered by the evidence that a significant change occurs prenatally in the temporal organization of the more complex movements, particularly *GMs*. They begin to assume conspicuous *rest-activity cycles* that become increasingly synchronized with each other. Toward the end of pregnancy, the coincidence of these cycles gives rise to stable *behavioral states*. This apparently late-occurring event in human pregnancy is a crucial achievement that equips the fetus for the markedly different demands of the extra-uterine environment. What also increases is the variability and complexity with which *jaw movements* are performed, occurring first as isolated events and then becoming integrated into *sucking and swallowing*, and subsequently with *non-nutritive sucking*. Such variability can also be seen as another essential ingredient in being able to adapt to the postnatal environment.

Findings on the development of fetal movements during the last twenty years or so have convincingly dismissed the long-held notion that the origins of human development reside in "primitive reflexes," somehow triggered by sequences of regularly timed stimuli. The fact that the diverse movement patterns emerge within such a short age period, and then are performed so frequently that periods of rest are relatively brief, speaks against their establishment as being dependent on external sources of stimulation. Certainly, once inaugurated, they are susceptible to modifying influences emanating from maternal behavior and dietary constituents, as well as from marked changes in the intrauterine environment such as a reduction in *amniotic fluid* (Sival, Visser, & Prechtl, 1990). Thus, for example, maternal activity (e.g., coughing) induces larger and more abrupt changes in orientation and posture than the fetus alone can produce.

Despite incontrovertible evidence that fetal motility does not consist of reflexes chained together by some exogenous *zeitgeber*, the precise nature of how the developing nervous system spontaneously generates such an array of complex movement patterns remains unclear. The scarcity of research on the ultrastructural development of the *spinal cord* in the human continues to hinder progress in this respect, as does the lack of knowledge about the timing of *supraspinal influences* on spinal motor centers. To complicate the picture still further, contrasting changes in both the incidence and temporal organization of movements suggest that different pattern generating mechanisms are involved. Such changes raise the possibility that interactions between the *functional dynamics* of different movements are one possibility through which developmental transformations are achieved. Accordingly, modification in the incidence and temporal arrangement of one movement by another leads to the emergence of a qualitatively new pattern with short- or long-term adaptive functions for postnatal life. Change achieved in this way is a *modus operandi* of *self-organizing systems* (Ball, 1999).

The functional significance of fetal movements remains a matter of educated speculation. In this regard, there are seemingly movement patterns that do not appear to have *specific* functions prior to postnatal life (e.g., *breathing movements, eye movements, yawns*). After birth, they become linked to particular conditions of elicitation in the postnatal environment. The achievement of stable behavioral states toward the end of gestation is an important event in this respect, in that they provide the necessary coupling between perception and action so that responses can be attuned to the particulars of elicitation. Stable *waking states*, however, which are so crucial for psychological development, seem to be minimally present before birth. Their development then is largely a postnatal phenomenon and, in contrast to the striking continuity in movement patterns and sleep states before and after birth, they may represent a more discontinuous change. Set against this suggestion is the finding that when the fetus remains in the uterus after forty-one weeks of gestation, increases to that comparable with active wakefulness in the newborn occur (van der Pas, Nijhuis, & Jongsma, 1994). The further differentiation of wakefulness after birth is dependent not only on improvements in movement coordination, but also on the acquisition of active, anti-gravity *postural control*. These two sets of changes are inextricably linked, such that changes in one lead to changes in the other (Hopkins, 2001) and ultimately to the emergence of goal-directed behaviors, such as reaching (Hopkins & Rönnqvist, 2002).

Staying with the theme of continuities between pre- and postnatal life, there is another, less obvious one, to consider. Here, we refer to the *maternal perception of fetal movements* that begins around seventeen weeks of pregnancy with the onset of "quickening." Perceptions of the amount of fetal activity as well as the vigor of movements are potential sources of information by which parents can categorize or "individualize" their newborns. Thus, a "hidden agenda" of fetal movements could be the contribution they make toward individual differences in *parenting*, at least in the early months of postnatal life. While a plausible proposition, recent evidence suggests that this may not be the case, as in one study there was a lack of association between fetal activity and early postnatal measures of personality (Niederhofer & Reiter, 2004).

In recent years, the claim has been made that the observation of fetal movements provides an entry point for the derivation of a *prenatal neurological examination* (Prechtl, 1999). What needs to be accounted for in this endeavor is that the quality, rather than the quantity, of fetal motility discriminates between the abnormal and compromised fetus and its healthy coeval. However, the detection of possible neurological abnormalities should be seen in the light of the hypothesis that there is a continuity of neural functions from pre- to postnatal life, with a major transformation at two to three months after birth. Consequently, particular dysfunctions in the newborn period such as "chaotic" GMs with abrupt onsets and offsets could be associated with fetal brain mechanisms, and may therefore disappear as a consequence of the transformation (Bos et al., 1997). Should neurological abnormalities persist beyond three months, then one may expect an increased likelihood of a deviant developmental outcome, ranging from mild (e.g., developmental coordination disorder) to major (e.g., cerebral palsy) disabilities.

In conclusion, it appears that the human newborn resembles an extrauterine fetus in terms of many non-vital functions. Birth in this state is matched by a suite of caretaking behaviors more or less unique to humans, such that they serve to bridge the gap between the relatively "helpless" newborn and the three-month-old infant who is more equipped to deal with the demands of the extrauterine environment. Nevertheless, a considerable amount of neuromuscular "groundwork" has been laid down during fetal development that allows an exquisite fit to be made with a decidedly different environment, cr what Bowlby (1969) referred to as the "environment of evolutionary *adaptedness*" (namely, the body of the mother). Thus, a movement repertoire adapted to life *within* the mother can with little modification be used for living *on* the mother. This double-edged form of adaptation constitutes an essential feature of any functional continuity between pre- and postnatal life.

REFERENCES

Anokhin, P.K. (1964). Systemogenesis as a general regulator of brain development. *Progress in Brain Research, 9,* 54–86.

Argiolis, A., & Melis, M.R. (1998). The neuropharmacology of yawning. *European Journal of Pharmacology, 343,* 1–16.

Ball, P. (1999). *The self-made tapestry: Pattern formation in nature.* Oxford, UK: Oxford University Press.

Bekoff, A. (1981). Essays in honor of Viktor Hamburger. In W.M. Cowan (Ed.), *Studies in developmental neurobiology* (pp. 134–170). Oxford, UK: Oxford University Press.

Bekoff, A. (2001). Development of motor behaviour in chick embryos. In A.F. Kalverboer & A. Gramsbergen (Eds.), *Handbook of brain and behaviour in human development* (pp. 429–445). Dordrecht: Kluwer.

Birnholz, J.C. (1981). The development of fetal eye movement patterns. *Science, 213*, 679–681.

Birnholz, J.C., & Farrell, E.E. (1984). Ultrasound images of the human fetal development. *American Scientist, 72*, 608–613.

Blechschmidt, E. (1977). *The beginnings of human life.* New York: Springer.

Bos, A.F., van Loon, A.J., Hadders-Algra, M., Martijn, A., Okken, A., & Prechtl, H.F.R. (1997). Spontaneous motility in preterm, small-for-gestational-age infants. II. Qualitative aspects. *Early Human Development, 50*, 131–147.

Bots, R.S.G.M., Nijhuis, J.G., Martin, C.B., & Prechtl, H.F.R. (1981). Human fetal eye movements: Detection in utero by ultrasonography. *Early Human Development, 5*, 87–94.

Bowlby, J. (1969). *Attachment.* New York: Basic Books.

Brace, R.A. (1997). Physiology of amniotic fluid regulation. *Clinical Obstetrics and Gynecology, 40*, 280–289.

Bradley, N.S. (2001). Age-related changes and condition-dependent modifications in distribution of limb movements during embryonic motility. *Journal of Neurophysiology, 86*, 1511–1522.

Brown, T.G. (1914). On the nature of the fundamental activity of the nervous centres, together with an analysis of the conditioning of rhythmic activity in progression, and a theory of evolution of function in the nervous system. *Journal of Physiology, 48*, 18–46.

Colling-Saltin, A.F. (1978). Enzyme histochemistry on skeletal muscle of the human fetus. *Journal of Neurological Sciences, 39*, 61–66.

Crelin, E.S. (1969). *Anatomy of the newborn: An atlas.* Philadelphia: Lea & Febiger.

de Vries, J.I.P (1997). De normale ontwikkeling van foetale bewegingspatronen [The normal development of fetal movement patterns]. *Journal for Obstetricians, 22*, 6–10.

de Vries, J.I.P., & van Geijn, H. (1994). The rationale and irrationale of fetal stimulation. In H.P. van Geijn & F.J.A. Copray (Eds.), *A critical appraisal of fetal surveillance* (pp. 188–192). Amsterdam: Elsevier.

de Vries, J.I.P., Visser, G.H.A., Mulder, E.J.H., & Prechtl, H.F.R. (1987). Diurnal and other variations in fetal movement and heart rate patterns at 20–22 weeks. *Early Human Development, 15*, 333–348.

de Vries, J.I.P., Visser, G.H.A., & Prechtl, H.F.R. (1982). The emergence of fetal behaviour. I. Qualitative aspects. *Early Human Development, 7*, 301–322.

de Vries, J.I.P., Visser, G.H.A., & Prechtl, H.F.R. (1985). The emergence of fetal behaviour. II. Quantitative aspects. *Early Human Development, 15*, 333–348.

de Vries, J.I.P., Visser, G.H.A., & Prechtl, H.F.R. (1988). The emergence of fetal behaviour. III. Individual differences and consistencies. *Early Human Development, 16*, 85–103.

de Vries, J.I.P., Wimmers, R.H., Ververs, I.A.P., Hopkins, B., Savelsbergh, G.J.P., & van Geijn, H.P. (2001). Fetal handedness and head preference: A developmental study. *Developmental Psychobiology, 39*, 171–178.

Dubowitz, V. (1966). Histochemistry, enzyme histochemistry of developing human muscle. *Nature, 211*, 884–885.

Eyre, J.A., Miller, S., Clowry, G.J., Conway, E.A., & Watts, C. (2000). Functional corticospinal connections are established prenatally in the human foetus permitting involvement in the development of spinal motor centres. *Brain, 123*, 51–64.

Eyre, J.A., Miller, S., & Ramesh, V. (1991). Constancy of central conduction delays during development in man: Investigation of motor and somatosensory pathways. *Journal of Physiology, 434*, 441–452.

Finlay, B.L., Clancy, B., & Kingsbury, M.A. (2003). The developmental neurobiology of early vision. In B. Hopkins & S.P. Johnson (Eds.), *Neurobiology of infant vision* (pp. 1–41). Westport, CT: Praeger.

Gasser, R.F. (1967). The development of facial muscles in man. *American Journal of Anatomy, 120*, 357–375.

Gilles, F.H., Shankle, W., & Dooling, E.C. (1983). Myelinated tracts: Growth patterns. In F.H. Gilles, A. Leviton, & E.C. Dooling (Eds.), *The developing human brain* (pp. 117–183). Boston: John Wright.

Griffin, R.L., Caron, F.J.M., & van Geijn, H.P. (1985). Behavioral states in the Human fetus during labor. *American Journal of Obstetrics and Gynecology, 152*, 828–833.

Hadders-Algra, M., & Prechtl, H.F.R. (1992). Developmental course of general movements in early infancy: I. Descriptive analysis of change in form. *Early Human Development, 28*, 201–213.

Hannah, M.E., Hannah, W.J., Hewson, S.A., Saigal, S., & Willan, A.R. (2000). Planned caesarian section versus planned vaginal birth for breech presentation at term: A randomized multicentre trial. Term Breech Trial Collaborative Group. *Lancet, 356*, 1375–1383.

Hepper, P.G., McCartney, G.R., & Shannon, E.A. (1998). Lateralized behavior in first trimester fetuses. *Neuropsychologica, 36*, 531–534.

Hertz, R.H., Timor-Tritsch, I.E., Dierker, L.J., Chick, L., & Rosen, H.G. (1979). Continuous ultrasound and fetal movement. *American Journal of Obstetrics and Gynecology, 135*, 152–154.

Hooker, D. (1952). *The prenatal origin of behavior.* Lawrence, KS: University of Kansas Press.

Hopkins, B. (2000). Development of crying in normal infants: Method, theory and some speculations. In R.G. Barr, B. Hopkins, & J.A. Green (Eds.), *Crying as a sign, a symptom, and a signal* (pp. 176–209). London: MacKeith Press.

Hopkins, B. (2001). Understanding motor development: Insights from dynamical systems approaches. In A.F. Kalverboer & A. Gramsbergen (Eds.), *Handbook of brain and behaviour in human development* (pp. 591–620). Dordrecht: Kluwer.

Hopkins, B. (2003). Developmental disorders: An action-based account. In J. Valsiner & K. Connolly (Eds.), *Handbook of developmental psychology* (pp. 292–329). London: Sage.

Hopkins, B., Lems, W., Jansen, B., & Butterworth, G. (1987). Postural and motor asymmetries in newlyborns. *Human Neurobiology, 6*, 153–156.

Hopkins, B., & Prechtl, H.F.R. (1984). A qualitative approach to the development of movements during early infancy. In H.F.R. Prechtl (Ed.), *Continuity of neural functions from prenatal to postnatal life* (pp. 179–197). Oxford, UK: Blackwell.

Hopkins, B., & Rönnqvist, L. (1998). Human handedness: Developmental and evolutionary perspectives. In F. Simion & G. Butterworth (Eds.), *The development of sensory, motor, and cognitive capacities in early infancy* (pp. 191–236). Hove, UK: Psychology Press.

Hopkins, B., & Rönnqvist, L. (2002). Facilitating postural control: Effects on the reaching behavior of 6-month-old infants. *Developmental Psychobiology, 40*, 168–182.

Humphrey, T. (1960). The development of the pyramidal tracts in human fetuses, correlated with cortical differentiation. In D.B. Tower & J.P. Schadé (Eds.), *Structure and function of the cerebral cortex* (pp. 413–441). Amsterdam: Elsevier.

Ianniruberto, A., & Tajani, E. (1981). Ultrasonographic study of fetal movements. *Seminars in Perinatology, 5*, 175–181.

Junge, H.D. (1979). Behavioural states and state related heart rate and motor activity patterns in the newborn infant and the fetus antepartum: Comparative study. *Journal of Perinatal Medicine, 4*, 85–103.

Kumagai, T., Hakamada, S., Hara, K., Takeuchi, T., Miyazaki, S., Watanabe, K., et al. (1984). Development of human fetal muscles: A comparative histochemical analysis of the psoas and quadriceps muscles. *Neuropediatrics, 15*, 198–202.

Kuo, Y. (1967). *The dynamics of behavior development.* New York: Random House.

Kurjak, A., Azumendi, G., Vecek, N., Kupesic, S., Solok, M., Varga, D., et al. (2003). Fetal hand movements and facial expression in normal pregnancy studied by four-dimensional sonography. *Journal of Perinatal. Medicine, 31*, 496–508.

Langman, J. (1963). *Medical embryology: Human development—normal and abnormal.* Baltimore: Williams & Wilkins.

Larsen, W.J. (2001). *Human embryology* (3rd ed.). New York: Churchill Livingstone.

Lashley, K.S. (1952). The problem of serial behavior. In L.A. Jeffress (Ed.), *Cerebral mechanisms* (pp. 112–136). New York: Wiley.

Liggins, G.C., Vilos, G.A., Kitterman, J.A., & Lee, C.H. (1981). The effect of spinal cord transection on lung development in the fetal sheep. *Journal of Developmental Physiology, 3*, 267–274.

Meltzoff, A.N., & Moore, M.K. (1983). Newborn infants imitate adult facial gestures. *Child Development, 54*, 702–709.

Miller J.L., Sonies, B.C., & Macedonia, C. (2003). Emergence of oropharyngeal, laryngeal and swallowing activity in the developing upper aerodigestive tract: An ultrasound evaluation. *Early Human Development, 71*, 61–87.

Mulder, E.J.H., Morrsink, L.P., van der Schee, T., & Visser, G.H.A. (1998). Acute maternal alcohol consumption disrupts behavioural state organization in the near-term fetus. *Pediatric Research, 44*, 744–779.

Mulder, E.J.H., & Visser, G.H.A. (1991). Growth and motor development in fetuses of women with type I diabetes: II. Emergence of specific movement patterns. *Early Human Development, 25*, 107–115.

Müller, K., Homberg, V., & Lenard, H.G. (1991). Magnetic stimulation of motor cortex and nerve roots in children. *Electroencephalography and Clinical Neurophysiology, 81*, 63–70.

Mulvihill, S.J., Stone, M.M., Debes, H.T., & Fonkalrud, E.W. (1985). The role of amniotic fluid in fluid nutrition. *Journal of Pediatric Surgery, 20*, 668–672.

Niederhofer, H., & Reiter, A. (2004). Prenatal maternal stress, prenatal fetal movements and perinatal temperament factors influence behavior and school marks at the age of 6 Years. *Fetal Diagnosis and Therapy, 19*, 160–162.

Nijhuis, J.G., Prechtl, H.F.R., Martin, C.B., & Bots, R.S.G.M. (1982). Are there behavioural states in the human fetus? *Early Human Development, 6*, 177–195.

Okada, N., & Kojima, T. (1984). Ontogeny of the central nervous system: Neurogenesis, fibre connection, synaptogenesis and myelination in the spinal cord. In H.F.R. Prechtl (Ed.), *Continuity of neural functions from prenatal to postnatal life* (pp. 31–45). Oxford, UK: Blackwell.

Oppenheim, R.W. (1981). Ontogenetic adaptations and retrogressive processes in the development of the nervous system and behavior: A neuroembryological perspective. In K. Connolly & H.F.R. Prechtl (Eds.), *Maturation and development: Biological and psychological perspectives* (pp. 73–109). London: Heinemann.

Oppenheim, R.W. (1995). Conceptions and misconceptions about embryonic development. In B. Hopkins (Ed.), *Cambridge encyclopedia of child development* (pp.159–165). Cambridge, UK: Cambridge University Press.

Oster, H. (1978). Facial expression and affect development. In M. Lewis & L.A. Rosenblum (Eds.), *The development of affect* (pp. 43–75). New York: Plenum Press.

Parson, S., & Ribchester, R. (2005). Prenatal development of the human musculoskeletal system. In B. Hopkins (Ed.), *Cambridge encyclopedia of child development* (pp. 166–172). Cambridge, UK: Cambridge University Press.

Prechtl, H.F.R. (Ed.). (1984). *Continuity of neural functions from prenatal to postnatal life*. Oxford, UK: Blackwell.

Prechtl, H.F.R. (1999). How can we assess the integrity of the fetal nervous system? In P. Arbeille, D. Manlik, & R.N. Laurini (Eds.), *Fetal hypoxia* (pp. 109–115). New York: Parthenon.

Previc, F. (1991). A general theory concerning the prenatal origin of cerebral lateralization in humans. *Psychological Review, 98,* 299–334.

Roodenburg, P.J., Wladimiroff, J.W., van Es, A., & Prechtl, H.F.R. (1991). Classification and quantitative aspects of fetal movement during the second half pregnancy. *Early Human Development, 25,* 19–35.

Sandyk, R. (1999). Yawning and stretching induced by transcranial application of AC pulsed electromagnetic fields in Parkinson's disease. *International Journal of Neuroscience, 97,* 139–145.

Schloon, H., Schlottmann, J., Lenard, H.G., & Goebel, H.H. (1979). The development of skeletal muscles in premature infants: I. Fibre size and histochemical differentiation. *European Journal of Pediatrics, 131,* 49–60.

Schulte, F.J. (1970). Neonatal brain mechanisms and the development of motor behavior. In U. Stave (Ed.), *Perinatal physiology* (pp. 685–713). New York: Plenum Press.

Sival, D.A., Visser, G.H.A., & Prechtl, H.F.R. (1990). Does reduction of amniotic fluid affect fetal movements? *Early Human Development, 23,* 233–246.

Smotherman, W.P., & Robinson, S.R. (Eds.). (1988). *Behavior of the fetus.* Caldwell, NJ: Telford Press.

Sparling, J.W., van Tol, J., & Chescheir, N.C. (1999). Fetal and neonatal hand movement. *Physical Therapy, 79,* 24–39.

Suzue, T., & Shinodo, Y. (1999). Highly reproducible spatiotemporal patterns of mammalian movements in the development stage of the earliest spontaneous motility. *European Journal of Neuroscience, 11,* 2697–2710.

Thornell, L.E., Billeter, R., Bulter-Browne, G.S., Eriksson, P.O., Rinqqvist, M., & Whalen, R.G. (1984). Development of fiber types in human fetal muscle: An immunocytochemical study. *Journal of Neurological Sciences, 66,* 107–115.

Trudinger, B.J., Aust, F., & Knight, P.C. (1980). Fetal age and patterns of human breathing movements. *American Journal of Obstetrics and Gynecology, 137,* 724–728.

van der Pas, M., Nijhuis, J.G., & Jongsma, H.W. (1994). Fetal behaviour in uncomplicated pregnancies after 41 weeks of gestation. *Early Human Development, 40,* 29–38.

van Woerden, E.E., van Geijn, H.P., Caron, F.J., van der Valk, A.W., Swartjes, J.M., & Arts, N.F. (1988). Fetal mouth movements during behavioural states 1F and 2F. *European Journal of Obstetrics, Gynecology and Reproductive Biology, 29,* 97–105.

Ververs, I.A.P., de Vries, J.I.P., van Geijn, H.P., & Hopkins, B. (1994a). Prenatal head position from 12–38 weeks: I. Developmental aspects. *Early Human Development, 39,* 83–91.

Ververs, I.A.P., de Vries, J.I.P., van Geijn, H.P., & Hopkins, B. (1994b). Prenatal head position from 12–38 weeks: II. The effects of fetal orientation and placental localization. *Early Human Development, 39,* 93–100.

Ververs, I.A.P., van Gelder-Hasker, M.R., de Vries, J.I.P., Hopkins, B., & van Geijn, H.P. (1998). Prenatal development of arm posture. *Early Human Development, 51,* 61–70.

Visser, G.H.A., Laurini, R.N., de Vries, J.I.P., Bekedam, D.J., & Prechtl, H.F.R. (1985). Abnormal behaviour in anencephalic fetuses. *Early Human Development, 12,* 173–182.

Visser, G.H.A., Poelman-Weesjes, G., Cohen, T.M.N., & Bekedam, D.J. (1987). Fetal behavioural states at 30–32 weeks. *Pediatric Research, 22,* 655–658.

Wilson, J.G. (1973). *Environment and birth defects.* New York: Academic Press.

Wolff, P.H. (1986). The maturation and development of fetal motor patterns. In M.G. Wade & H.T.A. Whiting (Eds.), *Motor development in children: Aspects of coordination and control* (pp. 65–74). Dordrecht: Martinus Nijhoff.

FURTHER READING

England, M.A. (1996). *Life before birth* (2nd ed.). London: Mosby-Wolfe.

Flanagan, G.L. (1996). *Beginning life.* London: Dorling Kindersley.

Lecanuet, J.-P., Fifer, W.P., Krasnegor, N.A., & Smotherman, W.P. (Eds.). (1995). *Fetal development: A psychobiological perspective.* Hillsdale, NJ: Erlbaum.

Nathanielz, P.W. (1999). *Life in the womb: The origin of health and disease.* Ithaca, NY: Promethean Press.

Nijhuis, J.G. (Ed.). (1992). *Fetal behavior: Developmental and perinatal aspects.* Oxford, England: Oxford University Press.

Preyer, W.T. (1937). Embryonic motility and sensitivity. *Monographs of the Society for Research in Child Development, 2* (6, Serial No. 13).

Robles de Medina, P.G., Visser, G.H., Huizink, A.C., Buitelaar, J.K., & Mulder, E.J. (2003). Fetal behaviour does not differ between boys and girls. *Early Human Development, 73,* 17–26.

Sjostrom, K., Thelin, T., Marsal, K., & Valentin, L. (2003). Effects of maternal anxiety on perception of fetal movements in late pregnancy. *Early Human Development, 72,* 111–122.

Sparling, J.W. (Ed.). (1993). Concepts in fetal movement research [Special issue]. *Physical and Occupational Therapy in Pediatrics, 12.*

ten Hof, J., Nijhuis, I.J.M., Mulder, E.J.H., Nijhuis, J.G., Narayan, H., Taylor, D.J., Westers, P., & Visser, G.H.A. (2002). Longitudinal study of fetal body movements: Normograms, intrafetal consistency, and relationship with episodes of heart rate patterns A and B. *Pediatric Research, 52,* 568–575.

CHAPTER 7

EFFECTS OF ANTENATAL MATERNAL STRESS OR ANXIETY: FROM FETUS TO CHILD

Vivette Glover and Thomas G. O'Connor

ABSTRACT

There is very strong evidence from animal studies showing that if the mother is stressed during pregnancy that it has a direct effect on the fetus and long-term effects on the child. In particular, the offspring show behavioral abnormalities including more anxiety and shorter attention span. There are also changes in sexual behavior and in laterality. Such studies have also demonstrated that these effects are due to the altered hormonal milieu in the mother having a permanent effect on the development of the fetal brain. In humans, this type of research is just beginning. While there is a substantial literature linking antenatal maternal stress or anxiety with adverse birth outcome, which in turn can affect the long-term development of the child, there are few published studies on antenatal programming effects on the fetus. Using a large prospective, cohort, we have shown that antenatal maternal anxiety is linked with behavioral problems in the four-year-old child. In an attempt to control for both genetic and parenting effects, post-natal anxiety was co-varied out, and the same outcome still obtained. We also found a link between antenatal anxiety and mixed handedness in the child, after allowing for parental handedness, which is another possible example of fetal programming. Other studies are starting to report similar findings. Some possible mechanisms for the links between antenatal maternal anxiety and effects on the fetus are discussed. These include impaired maternal uterine blood flow and the transplacental passage of cortisol from mother to fetus.

INTRODUCTION

Recent research suggests several ways in which *maternal stress* or anxiety during pregnancy may influence the development of the fetus and child, with potentially long-lasting effects. The aim of this chapter is to review these findings and address some of the key outstanding conceptual and methodological issues. First, we begin with a discussion of the animal findings as a starting point for research on humans. Second, we consider measurement issues—especially how stress and anxiety in pregnancy have been measured—and what current data suggest may be the nature of the risk in the antenatal period. Third, we review the findings that link antenatal stress or anxiety with obstetrical, behavioral, and neurological outcomes in children. Fourth, we examine possible mechanisms that may underlie these reported associations in humans.

ANIMAL STUDIES

Long-term effects of prenatal stress on the progeny have been well described in rats. One common finding is increased anxiety in the offspring, as shown by an increased startle response, decreased social interaction, or freezing (Weinstock, 2001). This is associated with an increased *hypothalamus-pituitary axis* (HPA) reactivity (Barbazanges, Piazza, Le Moal, & Maccari, 1996; Henry, Kabbaj, Simon, Le Moal, & Maccari, 1994). *Maternal stress* has been shown to cause a permanent reduction in the number of *corticosterone receptors* in the rat fetal brain (Henry et al., 1994), which could explain the long-term increase in stress responses through reducing the effect of negative feedback control. Male offspring of stressed mothers have been reported to show reduced sexual behavior (e.g., diminished initiation of copulation and failure to ejaculate), and female offspring have shown impaired maternal behavior, together with changes in exploration and aggression (Insel, 1990; Ward, 1972). Research on rats has revealed that the effects of antenatal stress persist into adulthood, and are frequently gender specific (Shalev & Weiner, 2001). Nevertheless, manipulating the postnatal environment can prevent some of the behavioral effects of antenatal stress, at least in the immediate postpartum period (Barbazanges et al., 1996). Rats whose mothers were stressed during gestation also have some permanent neurological deficits and altered *laterality* (Fride & Weinstock, 1989; Weinstock, 2001).

When pregnant monkeys were stressed by exposure to unpredictable noise (there was no difference in gestational age), their offspring had lower birthweights, worse neuromotor maturity, and impaired attention (Schneider, Roughton, Koehler, & Lubach, 1999). Studies in which control and intervention progeny were reared together showed that the effects were specifically due to antenatal maternal stress, rather than resultant impaired parenting (Clarke & Schneider, 1993; Schneider & Suomi, 1992). The effects were more marked if the mothers were stressed early in pregnancy, rather than in mid- to late-gestation, with the mean birthweight of males exposed to early stress being 468 grams (compared to 550 grams for those not subjected to stress). However, behavioral effects were also observable after stress solely at these later stages. The effects of prenatal stress could be mimicked by giving the pregnant mother *ACTH*, thus confirming the mediating role of the *HPA* (see Fig. 7.1). Offspring of prenatally stressed *rhesus monkeys* had heightened responses to stressful situations, producing elevated levels of *cortisol*, indicative of enhanced HPA reactivity (Clarke, Wittwer, Abbott, & Schneider, 1994). They were also less adaptable to novel situations. The authors concluded that the behavior of these monkeys was similar to that of children classed as difficult (Clarke & Schneider, 1997).

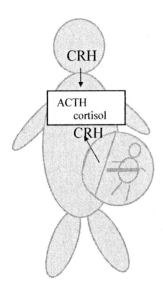

Figure 7.1. The HPA axis during pregnancy. CRH is released from the hypothalamus and stimulates the release of ACTH from the pituitary gland, which in turn stimulates the release of cortisol from the adrenal. During pregnancy the placenta also releases CRH into the maternal and fetal blood streams. ACTH: adrenocorticotropic hormone. CRH: corticotropin-releasing hormone.

The animal findings provide a convincing picture of the long-term effects of antenatal stress and some of the biological mechanisms involved. They also suggest a possible role for the early postnatal environment in attenuating the effects of antenatal stress, although it must be remembered that rodents are born at a much less mature stage than humans. Issues still to be resolved with animal studies concern the effects of timing of exposure to antenatal stress, or *critical periods*; the specificity of the effects on development; and the factors that moderate individual differences in response, such as genetics. It is likely that individual genetic differences will modify the effects of antenatal stress, with some individuals showing extra vulnerability and some being protected. Despite the robustness of the animal findings, their application to studies of humans is only just beginning.

THE NATURE OF THE ANTENATAL RISK

In the animal studies reported above, the experimentally imposed risk was stress. The specific risk varied across studies and species from, for example, brief unpredictable noise in the primate (Schneider, Moore, Roberts, & Dejesus, 2001) to crowding in the rat (Thompson, 1957). Nevertheless, each study imposed what could be broadly defined as stress. In several studies, this was shown to activate the *HPA axis* in the mother or be mimicked by direct activation such as injection of *ACTH* (e.g., Schneider, Moore, Roberts, & Dejesus, 2001). If there is concordance in the effects of *fetal programming* between animals and humans, then stress is an obvious focus for the human studies,

To date, studies of humans have assessed both antenatal stress and anxiety. These are different but overlapping concepts, and they involve different biochemical and hormonal correlates under different conditions. Both can be associated with activation of the *sympathetic-adrenal axis* and with the *HPA axis*, although the biological response can change with many other factors, such as whether the stress is acute or chronic. One cannot assume that because a person says that they are stressed or anxious that a particular chemical system is activated. This assumption needs independent demonstration, especially during pregnancy when it is known that the HPA axis and its responses are dampened (Schulte, Weisner, & Allolio, 1990), presumably due to placental release of the *corticotrophic hormone* (Petraglia et al., 1993), as depicted in Figure 7.1.

One set of studies examined stress using *life-event inventories*, a common procedure in psychological research (Hansen, Lou, & Olsen,

2000; Lou et al., 1994; Meijer, 1985). Using this strategy, researchers presume that the experience of certain specified life events induces physiological effects that may directly affect the fetus. However, they do not measure the impact of the life event on the mother. It may be significant that some of the studies using the life-event approach consider very severe stresses that are outside the control of the individual (see Hansen et al., 2000; Meijer, 1985).

A separate set of studies measured anxiety directly, which may or may not be secondary to stressful life events. Most of these studies measure general anxiety, typically with self-rating questionnaires (e.g., O'Connor, Heron, Golding, Beveridge, & Glover, 2002). It is important to note, however, that several sub-types of anxiety are recognized by psychiatric nosologies, and that some of these involve different physiological processes. For example, if the mechanism linking maternal anxiety and fetal/child outcomes is maternal hyper-responsiveness of the *HPA* and the consequent transfer of *cortisol* to the fetus (Gitau, Cameron, Fisk, & Glover, 1998), then we would expect more adverse child outcomes in women with *general anxiety disorder*, but not in women with *post-traumatic stress disorder*. Whereas the former involves a *hyper*-reactive HPA response, the latter consists of a *hypo*-response (Gold & Chrousos, 2002).

One question yet to be adequately addressed is whether or not the risk for fetal and child development derives from stress and/or anxiety specifically, or instead from a range of psychological disorders associated with, for example, hyper-responsiveness of the HPA (e.g., both depression and anxiety). Current findings suggest that the former may be more likely (see next section), but the current evidence is far too limited to make any firm conclusions.

A related point is that it is far from certain how well the constructs of stress and anxiety can be differentiated, either psychologically or physiologically. For example, in the *Spielberger State Anxiety* questionnaire (Spielberger, 1983), representative statements to be rated on a scale from "not at all" to "very much," are "I feel calm," "I feel secure," "I am relaxed," and "I feel pleasant." These statements would also be appropriate in a questionnaire to measure how stressed someone was feeling. Reciprocally, the experience of stress in the form of major life events is linked to increased rates of anxiety and depression. Complicating matters further is the fact that the anxiety disorders co-occur at very high rates, and also that there is substantial overlap between anxiety and other psychological disorders, notably depression and substance use. The implication of this is that it may be difficult to identify a group of pregnant women who exhibit a pure antenatal risk for obstetrical or developmental problems with their infants. Future research in this area will benefit from clear phenotypic descriptions and physiological profiles.

STUDIES OF THE EFFECTS OF ANTENATAL STRESS OR ANXIETY IN HUMANS

There are several ways in which maternal stress or anxiety during pregnancy may permanently affect the child. There may be a gross effect on organ formation, an effect on birth outcome such as *prematurity*, or there can be an independent effect on the later behavior of the child. There is some evidence for all of these effects.

Organ Formation and Neurological Development

Some studies have found that mothers of children with congenital abnormalities had more stress during pregnancy than controls (e.g., Nimby, Lundberg, Sveger, & McNeil, 1999). A very large study found that severe stress, as assessed by severe life events in the first trimester of pregnancy, caused an increased risk of congenital abnormalities in neural crest derived organs (e.g, *cleft palate*), with an odds ratio (OR) of 1.54 (Hansen et al., 2000). The most severe stress, associated with the unexpected death of a child, was associated with an increased OR of 8.36 for *cranial-neural crest malformations* and 3.64 for other malformations. It is likely that stress at different times in gestation has contrasting long-term effects, with *gross organ development* being affected by stress in the first trimester.

Studies on Birth Outcome

Most of the human studies have focused on birth outcome. In general, the results point in the same direction; namely, that antenatal stress or anxiety is linked with babies who are small-for-gestational age (SGA) and born earlier. Several studies have shown that antenatal distress (anxiety or stress) is associated with *preterm delivery* (Copper et al., 1996; Hedegaard, Henriksen, Sabroe, & Secher, 1993; Nordentoft et al., 1996). However, Perkin, Bland, Peacock, & Anderson (1993), in a study of 1,860 white London women, failed to find any substantial link between antenatal maternal anxiety or depression and the obstetrical complications examined, including preterm delivery and induced labor. The only significant association was between ante-natal anxiety and the amount of analgesia/anaesthesia used in the second stage of labor. In contrast, Hedegaard et al. (1993) studied 8,719 women, using the *General Health Questionnaire* score as an index of psychological distress. They found a significant association between scores at thirty weeks, and the risk of preterm delivery (<37 weeks). The relative risk for *preterm delivery* was 1.22 for moderate and 1.75 for high distress, compared to low levels of distress. There was no relation with distress early in pregnancy. The authors concluded that future intervention studies should aim to lower psychological stress in late pregnancy.

Another study assessed anxiety, perceived stress, depression, self-esteem, and mastery in relation to spontaneous preterm birth (<35 weeks) in a sample of 2,593 women (Copper et al., 1996). After con-trolling by multivariate analysis for smoking, social status, race, and so on, they found that among psychological factors, perceived stress was a risk factor for spontaneous preterm birth and for low (below 2,500 grams) birthweight. Nordentoft et al. (1996) studied 2,432 women using a psychosocial stress questionnaire, and they found stress to be associated with preterm delivery, and smoking with *intra-uterine growth restriction.*

Preterm delivery is a major cause of both mortality and morbidity in the child, the latter including behavioral problems, but especially if it occurs at the earlier gestational age (namely, before thirty-two weeks). In general, these studies have looked at later preterm delivery between thirty-two and thirty-seven weeks. However, Lou et al. (1992) have shown that seriously psychological stressful events contributed 11% to *severe prematurity,* using a cut-off of below thirty-four weeks.

More research is needed to assess the role of *psychosocial stress* on early preterm delivery. It would also be of value to distinguish between spontaneous preterm delivery with labor, and preterm deliv-ery that is induced due to some other cause, such as *pre-eclampsia.* These may well be caused by different mechanisms. A recent study (Dayan et al., 2002) has shown that both anxiety and depression can contribute to early *preterm labor* (namely, mean gestation of thirty-two weeks), when combined with other factors such as vaginal bleed-ing or a previous preterm labor.

Several studies have found a link between *psychosocial stress* or *anxi-ety* and babies born *SGA* (e.g., Lobel, Dunkel-Schetter, & Scrimshaw, 1992; Wadhwa, Sandman, Porto, Dunkel-Schetter, & Garite, 1993), although a Scandinavian study failed to find such a link (Jacobsen,

Schei, & Hoffman, 1997). As lower birthweight, across the full range, appears to be a risk factor for disease in later life, such as coronary heart disease (Barker et al., 1993), these findings also have implications for the general health of the population. *Low birthweight* may also be linked with later mental health problems. A recent study (Hultman et al., 1999) has revealed that there was an increased risk of *schizophrenia* in boys who were SGA at birth (i.e., 2 SD below mean) with an OR of 3.2 compared with those with an average birthweight. Large babies (> 2 SD above mean) had only 0.6 of the average risk.

The mechanism or mechanisms linking small babies to predisposition to later disease is still unclear. Genetic factors could be involved that cause low birthweight and are a later risk factor. It is known that *glucocorticoids*, including *cortisol*, cause slowing of growth (Mosier, Dearden, Jansons, Roberts, & Biggs, 1982; Novy & Walsh, 1983; Reinisch, Simon, Karow, & Gandelman, 1978; Seckl, 1994). It is thus possible that, at least in a proportion of cases, the mother has high cortisol in pregnancy due to a hyper-responsive *HPA*, and that her child inherits both this and a predisposition to disease. The low birthweight, then, would not be part of the causal pathway.

Birth

An important discontinuity between the fetal period and the child is the event of *birth* itself. This is the most stressful event that most infants experience, and it varies considerably between them depending on different modes of delivery. Those born by *elective caesarean* have the lowest cord *cortisol* levels, and those born by assisted delivery have the highest levels (Gitau et al., 2001). These groups had different stress responses to their *inoculation jab* at eight weeks (Taylor, Fisk, & Glover, 2000). Those born by assisted delivery had the greatest saliva cortisol response, and those born by vaginal delivery had the least. It is not yet known how long these effects last. However, animal data has shown that stress during birth (Boksa, Krishnamurthy, & Sharma, 1996), or in the first weeks following birth (Meaney et al., 1993), can have very long-term behavioral effects.

Effects on Child Behavior

There is much less evidence concerning the effect of antenatal stress or anxiety on the behavioral development of the child. A Danish study

(Lou et al., 1994), using the same cohort as Nordentoft et al. (1996), examined links between life events and *fetal brain development*. The authors followed 3,021 women through pregnancy, obtaining information about life-event stress by questionnaire. They found that both antenatal stress and *smoking* contributed independently to a lower gestational age at delivery, lower birthweight, and smaller head circumference corrected for birthweight, which suggests a specific effect of stress on brain growth. The effect of stress on birthweight, a mean reduction of about 250 grams, was comparable to that of smoking. Prenatal stress also significantly reduced the scores on the neonatal neurological examination. Based on this outcome, these authors have suggested the existence of a *Fetal Stress Syndrome*, analogous to the *Fetal Alcohol Syndrome*.

The hypothesis that antenatal stress predisposes to behavioral disturbance in human offspring (Glover, 1997; Glover & O'Connor, 2002) was first suggested many years ago (Stott, 1973), but the few studies in this area are of small sample size, lack statistical control of confounding variables, rely on retrospective reports, and fail to distinguish pre- from postnatal stress (McIntosh, Mulkins, & Dean, 1995; Meijer, 1985; Stott, 1973).

The ALSPAC Studies

To overcome the problems mentioned above, we have taken advantage of the *Avon Longitudinal Study of Parents and Children* (ALSPAC) cohort (O'Connor et al., 2002). This is a longitudinal, prospective study of women, their partners, and an index child (Golding, Pembrey, Jones, & the ALSPAC Study Team, 2001). The study design included recruitment of all pregnant women living in the geographical area of Avon, England, who were to deliver their baby between April 1, 1991 and December 31, 1992. It was estimated that 85%–90% of the eligible population took part. All data were collected via postal questionnaires. The information available for our study was based on an N of 7,448.

Data were collected during several assessments in the antenatal and postnatal period. Maternal anxiety and depression were assessed on two occasions in the antenatal period (eighteen weeks and thirty-two weeks gestation), and at eight weeks, eight months, and twenty-one months and thirty-three months postnatally. Data on covariates used in the analyses were assessed during pregnancy and shortly after birth. Data on children's behavioral/emotional problems were collected at forty-seven months. Maternal anxiety was measured using the anxiety items from the *Crown-Crisp Experiential Index*, a validated self-rating inventory (Birtchnell, Evans, & Kennard, 1988). As there is no well-established clinical cut-off for this measure, we identified as anxious those mothers who scored in the top 15% at each assessment. Maternal depression was assessed using the *Edinburgh Postnatal Depression Scale* (EPDS) at the same time points (Cox, Holden, & Sagovsky, 1987; Murray & Cox, 1990).

Key obstetrical factors likely to be directly or indirectly related to children's behavioral outcomes were included as covariates. Those included were gestational age, birthweight for gestational age (corrected for child sex, parity, and maternal age and weight), mode of delivery (cesarean or vaginal delivery), and first- or later-born status. Behavioral adjustment in children at age forty-seven months was based on parent reports (Goodman & Scott, 1999), using an adaptation of a previously widely used index of psychiatric symptoms in children (Elander & Rutter, 1996). This measure, which has three problem behavior sub-scales (conduct problems, emotional problems, hyperactivity/inattention), has established links with clinical levels of disturbance (Goodman & Scott, 1999). We identified children with difficulties based on statistically high scores, using a cut-off of 2 SD above the mean, which was approximately the top 5%. Cut-off scores were derived separately for male and females because of the sex differences in mean scores on these measures. Consequently, analyses are conducted separately for males and females.

Initial bivariate analyses indicated that mothers who scored in the top 15% of the sample on anxiety at eighteen or thirty-two weeks gestation were two to three times more likely to have a child who scored more than 2 SD above the mean in behavioral/emotional problems. The next set of analyses provide a stronger test of the effects of antenatal anxiety by including antenatal, obstetrical, and psychosocial covariates, together with postnatal assessments of anxiety and depression at eight weeks. The results for total problems for boys and girls showed that mothers who experienced markedly elevated anxiety at thirty-two weeks gestation were more than twice as likely to have children with markedly elevated behavioral/emotional problems at four years of age (OR = 2.14 for boys and 1.88 for girls). The effects of antenatal anxiety were equally strong for boys and girls, although the prediction from other covariates differed slightly for boys and girls. Mothers anxious at eighteen weeks gestation, but not later, did not show these predictions.

To determine whether or not the effect of antenatal anxiety could be distinguished from the cumulative effect of postnatal anxiety throughout the child's early years, we re-ran the models including maternal anxiety at eight, twenty-one, and thirty-three months postnatally. Analyses indicated that, for both boys and girls, the composite measure of total problems remained significantly associated with late antenatal anxiety, even when the effects of antenatal, obstetrical, and psychosocial covariates (as well as four measures of *postnatal anxiety*) were statistically controlled. In these models, the odds ratios for maternal anxiety at thirty-two weeks gestation were 1.56 (95% CI = 1.02–2.41) for boys and 1.51 (95% CI = 1.01–2.27) for girls. In addition, for males, late antenatal anxiety was significantly associated with *hyperactivity/inattention* at age forty-seven months, even after postnatal self-reports of anxiety at eight weeks and eight, twenty-one, and thirty-three months were included in the model (OR = 1.85, 95% CI = 1.22–2.81). These odds ratios refer to mothers who reached the cut-off for anxiety at thirty-two weeks gestation, but at none of the other measured time points, and it is a very stringent measure that is only achievable because of the large sample size.

Similar but somewhat weaker effects were found if antenatal depression, instead of antenatal anxiety, was included in the model. When both were included, the effect of antenatal anxiety reduced that of antenatal depression to non-significance. The effects of antenatal anxiety and postnatal depression on child behavioral problems at forty-seven months were independent and additive.

In summary, we have found strong and significant links between antenatal anxiety and children's behavioral/emotional problems at about four years of age. Associations were found for a range of disturbances in children, both boys and girls. The most impressive finding was that elevated levels of anxiety in late pregnancy were associated with hyperactivity/inattention in boys, and total behavioral/emotional problems in both boys and girls, even when the effects of multiple postnatal reports of anxiety were statistically controlled for. This makes it unlikely that this link is due to genetic transmission or to postnatal anxiety affecting parenting; rather, as in the animal models, it is likely due to a direct causal mechanism operating in the antenatal period.

The finding that the effects were strongest for antenatal anxiety at thirty-two weeks, rather than eighteen weeks, is of interest. While whole organs are formed in the first trimester, synaptic connections in the brain are formed in the second half of gestation. However, more evidence is need to be sure of exactly which part of gestation is most sensitive for these effects to occur.

Links between Maternal Antenatal Anxiety and Mixed-Handedness in the Child

In animal models, prenatal stress is associated both with behavioral alterations in the offspring and with changes in *laterality* (Alonso, Castellano, & Rodriguez, 1991; Fride & Weinstock, 1989; Weinstock, 2001). *Atypical handedness* in children has been associated with a range of conditions such as *attention deficit/hyperactivity, autism* (Baron Cohen & Hammer, 1997), *dyslexia* (Annett, Eglinton, & Smythe, 1996), and *altered sexual orientation.* Although it certainly has a genetic component (Annett, 1995) it has also has been suggested to be partly neurodevelopmental in origin (Geschwind & Galaburda, 1987). Thus, antenatal stress or anxiety may cause alterations in brain development and morphology, which both affect a range of behavioral problems in the child and laterality.

We have used the ALSPAC cohort of mothers and children to examine the link between antenatal maternal anxiety and *handedness* in the child (Glover et al., 2004). Child handedness was assessed by maternal report at forty-two months postnatally, from a scale developed by Coren (1992) based on six items (e.g., throwing a ball, using a toothbrush). Maternal handedness was assessed using a similar eleven-item scale. For child and mother measures, scores were scaled to distinguish right-, left-, and mixed- or non-dominant handedness. Information on the handedness of the father was based on maternal report of a single item, indicating left-, mixed-, or right-handedness. Several potentially relevant antenatal, obstetrical, and psychosocial variables were included as covariates, as in the behavioral study previously described. The final sample for whom full data were available consisted of 7,016 mother and children pairs.

Multivariate analysis showed that *laterality* was linked with maternal anxiety in the antenatal but not the postnatal period, and it was *mixed-handedness* rather than left-handedness that was affected. Further analyses were conducted to assess the joint effect of the multiple measures of maternal anxiety simultaneously, together with a multivariate analysis using all the variables used. The findings suggest that the effect of antenatal anxiety at eighteen weeks gestation on mixed-handedness in the child was independent of later antenatal anxiety (OR = 1.39, 95% CI = 1.16–1.66, p = 0.001). The effects were similar for the two sexes: the ORs for antenatal anxiety at eighteen weeks were 1.40 (1.09–1.78, p < 0.01) for boys, and 1.38 (1.06–1.80, p < 0.05) for girls.

These results provide new evidence for *fetal programming* in humans. They suggest that a proportion of mixed-handedness may be neuro-developmental in origin and affected by the uterine environment, which in turn may be affected by hormonal levels in the mother. It is an interesting possibility that a range of learning and behavioral disorders, such as *dyslexia* (Annett et al., 1996), *autism* spectrum (Baron-Cohen & Hammer, 1997) and *hyperactivity/attention deficit* (Reid & Norvilitis, 2000) linked with mixed-handedness, have a neurodevelopmental component that is also exacerbated by antenatal maternal stress or anxiety.

Related Studies

There are several other recent studies that are generating similar findings. In general, they are with much smaller cohorts but have the advantage of direct observations, rather than results from question-naires. However, the small sample size makes it hard to separate direct antenatal effects from genetic links, and to separate older infants and children from the effects of parenting. One study followed 170 nulliparous women through pregnancy and up to eight months postpartum (Huizink, de Medina, Mulder, Visser, & Buitelaar, 2002). Higher levels of maternal stress and anxiety during the first trimester of pregnancy were associated with low psychomotor scores on the Bayley developmental test at eight months. van den Bergh & Marcoen (2004) followed up seventy mother-infant pairs to nine years. During the first seven moths the infants of the more anxious women cried more and had a more difficult temperament. At nine years old, the children (boys in particular) were more active, showed more attention deficits, and were more aggressive. Brouwers, van Baar, & Pop (2001) followed a cohort of 105 mothers through pregnancy. They found links between high maternal anxiety at thirty-two weeks gestation and lower mental developmental scores at two years, and impaired attention-related processes. Problems with attention are thus a finding common to all the studies that examined it. However, the different studies disagree as to which is the most sensitive period of gestation. This may be partly because all have used different windows and only located part of the sensitive time.

Obel et al. (2003) have also found a link between maternal antenatal anxiety and *handedness*. They also reported that it is mixed-
rather than left-handedness that is most affected, but that the most
sensitive period is later in gestation (thirty as opposed to sixteen
weeks).

MECHANISMS BY WHICH MATERNAL STRESS
MAY EFFECT THE FETUS

Two mechanisms of transmission of stress from mother to fetus
in humans have been suggested (Gitau, Fisk, & Glover, 2001). One
hypothesis is that maternal stress hormones, and, in particular,
glucocorticoids, are transmitted across the placenta. A second possible mechanism is via an effect on uterine artery blood flow
(Fig. 7.2).

Transfer of Hormones across the Placenta

In utero exposure to abnormally high levels of maternal *glucocorticoids* is one plausible mechanism by which maternal stress may affect
the fetus. It is known that excess glucocorticoids retard fetal growth
in animals and humans (Mosier et al., 1982; Novy & Walsh, 1983;

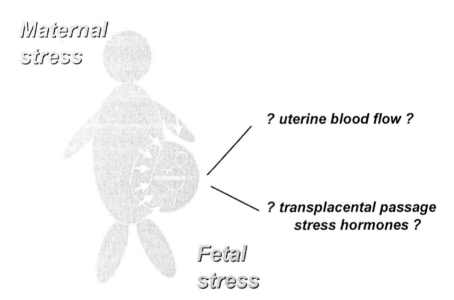

Maternal stress

? uterine blood flow ?

? transplacental passage
stress hormones ?

Fetal stress

Figure 7.2. Possible mechanisms by which changes in maternal mood
may be communicated to the fetus.

Reinisch et al., 1978; Seckl, 1994), and that fetal *cortisol* levels are increased in human fetuses showing *intrauterine growth restriction* (Goland et al., 1993). *In utero* exposure to synthetic glucocorticoids in laboratory animals can have neurotoxic effects on the brain development of the offspring (Epstein et al., 1977; Uno et al., 1990) and also cause organ malformation early in gestation (Fraser & Fainstat, 1951). However, the placenta is generally viewed as an effective barrier between the maternal and fetal hormonal environments in humans, being rich in protective enzymes such as monoamine oxidase A, peptidases, and 11-hydroxysteroid dehydrogenase type 2, which converts cortisol to inactive products (Lopez-Bernal, Flint, Anderson, & Turnbull, 1980; Murphy, Clark, Donald, Pinsky, & Vedady, 1974).

We have shown that maternal *cortisol* plasma concentration is directly correlated with fetal levels. Comparing basal levels of cortisol in paired maternal and fetal plasma samples taken at the same time, fetal concentrations were linearly related to maternal levels (r = 0.58, n = 51, p < 0.001) (Gitau et al., 1998). As maternal concentrations are substantially higher than fetal ones (over ten-fold), this is compatible with substantial (80%–90%) metabolism of maternal cortisol during passage across the placenta, and is in accord with *in vivo* (Murphy et al., 1974) and *ex vivo* studies (Benediktsson, Calder, Edwards, & Seckl, 1997).

With both *β-endorphin* and *noradrenaline*, there was no significant correlation between maternal and fetal plasma levels (Giannakoulopoulos, Teixeira, Fisk, & Glover, 1999). Neither β-endorphin nor noradrenaline is lipophilic, and neither would be expected to cross cell membranes as readily as *cortisol*.

Impaired Uterine Blood Flow

We have tested the hypothesis that anxiety in pregnant women is associated with abnormal blood flow in the *uterine arteries* (Teixeira, Fisk, & Glover, 1999). *Color Doppler ultrasound* was used to measure the blood flow pattern, and the Resistance Index (RI) was calculated from the recordings by standard procedures. A high RI indicates a greater resistance to blood flow, and it is known to be associated with adverse obstetrical outcome, particularly intrauterine growth restriction and pre-eclampsia.

We studied 100 women with singleton pregnancies between twenty-eight and thirty-two weeks of gestation. Mothers completed the *Spielberger Anxiety questionnaire* (Spielberger, 1983), which measures both State (how you feel right now) and Trait (how you generally feel).

There was a significant association between the RI in the uterine artery and both State and Trait Anxiety ($r_s = 0.31$, p < 0.002 and 0.28, p < 0.005, respectively). When the groups were divided according to their Spielberger Anxiety scores of 20–29, 30–39, or 40 and more, women in the highest State and Trait Anxiety groups had significantly worse uterine flow velocity waveform patterns than those in the lower anxiety groups. This study demonstrated that women with raised anxiety are more likely to have abnormal uterine blood flow parameters than those with lower anxiety.

These findings have recently been confirmed in a larger cohort. The association between maternal anxiety and uterine blood flow was present at thirty weeks, but not at twenty weeks gestation (Jackson, Fisk, Adams, & Glover, raw data, 2001). However, we do not know whether these associations between anxiety and Doppler pattern are acute or chronic. Further work is needed to determine whether overall anxiety during pregnancy, or even prior to or at conception, might affect uterine artery blood flow patterns, or instead, whether the association is only with the current emotional state.

It has been shown in a rat model study that cold stress early in pregnancy decreased trophoblastic invasion, and this was followed by increased blood pressure, raised blood catecholamine levels, and proteinuria in later pregnancy (Kanayama, Tsujimura, She, Maehara, & Terao, 1997). The authors suggest that they have produced a model for *pre-eclampsia*, mediated by increased *catecholamines* causing decreased trophoblastic invasion. These results raise the possibility that maternal stress or anxiety early in gestation might affect the outcome of pregnancy.

It is also possible that anxiety causes acute changes in uterine artery blood flow. Infusion of *noradrenaline* decreases uterine blood flow in pregnant sheep (Rosenfeld & West, 1977). In sheep, reproductive tissues, including the uterus, are more sensitive to the vasoconstrictive effects of noradrenaline than other body tissues.

To summarize, we have found two distinct mechanisms—placental transfer of *cortisol* and constriction of uterine blood flow—by which maternal anxiety or stress during pregnancy may affect the fetus. We have also recently found (Gitau, Fisk, Adams, & Glover, raw data, 2001) that the most anxious pregnant women, at twenty weeks gestation, had both raised plasma cortisol and raised corticotropin-releasing hormone (CRH). *CRH* is released from the placenta into the maternal circulation (Fig. 7.1), and this has been shown to be positively driven by cortisol. It is also known that raised CRH at this stage is associated with *preterm delivery* (Smith, 1999). This may begin to explain the mechanism of the link between maternal stress/anxiety and preterm labor.

Much remains, however, to be understood. We need to know more about the biochemical correlates of anxiety, stress, and the response to life events in the pregnant woman at different periods of gestation. We also need to know the ways in which these factors may affect organ formation, infant growth, age at delivery, and later behavior, and we need to be aware that these may all be by different mechanisms. We know that the mother's *HPA* becomes desensitized as her pregnancy develops (Kammerer, Adams, von Castelberg, & Glover, 2002; Schulte et al., 1990), presumably due to the large amounts of *CRH* that are released from the placenta, but we do not know exactly when and how much. A summary of some of the different mechanisms involving the HPA is given in Figure 7.3.

Possible mechanisms

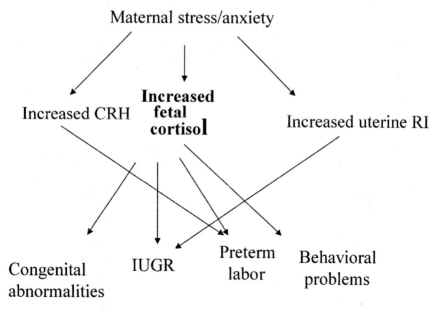

Figure 7.3. Possible mechanisms by which maternal mood may affect fetal development via the HPA.

Table 7.1: **Links between Maternal Antenatal Stress or Anxiety and Adverse Outcome**

Adverse Outcome	References
Organ malformation	Nimby et al. (1999)
	Hansen et al. (2000)
Preterm delivery	Lou et al. (1992)
	Hedegaard et al. (1993)
	Copper et al. (1996)
	Nordentoft et al. (1996)
	Dayan et al. (2002)
	Perkin et al. (1993)-negative*
Low birthweight for gestational age	Lobel et al. (1992)
	Wadhwa et al. (1993)
	Jacobsen et al. (1997)-negative
Behavioral problems	O'Connor et al. (2002)
	Huizink et al. (2002)
	Obel et al. (2003)
	van den Berg & Marcoen (2004)
	Brouwers et al. (2001)
Mixed-handedness	Glover et al. (2004)
	Obel et al. (2003)

* No adverse outcome was found.

CONCLUSIONS

In thinking about the effects of the environment, we now have to start with the uterine environment. There is considerable evidence from animal studies that maternal antenatal stress can have long-term effects on the behavioral development of the offspring. We are used to the idea that there can be external teratogens, and that the first few months of gestation are a vulnerable time for brain development. It increasingly seems likely that there are also more subtle long-term effects caused by the hormonal environment, perhaps also acting later in gestation. In humans, maternal stress may have effects on the immediate obstetrical outcome. Possible adverse outcomes include babies born SGA and those born early (see Table 7.1 for further details). Both of these conditions are known risk factors for vulnerability to later disease (Barker, 1999; Barker et al., 1993). There is also increasing evidence that maternal stress or anxiety during gestation can be influential in ways that can continue to have adverse impacts on the behavior of the child (Brouwers et al., 2001; Huizink et al., 2002; O'Connor et al., 2002).

REFERENCES

Alonso, J., Castellano, M.A., & Rodriguez, M. (1991). Behavioral lateralisation in rats: Prenatal stress effects on sex differences. *Brain Research, 539*, 45–50.

Annett, M. (1995). The right shift theory of a genetic balanced polymorphism for cerebral dominance and cognitive processing. *Current Psychology of Cognition, 14*, 427–480.

Annett, M., Eglinton, E., & Smythe, P. (1996). Types of dyslexia and the shift to dextrality. *Journal of Child Psychology and Psychiatry, 37*, 167–180.

Barbazanges, A., Piazza, P., Le Moal, M., & Maccari, S. (1996). Maternal glucocorticoid secretion mediates long-term effects of prenatal stress. *Journal of Neuroscience, 16*, 3943–3949.

Barker, D.J. (1999). The fetal origins of type 2 diabetes mellitus. *Annals of Internal Medicine, 130*, 322–324.

Barker, D.J., Hales, C.N., Fall, C.H., Osmond, C., Phipps, K., & Clark, P.M. (1993). Type 2 (non-insulin-dependent) diabetes mellitus, hypertension and hyperlipidaemia (syndrome X): Relation to reduced fetal growth. *Diabetologia, 36*, 62–67.

Baron-Cohen, S., & Hammer, J. (1997). Is autism an extreme form of the "male brain"? *Advances in Infancy Research, 11*, 193–217.

Benediktsson, R., Calder, A.A., Edwards, C.R., & Seckl, J.R. (1997). Placental 11 beta-hydroxysteroid dehydrogenase: A key regulator of fetal glucocorticoid exposure. *Clinical Endocrinology, 46*, 161–166.

Birtchnell, J., Evans, C., & Kennard, J. (1988). The total score of the Crown-Crisp Experiential Index: A useful and valid measure of psychoneurotic pathology. *British Journal of Medical Psychology, 61*, 255–266.

Boksa, P., Krishnamurthy, A., & Sharma, S. (1996). Hippocampal and hypothalamic type 1 corticosteroid receptor affinities are reduced in adult rats born by a caesarean section procedure with or without an added period of anoxia. *Neuroendocrinology, 64*, 25–34.

Brouwers, E., van Baar, A.L., & Pop, V.J.M. (2001). Maternal anxiety during pregnancy and subsequent infant development. *Infant Behavior and Development, 24*, 95–106.

Clarke, A.S., & Schneider, M.L. (1993). Prenatal stress has long-term effects on behavioral responses to stress in juvenile rhesus monkeys. *Developmental Psychobiology, 26*, 293–304.

Clarke, A.S., & Schneider, M.L. (1997). Effects of prenatal stress on behavior in adolescent rhesus monkeys. *Annals of New York Academy of Sciences, 807,* 490–491.

Clarke, A.S., Wittwer, D.J., Abbott, D.H., & Schneider, M.L. (1994). Long-term effects of prenatal stress on HPA axis activity in juvenile rhesus monkeys. *Developmental Psychobiology, 27,* 257–269.

Copper, R.L. Goldenber, R.L., Das, A., Elder, N., Swain, M., Norman, G., et al. (1996). The preterm prediction study: Maternal stress is associated with spontaneous preterm birth at less than thirty five weeks gestation. *American Journal of Obstetrics and Gynecology, 175,* 1286–1292.

Coren, S. (1992). *The causes and consequences of left handedness.* London: John Murray.

Cox, J.L., Holden, J.M., & Sagovsky, R. (1987). Development of the Edinburgh Postnatal Depression Scale. *British Journal of Psychiatry, 150,* 782–786.

Dayan, J., Crevveuil, C., Herlicoviez, M., Herbel, C., Baranger, E., Savoye, C., et al. (2002). Role of anxiety and depression in the onset of spontaneous preterm labour. *Amercian Journal of Epidemiology, 155,* 293–301.

Elander, J., & Rutter, M. (1996). Use and development of the Rutter parents' and teachers' scales. *International Journal of Methods in Psychiatric Research, 16,* 63–78.

Epstein, M.F., Farrell, P.M., Sparks, J.W., Pepe, G., Driscoll, S.G., & Chez, R.A. (1977). Maternal betamethasone and fetal growth and development in the monkey. *American Journal Obstetrics and Gynecology, 127,* 261–263.

Fraser, F.C., & Fainstat, T.D. (1951). Production of congenital defects in the offspring of pregnant mice treated with cortisone. *Pediatrics, 8,* 527–533.

Fride, E., & Weinstock, M. (1989). Alterations in behavioral and striatal dopamine asymmetries induced by prenatal stress. *Pharmacology Biochemistry and Behavior, 32,* 425–430.

Geschwind, N., & Galaburda, A. (1987). *Cerebral lateralisation.* Cambridge, MA: MIT Press.

Giannakoulopoulos, X., Teixeira, J., Fisk, N., & Glover, V. (1999). Human fetal and maternal noradrenaline responses to invasive procedures. *Pediatric Research, 45,* 494–499.

Gitau, R., Cameron, A., Fisk, N.M., & Glover, V. (1998). Fetal exposure to maternal cortisol. *Lancet, 352,* 707–708.

Gitau, R., Fisk, N.M., & Glover, V. (2001). Maternal stress in pregnancy and its effect on the human foetus: An overview of research findings. *Stress, 4,* 195–203.

Gitau, R., Menson, E., Pickles, V., Fisk, N.M., Glover, V., & MacLachlan, N. (2001). Umbilical cortisol levels as an indicator of the fetal stress response to assisted vaginal delivery. *European Journal Obstetrics and Gynecology and Reproductive Biology, 98,* 14–17.

Glover, V. (1997). Maternal stress or anxiety in pregnancy and emotional development of the child. *British Journal of Psychiatry, 171,* 105–106.

Glover, V., & O'Connor, T.G. (2002). Effects of antenatal stress and anxiety: Implications for development and psychiatry. *British Journal of Psychiatry, 180,* 389–391.

Glover, V., O'Connor, T.G., Heron, J., Golding, J., & the ALSPAC Study Team (2004). Antenatal maternal anxiety is linked with atypical handedness in the child. *Early Human Development, 79,* 107–118.

Goland, R.S., Jozak, S., Warren, W.B., Conwell, I.M., Stark, R.I., & Tropper, P.J. (1993). Elevated levels of umbilical cord plasma corticotropin-releasing hormone in growth-retarded fetuses. *Journal of Clinical Endocrinology and Metabolism, 77,* 1174–1179.

Gold, P.W., & Chrousos, G.P. (2002). Organization of the stress system and its dysregulation in melancholic and atypical depression: High versus low CRH/NE states. *Molecular Psychiatry, 7,* 254–275.

Golding, J., Pembrey, M., Jones, R., & the ALSPAC Study Team. (2001). ALSPAC—The Avon Longitudinal Study of Parents and Children. I. Study methodology. *Paediatric and Perinatology Epidemiology, 15,* 74–87.

Goodman, R., & Scott, S. (1999). Comparing the strengths and difficulties questionnaire and the child behavior checklist: Is small beautiful? *Journal of Abnormal Child Psychology, 27,* 17–24.

Hansen, D., Lou, H.C., & Olsen, J. (2000). Serious life events and congenital malformations: A national study with complete follow-up. *Lancet, 356,* 875–880.

Hedegaard, M., Henriksen, T.B., Sabroe, S., & Secher, N.J. (1993). Psychological distress in pregnancy and preterm delivery. *British Medical Journal, 307,* 235–239.

Henry, C., Kabbaj, M., Simon, H., Le Moal, M., & Maccari, S. (1994). Prenatal stress increases the hypothalamo-pituitary-adrenal axis response in young and adult rats. *Journal of Neuroendocrinolology, 6,* 341–345.

Huizink, A.C., de Medina, P.G.R., Mulder, E.J.H., Visser, G.H.A., & Buitelaar, J.K. (2002). Psychological measures of prenatal stress as predictors of infant temperament. *Journal of American Academy of Child and Adolescent Psychiatry, 41,* 1078–1085.

Hultman, C.M., Sparen, P., Takei, N., Murray, R.M., Cnattingius, S., & Geddes, J. (1999). Prenatal and perinatal risk factors for schizophrenia, affective psychosis, and reactive psychosis of early onset: Case-control study. *British Medical Journal, 318,* 421–426.

Insel, T. (1990). Prenatal stress has long term effects on brain opiate receptors. *Brain Research, 511,* 93–97.

Jacobsen, G., Schei, B., & Hoffman, H.J. (1997). Psychosocial factors and small-for-gestational-age infants among parous Scandinavian women. *Acta Obstetrica et Gynecologica Scandinavica, 165*(Suppl.), 14–18.

Kammerer, M., Adams, D., von Castelberg, B., & Glover, V. (2002). Pregnant women become insensitive to cold stress. *BMC Pregnancy and Childbirth, 2*, 8.

Kanayama, N., Tsujimura, R., She, L., Maehara, K., & Terao, T. (1997). Cold-induced stress stimulates the sympathetic nervous system, causing hypertension and proteinuria in rats. *Journal of Hypertension, 15*, 383–389.

Lobel, M., Dunkel-Schetter, C., & Scrimshaw, S.C. (1992). Prenatal maternal stress and prematurity: A prospective study of socioeconomically disadvantaged women. *Health Psychology, 11*, 32–40.

Lopez-Bernal, A., Flint, A.P.F., Anderson, A.B.M., & Turnbull, A.C. (1980). 11b-hydroxysteroid dehydrogenase activity in human placenta and decidua. *Journal of Steroid Biochemistry and Molecular Biology, 13*, 1081–1087.

Lou, H.C., Nordentoft, M., Jensen, F., Pryds, O., Nim, J., & Hemmingsen, R. (1992). Psychosocial stress and severe prematurity. *Lancet, 340*, 54.

Lou, H., Hansen, D., Nordentoft, M., Pyrds, O., Jensenn, F., Nim, J., et al. (1994). Prenatal stressors of human life affect fetal brain development. *Developmental Medicine and Child Neurology, 36*, 826–832.

McIntosh, D.E., Mulkins, R.S., & Dean, R.S. (1995). Utilization of perinatal risk indicators in the differential diagnosis of ADHD and UADD. *International Journal of Neuroscience, 81*, 35–46.

Meaney, M., Bhatnager, S., Diorio, J., Larocque, S., Francis, D., O'Donnell, D., et al. (1993). Molecular basis for the development of individual differences in the hypothalamic-pituitary-adrenal stress response. *Cell Molecular Neurobiology, 13*, 321–347.

Meijer, A. (1985). Child psychiatric sequelae of maternal war stress. *Acta Psychiatrica Scandinavia, 72*, 505–511.

Mosier, H.D.J., Dearden, L.C., Jansons, R.A., Roberts, R.C., & Biggs, C.S. (1982). Disproportionate growth of organs and body weight following glucocorticoid treatment of the rat fetus. *Developmental Pharmacology and Therapeutics, 4*, 89–105.

Murphy, B.E.P., Clark, S.J., Donald, I.R., Pinsky, M., & Vedady, D. (1974). Conversion of maternal cortisol to cortisone during placental transfer to the human fetus. *American Journal of Obstetrics and Gynecology, 118*, 538–541.

Murray, D., & Cox, J.L. (1990). Screening for depression during pregnancy with the Edinburgh Depression scale (EPDS). *Journal of Reproductive and Infant Psychology, 8*, 99–107.

Nimby, G.T., Lundberg, L., Sveger, T., & McNeil, T.F. (1999). Maternal distress and congenital malformations: Do mothers of malformed fetuses have more problems? *Journal of Psychiatric Research, 33*, 291–301.

Nordentoft, M., Lou, H.C., Hansen, D., Nim, J., Pryds, O., Rubin, P., et al. (1996). Intrauterine growth retardation and premature delivery: the influence of maternal smoking and psychosocial factors. *American Journal of Public Health, 86*, 347–354.

Novy, M.J., & Walsh, S.W. (1983). Dexamethasone and estradiol treatment in pregnant rhesus macaques: Effects on gestational length, maternal plasma hormones, and fetal growth. *American Journal of Obstetrics and Gynecology, 145*, 920–931.

Obel, C., Hedegaard, M., Henriksen, T.B., Secher, N.J., & Olsen, J. (2003). Psychological factors in pregnancy and mixed-handedness in the offspring. *Developmental Medicine and Child Neurology, 45*, 557–561.

O'Connor, T., Heron, J., Golding, J., Beveridge, M., & Glover, V. (2002). Maternal antenatal anxiety and children's behavioral/emotional problems at 4 years. *British Journal of Psychiatry, 180*, 502–508.

Perkin, M.R., Bland, J.M., Peacock, J.L., & Anderson, H.R. (1993). The effect of anxiety and depression during pregnancy on obstetric complications. *British Journal of Obstetrics and Gynaecology, 100*, 629–634.

Petraglia, F., Potter, E., Cameron, V.A., Sutton, S., Behan, D.P., Woods, R.J., et al. (1993). Corticotropin-releasing factor-binding protein is produced by human placenta and intrauterine tissues. *Journal of Clinical Endocrinology and Metabolism, 77*, 919–924.

Reid, H.M., & Norvilitis, J.M. (2000). Evidence for anomalous lateralisation across domain in ADHD children as well as adults identified with the Wender Utah rating scale. *Journal of Psychiatric Research, 34*, 311–316.

Reinisch, J.M., Simon, N.G., Karow, W.G., & Gandelman, R. (1978). Prenatal exposure to prednisone in humans and animals retards intrauterine growth. *Science, 202*, 436–438.

Rosenfeld, C.R., & West, J. (1977). Circulatory response to systemic infusion of norepinephrine in the pregnant ewe. *American Journal of Obstetrics and Gynecology, 127*, 376–383.

Schneider, M., Moore, C.F., Roberts, A.D., & Dejesus, O. (2001). Prenatal stress alters early neurobehavior, stress reactivity and learning in nonhuman primates: A brief review. *Stress, 4*, 183–193.

Schneider, M.L., Roughton, E.C., Koehler, A.J., & Lubach, G.R. (1999). Growth and development following pernatal stress exposure in primates: An examination of ontogenetic vulnerability. *Child Development, 70*, 263–274.

Schneider, M.L., & Suomi, S.J. (1992). Neurobehavioral assessment in rhesus monkey neonates (*Macaca mulatta*): Developmental changes, behavioral stability, and early experience. *Infant Behavior Development, 15*, 155–177.

Schulte, H.M., Weisner, D., & Allolio, B. (1990). The corticotrophin releasing hormone test in late pregnancy: Lack of adrenocorticotrophin and cortisol response. *Clinical Endocrinology, 33*, 99–106.

Seckl, J.R. (1994). Glucocorticoids and small babies [Editorial]. *Quarterly Journal of Medicine, 87*, 259–262.

Shalev, U., & Weiner, I. (2001). Gender-dependent differences in latent inhibition following prenatal stress and corticosterone administration. *Behavioral Brain Research, 126*, 57–63.

Smith, R. (1999). The timing of birth. *Scientific American, 280*, 68–75.

Spielberger, C.D. (1983). *State-trait anxiety inventory for adults. Sampler set, manual test, scoring key.* Palo Alto, CA: Consulting Psychologists Press.

Stott, D.H. (1973). Follow-up study from birth of the effects of prenatal stresses. *Developmental Medicine and Child Neurology, 15,* 770–787.

Taylor, A., Fisk, N.M., & Glover, V. (2000). Mode of delivery and later stress response. *Lancet, 355,* 120.

Teixeira, J.M., Fisk, N.M., & Glover, V. (1999). Association between maternal anxiety in pregnancy and increased uterine artery resistance index: Cohort based study. *British Medical Journal, 318,* 153–157.

Thompson, W.R. (1957). Influence of prenatal maternal anxiety on emotionality in young rats. *Science, 15,* 698–699.

Uno, H., Lohmiller, L., Thieme, C., Kemnitz, J.W., Engle, M.J., Roecker, E.B., et al. (1990). Brain damage induced by prenatal exposure to dexamethasone in fetal rhesus macaques. I. Hippocampus. *Developmental Brain Research, 53,* 157–167.

van den Bergh, B.R.H., & Marcoen, A. (2004). High antenatal maternal anxiety is related to ADHD symptoms, externalizing problems, and anxiety in 8- and 9-year-olds. *Child Development, 75,* 1085–1097.

Wadhwa, P.D., Sandman, C.A., Porto, M., Dunkel-Schetter, C., & Garite, T.J. (1993). The association between prenatal stress and infant birth weight and gestational age at birth: A prospective investigation. *American Journal of Obstetrics and Gynecology, 169,* 858–865.

Ward, I.L. (1972). Prenatal stress feminizes and demasculanizes the behavior of males. *Science, 175,* 82–84.

Weinstock, M., (2001). Alterations induced by gestational stress in brain morphology and behavior of the offspring. *Progress in Neurobiology, 65,* 427–451.

FURTHER READING

Austin, M.P., & Leader, L. (2000). Maternal stress and obstetric and infant outcomes: epidemiological findings and neuroendocrine mechanisms. *Australian and New Zealand Journal of Obstetrics and Gynaecology, 40,* 331–337.

Barker, D.J. (1995). The fetal origins of adult disease. *Proceedings of the Royal Society London B Biological Sciences, 262,* 37–43.

Bateson, P., & Martin, P. (1999). *Design for a life. How behavior develops.* London: Cape.

Cicchetti, D., & Nurcombe, B. (Eds.). (2001). Stress and development: Biological and psychological consequences. *Development and Psychopathology, 13,* Special Issue.

Gitau, R., Fisk, N., Teixeira, J., Cameron, A., & Glover, V. (2001). Fetal HPA stress responses to invasive procedures are independent of maternal responses. *Journal of Clinical Endocrinology and Metabolism, 86,* 104–109.

Nathanielsz, P.W. (1992). *Life before birth: The challenges of fetal development.* New York: Freeman.

Nathanielsz, P.W. (1999). *Life in the womb: The origin of health and disease.* Ithaca, NY: Promethean Press.

Sapolsky, R.M. (1998). *Why zebras don't get ulcers: An updated guide to stress, stress-related diseases and coping.* New York: Freeman.

AUTHOR INDEX

Subject Index

About the Editors and Contributors

ANTHONY DECASPER is Professor of Psychology at the University of North Carolina–Greensboro. After receiving his PhD from Emory University in 1974, he studied perception and learning in human newborns, and since 1986 perception and learning in human fetuses. His fetal research resulted from collaboration with French colleagues, including the late Jean-Pierre Lecanuet. Among his research publications are those showing that fetuses register, with good fidelity, maternal voice and speech sounds that reach their ears during the normal course of gestation, and that this experience has a significant effect on their postnatal perception of speech and voice sounds as well as on postnatal instrumental learning when they serve as discriminative or reinforcing stimuli. He has also served as Head of Department while continuing his developmental research on early perception and learning.

JOHANNA I.P. DE VRIES received her MD from the University of Groningen. After Medical School, she began to study the qualitative and quantitative emergence of specific human fetal movement patterns. In 1987, she obtained her PhD on this topic, and the year thereafter her registration as gynecologist. Since 1988, she has worked at the Medical Centre of the Vrije Universiteit Amsterdam (VUA). As a clinician, she performs research on fetal and maternal monitoring. Her publications on fetal monitoring are focused on fetal motility, posture, and brain development. From the beginning, this research has involved a close collaboration with the Faculty of Human Movement Sciences at the VUA, and which is formalized within the Institute for Fundamental and Clinical Human Movement Sciences. This unique situation facilitates the study of the further development of fetuses after birth. In 2003, she was awarded a special Professorship in Fetal Developmental Neurology at the Faculty of Human Movement Sciences. Recently, she received two international prizes for the DVD *Fetal movements: Development of motility and posture before birth.*

VIVETTE GLOVER was trained as a biochemist at Oxford and did her PhD in neurochemistry at University College London. She then moved to Queen Charlotte's Maternity Hospital, where she worked in the field of biological psychiatry, especially on monoamine oxidase. In more recent years, she has applied this expertise to the problems of mothers and babies. She is currently Professor of Perinatal Psychobiology at Imperial College London. She has published over 380 papers. The current aims of her group are to study fetal and neonatal stress responses, methods to reduce them, and long-term effects. The effects of maternal psychopathology, both on the developing fetus and on the neonate, are also being studied. Recent projects of interest include studies showing that maternal antenatal anxiety doubles the risk for hyperactivity in boys, and studies showing possible mechanisms by which maternal anxiety may affect the development of the fetus.

CAROLYN GRANIER-DEFERRE is Associate Professor of Psychology at the Université René Descartes (Paris 5). She is the head of a research group on prenatal sensory perception and learning at the CNRS (Laboratoire Cognition et Développement, UMR 8605). After studying the behavioral and physiological effects of sound-enriched environments on the development of the auditory system in different strains of mice, she worked on prenatal hearing both in the guinea pig and the human. Since 1981, she has been associated with Marie-Claire Busnel and the late Jean-Pierre Lecanuet, first examining the properties of auditory response as a function of the acoustical characteristics of stimulus and fetal behavioral states, then sound discrimination in the near-term fetus. Her current research involves prenatal and neonatal sound categorization and learning and the consequence of stress and noisy environments on the developing ear.

BRIAN HOPKINS is Professor in the Department of Psychology at Lancaster University, where he has been for the last 10 years. Previously, he was Professor and Dean in the Faculty of Human Movement Sciences at the Vrije Universiteit Amsterdam for 10 years. His research interests cover the pre- and postnatal development of movement and posture, and within that context the developmental origins of laterality, all in relation to brain development. For a number of years, he has been editor of the journal *Infant and Child Development*.

SCOTT P. JOHNSON is at present Associate Professor in the Department of Psychology at New York University, having previously been Assistant Professor at Cornell University. His research interests concern infant perceptual and cognitive development, with an emphasis on visual perception, object concepts, and early learning, mainly using the head-free registration of eye movements.

GALE A. KLEVEN recently completed research in the Laboratory of Comparative Ethogenesis at the University of Iowa for which she was awarded a PhD in 2005. Her previous research focused on systematic exploration of patterns of early behavioral development, including the temporal organization of spontaneous movement in rodent fetuses and preterm human infants, and coordinated fetal responses related to suckling and grooming behavior in early infancy. Currently, she is developing an animal model of prenatal behavioral diagnostic methods that are predictive of postnatal outcomes of early neural insult or developmental disorders.

JEAN-PIERRE LECANUET was Research Director of three laboratories in Paris: Laboratoire de Physiologie Nerveuse (1972–1985), Laboratoire de Psychobiologie du Développement (1985–1995), and the Laboratoire Cognition et Développement (1996–2002). His research endeavors can be divided into two periods. During the first period, he worked on visual imprinting in the domestic chick, studying the processes involved in memory formation and consolidation. He was awarded the CNRS bronze medal (1982) for this work. In the second period, he continued investigating this issue in the near-term human fetus, with the hypothesis that analogous mechanisms could be present in fetal mammals. Working from the same theoretical approach in the auditory modality, he examined successfully the possibility of prenatal auditory learning and its impact *ex utero*.

THOMAS G. O'CONNOR is Associate Professor of Psychiatry and Psychology and Director of the Laboratory for the Prevention of Mental Disorders in the Department of Psychiatry at the University of Rochester Medical Center. His research interests include how early experiences may shape longer-term development, parent-child and family processes in diverse family forms, methodologies for studying family effects, behavioral genetics, and parenting interventions to improve child behavior. He has won several awards, including the Boyd McCandless Award from the American Psychological Association, Division 7 (2001), and the American Psychological Association Distinguished Scientific Award for Early Career Contribution to Psychology (2004).

SARAH L. PALLAS received her B.S. summa cum laude in Biology at the University of Minnesota in 1977. She completed a M.S. in Zoology/Neurobiology at Iowa State University in 1980, and a PhD in Neurobiology and Behavior from Cornell University in 1987. Her dissertation under Professor Barbara L. Finlay concerned compensation for perinatal damage within the retinocollicular pathway of mammals. Her postdoctoral work at M.I.T.'s Department of Brain and Cognitive Science was carried out under the direction of Professor Mriganka Sur on cross-modal plasticity in mammalian sensory cortex. After serving 5 years as an Assistant Professor of Neuroscience and Developmental Biology at Baylor College of Medicine in Houston, she joined the Department of Biology at Georgia State University as an Associate Professor in 1997. Her primary research interests are cortical development, sensory physiology, and developmental plasticity in sensory systems.

RICHARD H. PORTER is currently Director of Research at the Centre National de la Recherche Scientifique (CNRS). After receiving his PhD from Wayne State University, he spent two years at Leicester University as a post-doctoral fellow. He then moved to a faculty position at Vanderbilt University, where he conducted research and taught courses on ethology and developmental psychobiology. At present, he is studying chemosensory communication and the development of social recognition at a research center and a maternity hospital in the Loire Valley. During his career, he has worked with a variety of species, including bobwhite quail, domestic chicks, garter and water snakes, spiny mice, sheep, horses, and human neonates.

SCOTT R. ROBINSON received his PhD from Oregon State University in 1989, and is currently Associate Professor of Psychology at the University of Iowa, where he heads the Laboratory of Comparative Ethogenesis. Since 1982, his research has focused on the prenatal origins of behavior in the fetus. This research has sought evidence for the temporal and spatial organization of motor behavior, the prenatal expression of species-typical responses to sensory stimulation, the capacity to learn *in utero,* and the biological determinants of these abilities in rodent and sheep fetuses. His laboratory employs techniques for gaining experimental access to animal fetuses, manipulating neurochemical receptors in the fetal nervous system, and assessing the earliest forms of behavioral organization through quantitative and video-based kinematic analyses of fetal and neonatal movement. He serves on the Editorial Boards of *Developmental Psychobiology* and the *Journal of Comparative Psychology.*

BENOIST SCHAAL received his PhD from the University of Franche-Comté (1984), and his Habilitation from the Université Claude Bernard, Lyon (2000). He was a post-doctoral fellow at the University of Montréal, working with Richard E. Tremblay on the sensory and hormonal correlates of behavior in boys. Since 1988, he is a permanent researcher at the Centre National de la Recherche Scientifique (CNRS), working in several labs, including the Laboratoire de Psychobiologie du Développement, Paris, where he studied the olfactory abilities of the human fetus with Jean-Pierre Lecanuet, and the Animal Behaviour Unit of the French Agronomic Research Institute, Tours, where he investigated the sensory regulations of behavior in newborn sheep, pigs, rabbits, and humans. More recently, he moved to the Centre des Sciences du Goût, Dijon, of which he is the current director. He is presently investigating the role of odors between mothers and infants in various mammals, including humans.

HEILI VARENDI is Senior Pediatrician, Neonatal Unit, Children's Clinic of Tartu University, Senior Researcher in the Department of Pediatrics at the same university, and President of the Estonian Perinatal Society. She received both her MD and PhD from Tartu University, and a Dr. Med. Sci. from the Karolinska Institute in Stockholm. Her primary research interests are the behavior of neonates, mother-newborn interactions, and neonatal olfaction.

JAN WINBERG received both his MD and PhD from the Karolinska Institute in Stockholm. He was Professor and Chairman of the Departments of Pediatrics at the Universities of Gothenburg and Umeå from 1972 to 1974, and then again at the Karolinska Institute from 1974 to 1989, becoming an emeritus Professor from 1989 to 2003. Among his many honors, he was Physician in Order to the children of the King and Queen of Sweden, Fellow of the Infectious Diseases Society of America, and Honorary member of the British Association for Paediatric Nephrology and the International Pediatric Nephrology Association. He was also a member of the founding committees of the European Society for Pediatric Nephrology and the International Pediatric Nephrology Association. With more than 300 publications, his research interests covered urinary tract infections, physiology of lactation, nephrology, epidemiology of congenital malformations, infant nutrition, and neurobiology of mother-infant interactions.